Globalized Fruit, Local Entrepreneurs

Globalized Fruit, Local Entrepreneurs

How One Banana-Exporting Country
Achieved Worldwide Reach

Douglas Southgate and Lois Roberts

UNIVERSITY OF PENNSYLVANIA PRESS

PHILADELPHIA

Published by
University of Pennsylvania Press
Philadelphia, Pennsylvania 19104-4112

www.upenn.edu/pennpress

Printed in the United States of America on acid-free paper
1 3 5 7 9 10 8 6 4 2

Library of Congress Cataloging-in-Publication Data
ISBN 978-0-8122-4807-4

CONTENTS

List of Acronyms and Abbreviations   vii

Introduction   1

Chapter 1. The Octopus   7

Chapter 2. *El Pulpo*'s South American Rivals   20

Chapter 3. Never a Banana Republic   38

Chapter 4. Good Governance, for a Change   53

Chapter 5. South American Entrepreneurs Go Global   69

Chapter 6. Keeping Up with Technological Advances   89

Chapter 7. Agrarian Reform, Unionization, and a Policy Tilt
Against Agriculture   106

Chapter 8. Resurgence   125

Chapter 9. The Environmental Impact   145

Chapter 10. Continuing Challenges, New Risks   157

Chapter 11. Creative Destruction?   174

Appendix: Ecuadorian Banana Production and Exports, 1961 to 2013   181

Notes   183

References   201

Index   209

Acknowledgments   215

ABBREVIATIONS

A&P	Atlantic and Pacific supermarket chain
ACP	Africa, Caribbean, and Pacific
AEBE	Asociación de Exportadores de Banano del Ecuador
AGP	Associate Growers' Program
ANBE	Asociación Nacional de Bananeros Ecuatorianos
BCA	Banco Comercial y Agrícola
BFA	Banana Framework Agreement
BNF	Banco Nacional de Fomento
CAN	Conservation Agriculture Network
CIA	U.S. Central Intelligence Agency
CIF	cost insurance freight
COMB	Common Organization of the Market for Bananas
COPORESA	Corporación Ecuatoriana Europea
CTE	Confederación de Trabajadores Ecuatorianos
DBCP	dibromochloropropane
EEC	European Economic Community
EU	European Union
FAO	UN Food and Agriculture Organization
FDI	Foreign Direct Investment
FHIA	Fundación Hondureña de Investigación Agrícola
FOC	*Fusarium oxysporum* Schlect. f. sp. *Cubense* virus
GATT	General Agreement on Tariffs and Trade
GDP	gross domestic product
GM	genetically modified
HIV	human immunodeficiency virus
IERAC	Instituto Ecuatoriano de Reforma Agraria y Colonización
IESS	Instituto Ecuatoriano de Seguridad Social
IMF	International Monetary Fund
INC	Instituto Nacional de Colonización

INRA	Institut National de la Recherche Agronomique
IPR	intellectual property right
ISI	import substituting industrialization
PNB	Programa Nacional del Banano
Reybanpac	Rey Banano del Pacífico
SAFCO	South American Fruit Company
SICA	Servicio Interamericano de Cooperación para la Agricultura
TR4	Tropical Race Four
UBESA	Unión de Bananeros Ecuatorianos
UNIBAN	Unión de Bananeros de Urabá
UPEB	Unión de Países Exportadores de Banana
WHO	World Health Organization
WTO	World Trade Organization

Map of Colombia.

Map of Ecuador.

Map of Honduras.

Introduction

A tropical commodity bought and sold by the boatload throughout the world. Agribusinesses with worldwide reach, including a firm that has been a lightning rod for anti-corporate criticism since the Great Depression. Minor Latin American states on the receiving end of globalization. An uncomplicated, and oft-told, story of banana republics and the misfortunes visited on them by multinational companies. What more need be said?

Bananas are the ultimate nonlocal food. More tons of wheat are exported. Cross-border shipments of corn and soybeans are more sizable as well. Barley holds fourth place in a ranking of agricultural exports by weight because harvests in Europe are routinely sold to feedlots and breweries in neighboring countries. But bananas come next, in fifth place and far ahead of every other fruit and vegetable. International shipments of bananas are a full order of magnitude greater than the cross-border trade in rice, which is produced in enormous quantities in China, India, and other Asian nations though almost entirely for domestic consumption. Economists characterize the international rice market as thin, which is another way of saying that the staple grain of the world's most populous continent is primarily a local food. In contrast, countless bunches of fruit are purchased in the United States, Germany, and other places where few bananas grow. These places' imports come from countries where negligible shares of production are consumed domestically, thereby allowing practically all output to be dispatched overseas. Safe to say, no farm product is more globalized than bananas.

Likewise, no agricultural commodity is associated more closely with large corporations based in the United States. The banana business was largely the creation of the United Fruit Company, called The Octopus because of its near monopoly in the U.S. market and its control of supplies in Central America and other parts of the Caribbean Basin for many years after the firm's founding right before the turn of the twentieth century. The banana republic narrative derives from this period, when The Octopus overwhelmed its commercial rivals and controlled the fortunes of entire nations.

Chiquita Brands International (the current incarnation of United Fruit) has not had a lock on the production and marketing of bananas for decades. Nevertheless, corporate power and wrongdoing in Latin America are a recurring theme of books and articles about the tropical fruit industry—so much so that events and trends that do not fit with this theme are downplayed, if not ignored completely. Relatively little has been written, for instance, about the impact Colombians competing against United Fruit have had on banana development in their country. An even more striking example of neglect is Ecuador, which has been the world's leading exporter of bananas for sixty years and counting. In various ways, the country contradicts the two-dimensional tale so many authors relate of The Octopus and the tropical lands it plunders. The truth is that Ecuador's banana industry, which is the subject of this book, is independent, has been forged in competition, and ably serves customers wherever they are found.

Multinational enterprises have had a presence in Ecuador—an important presence, dating back to the 1930s and continuing today. However, the country has not achieved and sustained export leadership at the expense of turning itself into a corporate satrapy; to the contrary, its commercial accomplishments have gone hand in hand with its insistence on steering its own course. Still, the South American nation is treated as just another banana republic by authors bent on chronicling the power and abuses of The Octopus. Take Peter Chapman, who mentions Ecuador barely five times in a book titled *Bananas* that was published in 2007. Only once does Chapman distinguish the country from places that arguably have been under United Fruit's thumb, by acknowledging in passing that an unnamed Ecuadorian firm competes in the global marketplace against Chiquita and a couple of other multinational fruit businesses.[1] In a volume with a nearly identical title released a year after Chapman's book, Dan Koeppel goes so far as to mention the Ecuadorian brand (though never the name of the company, itself) on two separate pages.[2] No matter. One can read both books, which are supposed to be about the tropical fruit sector in its entirety, and still be unaware that the world's largest fruit exporter has never been a banana republic.

Many authors whose writings have a narrower geographic scope hew to the prevailing narrative every bit as much as Chapman and Koeppel do. Historian Marcelo Bucheli does not do so. His book underscores United Fruit's monopolization of Colombia's banana industry before World War II, yet details the achievements of national planters and exporters since the middle of the twentieth century.[3] In contrast, The Octopus looms very large in a book about Ecuador published in 2002. The author, Steve Striffler, is also dismissive of "local capitalists," whom he lumps together with "small-time con men."[4] Aside from describing their conflicts with peasants and workers, Striffler devotes little more attention than Chapman and Koeppel to Ecuadorian growers and exporters. As a result, opportunities are cast aside to examine the significant contributions these economic actors have made to agricultural trade and development.

Geography and history have mattered a lot in Ecuador's banana industry, including in terms of local entrepreneurship. The western part of the country, between the Andes Mountains and the Pacific Ocean, abounds in the natural resources needed for tropical fruit production: fertile soils, generous precipitation in some places and easy irrigation elsewhere, and a Caribbean climate though without hurricanes. The area also boasts a port city of long standing: something the Caribbean coast of Central America lacked at the turn of the twentieth century, when United Fruit and other U.S. companies started carving banana plantations out of the region's tropical forests. Remote from governmental authority for hundreds of years after its founding by Spanish conquistadors, Guayaquil was a hub for business long before opportunities arose to export tropical fruit.

With a commercial city in its midst, western Ecuador has a banana market worthy of the name, with dozens of exporters and other merchants purchasing and selling the harvests of hundreds of farms. Few of these farms are large enough to qualify as plantations. By the same token, no fruit buyer, either foreign or domestic, monopolizes the market. Under the pressure of competition, entrepreneurial innovation, such as sales of bananas in places where U.S. firms rarely if ever venture, is rewarded. Additionally, business skills are honed. Not least among these skills is a knack for mutually advantageous partnerships, of the sort Ecuadorian exporters have harnessed in their ascent to the very heights of the global banana business.

Some of the most rewarding partnerships have been with agribusinesses headquartered in the United States, thereby demonstrating that the relationship between Ecuador and companies such as United Fruit has always been a mix of the cooperative and the adversarial. The country's growers rely on the multinationals for technology, which those firms have been willing to share since they deal regularly in bananas grown in Ecuador. Similarly, many Ecuadorian exporters got their start by associating with foreign businesses that were already established in the banana trade. Even now that those exporters have gained experience and have cracked a number of overseas markets on their own, partnerships continue—whenever the benefits are mutual, that is.

By no means has the Ecuadorian government been a passive observer of banana development. Hoping for an infusion of technology and capital, national leaders courted United Fruit as long ago as the early 1920s. Investment by the company did not actually begin until a decade or so later, by which time the political temper of Ecuador was much more populist and nationalistic. Along with other restrictions, limits were placed on the foreign ownership of agricultural land. Aimed squarely at The Octopus, these limits and restrictions allayed fears of political and economic subservience without being so burdensome that the firm would give up on Ecuador. Accordingly, the government was free to facilitate a boom in banana exports, in which United Fruit played a major role and which began once normal transoceanic commerce resumed after World War II. For example, macroeconomic stability was maintained, which encouraged private investment. Ecuador's government also saw to the construction of roads and bridges, which accelerated the tropical fruit sector's geographic expansion.

But while foreign firms and the national government have furnished critical support, Ecuador's banana industry has been led by competitive, homegrown entrepreneurs and, thanks primarily to them, challenges consistently have been met and overcome. Some of these challenges have been microbial, as when pathogenic depredations required a wholesale switch after the mid-1960s from the traditional variety of bananas to a new, disease-resistant variety. Others have had to do with disadvantageous public policies on the far side of the world, such as trade barriers the European Union adopted during the 1990s to limit fruit imports from Latin America. Ecuadorian entrepreneurs have found ways to deal with these difficulties, sometimes with the government's involvement or the assistance of multinationals and at other times on their own.

There are no guarantees of similar success in the future. Importing nations regularly succumb to the protectionist temptation. The banana industry is harmed as well by policies with national, not foreign, origins. Thirty to forty years ago, for example, Ecuadorian authorities followed the lead of their counterparts elsewhere in Latin America by pursuing a strategy for economic development that stressed enlargement of the state, favoritism for the manufacturing sector, and weakening of agricultural incentives. The banana industry was not spared the consequences and fruit exports stagnated for many years. Even though the development strategy of the 1970s led to a severe economic crisis in the early 1980s, it has been resurrected in recent years and the tropical fruit sector is paying the price.

Plant pathogens also take a heavy toll. Already representing a large share of overall costs of production, pesticide expenditures are heading upward, mainly because chemical inputs grow less effective as harmful organisms evolve. Worse yet, there are no chemical countermeasures for some plant diseases, which can be overcome only through biotechnology—a tool for agricultural progress that is still not accepted in some quarters.

Notwithstanding pathogenic and other challenges, Ecuador's banana industry and its independent entrepreneurs continue to survive and prosper. The Octopus, in contrast, no longer does so, at least as a separate business entity headquartered in the United States. In October 2014, Brazilian investors announced they would be buying Chiquita, lock, stock, and bananas.[5] So The Octopus—an enduring symbol for many of multinational dominance south of the U.S. border—will henceforth be a Latin American possession.

A note on currency conversions. Ecuador's long-time currency, the sucre, disappeared in January 2000, when hyperinflation threatened and the U.S. dollar was adopted as the legal national tender. Throughout this book, historical values in sucres are converted into modern dollar equivalents by, first, applying the rate of exchange between Ecuadorian and U.S. currency that prevailed at the indicated date and, second, converting historical dollars into equivalent values in 2014 using the deflator for U.S. gross domestic product (GDP).

CHAPTER 1

====

The Octopus

Turned out in clean clothes, which his widowed mother insisted he wear while working, the juvenile street vendor stepped forward and addressed one of Guayaquil's most prominent businessmen: Juan F. Marcos. Twelve years old at the time, Luís Noboa was intent on selling "magic metal" polishing cloths, which he had peddled already to more than a few merchants and housewives in the port city. Making his pitch at the entrance to Marcos's business, the Sociedad General, Noboa observed, "This building has a lot of brass, but none of it is shiny." He seized a tarnished pot for an improvised demonstration, and in a few seconds the pot was glistening in the tropical sun.[1]

Marcos and Noboa might well have been passing acquaintances. Guayaquil, though more populous than any other settlement on the Pacific coast of Ecuador, was not a large city. Also, Noboa had received acclaim the previous year, 1927, for selling more copies of a popular magazine than any other newsboy. This feat related in part to personal deliveries of the magazine to the homes of wealthy subscribers, including Marcos. But whatever his previous contact with the businessman had been, the youngster made the sale. Handing over a few coins for the polishing cloths, Marcos also had something to offer: a job at the Sociedad General.[2]

Noboa did not accept on the spot. After all, he figured, the starting salary at the bank did not match his earnings as a street vendor. But his mother, left nearly penniless by her husband's death in August 1924, scolded him later for this hesitancy, emphasizing how much he could learn by working at a leading commercial establishment. Always obedient to her, the boy wasted little time returning to Marcos's office to take the job.[3]

So began the career of Ecuador's most successful businessman of all time. When Noboa died in 1994, he left his heirs more than 650 million dollars.[4]

However, an enormous fortune was not his only legacy, or indeed his most significant accomplishment. Noboa deserves much of the credit for his country's rise to the top of the tropical fruit industry. This ascent transformed Ecuador, the smallest Spanish-speaking republic aside from Uruguay in South America and about the size of the U.S. state of Colorado. The industry as a whole changed fundamentally as well.

Banana exports from Ecuador boomed after World War II, which ended the effective monopoly the United Fruit Company had enjoyed since its creation in 1899. The firm's unchallenged position had been secure as long as the Caribbean Basin, where United Fruit faced little competition, provided most of the bananas consumed in the United States and other importing nations. But once entrepreneurs such as Noboa tapped into Ecuador's enormous agricultural potential, monopolization of the banana market was beyond the reach of any single company, even the most powerful agribusiness the world has ever known.

Vertical Integration

United Fruit emerged out of a brisk trade in bananas launched after the U.S. Civil War by sea captains eager to profit from their countrymen's desire for fresh fruit year round—not just in the months when apples, peaches, and other crops are harvested north of the Tropic of Cancer. Before the days of refrigerated shipping, the only way to supply fruit before and after the harvest season was to bring in bananas from the Caribbean Basin—a line of commerce that was fraught with risk, and not only because of the speed at which the fruit ripens, then rots. Between 1885 and 1890, one of every seven sailing ships used to carry bananas to the United States ended up at the bottom of the ocean. Of the 114 banana-importing firms that operated in the United States from 1870 to 1899, 92 went out of business; of the 22 firms that remained at the end of the nineteenth century, all but four were small concerns.[5]

The largest firm of all, the Boston Fruit Company, was the product of an association between Captain Lorenzo Baker and Andrew Preston. Baker had helped introduce bananas to the United States in 1870 by purchasing 160 stems in Jamaica, catching a favorable wind to sail straight to New York harbor, then selling the odd, exotic fruit at a handsome price.[6] A year later, while delivering bananas to Boston, he met Preston, who had little formal schooling yet had a talent for sales, marketing, and distribution. Not long afterward, Preston quit his old job so that he could work full time selling the fruit imported by Baker up and down the eastern seaboard. This partnership was formalized in 1885, when the two men joined ten private investors to establish Boston Fruit.[7]

Another of the four large firms supplying bananas to the United States during the late 1800s, the Tropical Trading and Transport Company, was headed by Minor Keith, whose career in railroads included construction of a line linking the Caribbean coast of Costa Rica with the highland capital of San José. Yellow fever and other diseases cost the lives of thousands of men whom Keith had brought down from New Orleans to work on the project. All three of his brothers died in Costa Rica as well. Yet the reward for completing the railroad was a sprawling grant of land, some of which was cleared and planted to bananas.[8]

As the nineteenth century was drawing to a close, Boston Fruit possessed an impressive fleet of steam-powered vessels, which brought in most of the U.S. banana supply.[9] Due largely to Preston's efforts, it also had the best network of ice-cooled railcars and warehouses for delivering fruit far into the continental interior from coastal ports. But aside from 540 hectares that Baker had bought in Jamaica, Boston Fruit's holdings of tropical farmland were negligible.[10] In contrast, the holdings of Tropical Trading and Transport were extensive, far outstripping its assets for shipping and distribution. Each firm's shortcomings were overcome by the merger of Boston Fruit and Keith's business that created United Fruit less than a year before the turn of the twentieth century. Vertically integrated, the combined enterprise could grow bananas in the tropics, ship fruit across the ocean without delay, and dispatch produce quickly to customers throughout the United States.

Preston reinforced United Fruit's dominance of the U.S. market by arranging for the company to purchase shares in dozens of smaller competitors. To avoid being charged with violating the Sherman Antitrust Act of 1890, the company made sure never to control more than 49 percent of the banana business in any of the cities where it operated.[11] Tacit cooperation was routine between the commercial leviathan formed by Baker, Preston, and Keith and the other firms. But even as United Fruit came to be known as The Octopus for wrapping its figurative tentacles around those firms, their continuing existence helped create a legal defense that could be used in the event of antimonopoly litigation.

Among the many businesses United Fruit invested in was Elders and Fyffes, the leading supplier of bananas in Great Britain. Known as Fyffes after it became a wholly owned subsidiary of the U.S. multinational in 1910, the British enterprise previously had competed directly with The Octopus for bananas harvested by Jamaican growers.[12] United Fruit also took a stake in the Standard Fruit and Steamship Company. Established the same year as the industry leader, Standard Fruit had a foothold in the southern United States because one of its founders, an Italian immigrant named Joseph Vaccaro, had purchased or constructed a number of ice factories along the Gulf Coast.[13] Like its larger rival, the company owned plantations in northern Honduras: a Central American setting reached by sailing south from New Orleans or Mobile and then past the Yucatan Peninsula, which is too dry for banana production. These properties had been received from the Honduran government in return for building a railroad,[14] exactly like Keith's holdings in Costa Rica.

Aside from the construction of railroads, which were needed to transport harvested fruit speedily to coastal harbors, plantation development involved the clearing of jungles and the preparation of land. Vertically integrated firms invested in oceangoing vessels with refrigerated holds (commonly called reefer ships) and climate-controlled facilities for the distribution of perishable produce. Also, United Fruit pioneered the use of two-way radios for the careful orchestration of banana harvesting, transoceanic shipping, and offloading at import terminals.[15]

Thanks to all these investments and technological advances, fruit supplies multiplied in the United States, which caused prices to plummet. As historian Virginia Scott Jenkins observes, few Americans in 1880 had ever seen a banana. Thirty years later, the fruit had ceased to be a luxury item and was instead a dietary staple for the poor—especially their offspring, whose first food after weaning almost always consisted of mashed bananas.[16] The value of bananas coming in from Central America and the Caribbean, which was less than two million dollars in 1885 and amounted to six million dollars in 1899, doubled during the first decade of the twentieth century in spite of a dramatic price reduction.[17]

The dietary importance bananas acquired so quickly in the United States during this period was underscored when a duty of five cents a bunch was proposed in 1913. The tariff might have seemed a trivial matter in light of the ratification earlier that year of the constitutional amendment that established the federal income tax. Not so. The National Housewives' League urged its two million members to protest to President Woodrow Wilson, who had been inaugurated in March and supported the banana duty. By October, the idea had been dropped.[18]

Sam the Banana Man

Along with United Fruit and Standard Fruit, another vertically integrated enterprise, the Cuyamel Fruit Company, raised bananas in northern Honduras for the U.S. market. The driving force behind this firm was Samuel Zemurray, who had been born on a wheat farm in present-day Moldova in 1877. Having lost his father at a young age, Zemurray traveled with an aunt to New York in 1892 and from there to Selma, Alabama, to join an uncle who had a small store.[19]

Entrepreneurial derring-do had to wait until the adolescent immigrant had brought his widowed mother and all his younger siblings to the United States, paying their fares out of earnings from a series of menial jobs. But with the entire family reunited in Alabama by 1895, when Zemurray turned eighteen, there was no reason not to roll the dice. He staked $150 on bananas that were about to be discarded in the port of Mobile because they had ripened during the passage across the Caribbean Sea and the Gulf of Mexico.[20] With no money to spare, Zemurray offered a telegraph operator a percentage of sales revenues in return for lining up buyers along the route of the train he was to take with his perishable cargo. The operator accepted the deal, so all the ready-to-eat bananas found customers—at low prices, though still at a profit.[21] After three years of wholesaling "ripes," Sam the Banana Man (Zemurray's lifelong nickname) had $100,000 in the bank.[22]

In 1903, Zemurray sold 574,000 bananas, up from 20,000 in 1899. That same year, he met with Preston in Mobile and signed a contract with United Fruit to take bananas that were fully mature. In 1905, Zemurray and a local partner named Ashbell Hubbard purchased a financially troubled steamship company, with partial backing from United Fruit.[23] The two businessmen also bought Cuyamel and its 2,000 hectares planted to bananas in northern Honduras from the American who had founded the firm and had received agricultural real estate as a reward for railroad construction.[24] Around this time, Zemurray relocated to New Orleans, still shy of his thirtieth birthday.

The acquisition of Cuyamel and its Honduran farms coincided with an upswing in the U.S. government's interest in Central America. During the nineteenth century, official Washington had paid little attention to the region—even after its economic isolation had been alleviated by the completion of a railroad across the Panamanian Isthmus in 1854, which made it profitable to ship coffee produced in the Central American highlands to Europe and the eastern United States from Punta Arenas, Costa Rica, and other harbors along the Pacific coast. But circumstances were different after 1903, when the United States facilitated Panama's separation from Colombia and started excavating an interoceanic canal across the narrow country. U.S. leaders were concerned that past borrowing by Central American governments in Europe had rendered them susceptible to influence from outside the Western Hemisphere. To keep this influence in check, the United States engaged in Dollar Diplomacy, with U.S. financiers purchasing unpaid debts from their European counterparts and the U.S. government guaranteeing loan payments by taking over the collection of export and import duties in the indebted countries.

Dollar Diplomacy was put into practice in Nicaragua in 1911, which marked the beginning of more than two decades of colonial-style administration of the country by the United States.[25] The policy's application around the same time in Honduras derived from bonds that national authorities had sold to London investors during the 1860s to finance a railroad. Due mainly to fraud, the railroad was never completed, which severely impeded coffee development and overall economic progress. However, these difficulties did not prevent the British government from insisting that all debts be settled. Stepping in to resolve the dispute, U.S. officials arranged for J. P. Morgan to buy the old bonds for 15 percent of their face value. The Wall Street tycoon then issued five million dollars in new securities to the Honduran government, which agreed to meet its financial obligations by instituting a tax on exported bananas to be collected by U.S. customs officials stationed in the country's ports.[26]

By adding a penny to the cost of every bunch of Honduran bananas, this arrangement put Cuyamel, which lacked agricultural holdings elsewhere, at a competitive disadvantage vis-à-vis United Fruit, which had a large operation in Honduras but also grew or purchased fruit in other countries where exports were not taxed. Zemurray protested, including in person to the U.S. secretary of state, though to no avail. Unwilling to knuckle under, he then recruited and financed a small band of mercenaries to topple the government in Tegucigalpa, with which he had a number of quarrels.[27] The government fell and its successor rescinded the export tax and other elements of the arrangement with Morgan and the U.S. government—an arrangement few Hondurans supported.[28] Cuyamel and Zemurray subsequently prospered.

Big Mike's Vulnerabilities and a Corporate Coup

In a political and economic history of Central America, Victor Bulmer-Thomas wonders how U.S. fruit companies "could have resisted the temptation to meddle in (the region's) internal politics" during the early 1900s.[29] At the time, however, their actions in places such as Honduras aroused little public comment in the United States, where banana sales continued to grow rapidly. Instead, U.S. observers were impressed mainly by the companies' ability to supply perishable goods reliably to customers across great distances. The difficulties of this task are illustrated in John Steinbeck's *East of Eden*, which is set in California's Salinas Valley during World War I, when a failed attempt to transport lettuce in ice-cooled boxcars to New York City almost ruins the story's protagonists. Well aware that shipping bananas from the Caribbean Basin to the United States was even harder than enterprises of the sort depicted in Steinbeck's novel, authors during the first part of the twentieth century were unstinting in their praise of all that firms like United Fruit were doing to the benefit of U.S. consumers.[30]

What was not understood a hundred years ago was that the environmental underpinnings of the banana business were fragile. Practically all the fruit imported by the United States was of the same cultivar: Gros Michel, which translates from French as Big Mike. Moreover, the standard practice in the industry, today as in the past, has been to propagate bananas asexually, which means there is no genetic variation from plant to plant.[31] Agricultural estates encompassing hundreds or even thousands of hectares planted to a genetically identical crop represent monoculture on a scale that would have awed a pharaoh. Factor in tropical heat and humidity, and banana plantations comprise an ideal arena for microbial mayhem.

The opening salvo in the microbes' assault on the tropical fruit business occurred in the 1890s, when the leaves on large numbers of banana plants in Panama started wilting and then dying and falling to the ground. The culprit turned out to be a single strain of a soil-borne fungus, *Fusarium oxysporum* Schlect. f. sp. *cubense* (FOC), against which the Gros Michel had no resistance at all.[32] Tens of thousands of hectares planted to that variety were lost during the next six to seven decades. Not until the late 1950s was Standard Fruit able to solve the problem by planting a disease-resistant banana variety called Cavendish, which the company's scientists had spent many years developing.[33]

For much of the twentieth century, however, the primary response of

United Fruit and its competitors to Fusarium Wilt—or Panama Disease, as the malady was known for many years after it was first detected and as many in the banana industry still call it—was not to undertake the sort of research and development that leads to better varieties. Instead, they moved their operations to places not yet infected by the FOC fungus. Some tropical countries, most notably Ecuador, gained from this relocation. But when thousands of hectares were locked up as reserves, which could be cleared and brought into production if and when existing plantations had to be abandoned because of Panama Disease, the results could be disadvantageous for host nations. Thomas McCann, who spent his career at United Fruit, admitted that real estate acquisition by his former employer went well beyond what was required for "shifting plantation agriculture"—to use a term coined by John Soluri, a historian of the banana industry.[34] In 1952, the industry leader

> owned or controlled three million acres of land. Only 139,000 of those acres were actually planted in bananas; the rest were euphemistically carried on the books as "reserves," although one of the most important reasons they were held was to guarantee that they would not become farmland for our competitors.[35]

Due to strategic behavior of this sort, competition was stifled in a key sector of the Central American economy as well as the banana industry as a whole.

Territorial acquisition could even provoke international conflicts. A case in point was a dispute that arose in 1915 over a productive region on the border between Guatemala, where United Fruit had secured extensive territorial concessions in 1906, and Honduras, which was always the leading source of bananas for Zemurray's firm. Each of the two governments rattled sabers occasionally at the urging of private interests, and U.S. mediation was needed twice during the next thirteen years to avert declarations of war.

Final resolution of the dispute had to wait until 1929, when the Boston Brahmins who had assumed control of United Fruit after the departure of Baker, Keith, and Preston decided to deal once and for all with the company's pesky rival. A merger was proposed, which Zemurray accepted on being offered 300,000 shares of United Fruit stock.[36] The buy-out made him the firm's leading investor, which distressed him enormously as the value of his holdings shrank. Worth $31,500,000 (or $105 per share) when the merger was effected, in early 1930, Zemurray's stake in United Fruit had lost more than 90 percent of its value by December 1932, when shares in the company were being bought and sold for $10.25. The stock collapse was in large measure the result of poor corporate administration, not simply a consequence of the Great Depression.

In January 1933, Sam the Banana Man traveled to Boston for one of the most storied confrontations in the annals of U.S. business. According to McCann, "Zemurray presented an incisive review of the company's mismanagement." The patrician chairman of the board responded by smiling thinly and drawing attention to his stockholder's accent: "Unfortunately, Mr. Zemurray, I can't understand a word you say." The former immigrant stepped out of the room, but only to return a few moments later clutching the majority share of proxies he had collected beforehand. "You gentlemen have been f---ing up this business long enough," Zemurray informed the board slowly and precisely. "I'm going to straighten it out."[37]

The investing public was more than pleased; the price of United Fruit stock shot up, doubling during the fortnight after the corporate coup.[38] Confidence in Zemurray's leadership turned out to be entirely justified. For example, he had learned from conversations with the company's ship captains prior to the January 1933 takeover that all vessels had been ordered to cruise at half speed. While this measure reduced expenditures on fuel, it also caused much more fruit to spoil while in transit, so the policy was reversed and all ships were authorized to travel at full speed soon after United Fruit's old president and former chairman of the board were sacked.[39] Changes of this sort not only had a positive impact on United Fruit's bottom line, but probably saved the company from going under in the 1930s.

Latin Americans Take On *El Pulpo*

Just as United Fruit acquired agricultural land and strove to dominate its commercial rivals, every firm in the industry sought to exercise tight control over agricultural labor. Wages offered by the multinationals and benefits such as food sold in company stores at below-market prices and medical care provided free of charge in company hospitals were superior to the rural norm in countries such as Ecuador and Honduras.[40] But at the same time, unionization was opposed vigorously.

Transnational firms did not win every battle with organized labor. For example, plantation workers in Honduras struck successfully in 1920 for a daily wage of $1.75, with double pay for overtime;[41] this level of compensation was well above the sixteen to fifty cents per day earned by laborers on coffee farms elsewhere in the same country.[42] However, workers and unions also suffered crushing defeats. An unusually bloody confrontation occurred in 1928 in northeastern Colombia, where United Fruit had arrived at the turn of the twentieth century. Opposed to the labor-contracting system the company used not just in Colombia but on all its plantations, strikers demanded regular employment and recognition of their union. The authorities in Bogotá responded by deploying a military force, which on 6 December 1928 killed sixty to seventy-five protesters in the city of Ciénaga.[43] This woeful incident achieved lasting notoriety once Gabriel García Márquez featured the confrontation and a wildly exaggerated death count in his novel, *One Hundred Years of Solitude.*

Events such as the Ciénaga massacre caused opinions about the tropical fruit industry to shift. Gone were the encomia published during the early 1900s. In their place were indictments consistent with the anti-corporate attitudes that gained wide circulation in the United States during the 1930s. Representative of the new literature was a frequently-quoted denunciation of United Fruit penned by Charles D. Kepner and Jay Soothill:

> [This] powerful company has throttled competitors, dominated governments, manacled railroads, ruined planters, choked cooperatives, domineered over workers, fought organized labor, and exploited consumers. Such usage of power by a corporation of a strongly industrialized nation in relatively weak foreign countries constitutes a variety of economic imperialism.[44]

This denunciation, which did not even concede that cheap bananas were a boon to consumers, resonated in Latin America. Most famously, Chilean poet Pablo Neruda condemned *El Pulpo* (The Octopus) in his *Canto General* of 1950 for "reserving for itself the juiciest part" of the Western Hemisphere, staging an "opera buffa" in the banana republics it spawned, and making off with "the treasure of our sunken lands."[45]

However, exercises of power by the company or its local allies did not cement the multinational's hegemony over the tropical lands that were the source of its produce. To the contrary, opposing forces were often galvanized. As Marcelo Bucheli notes in his history of Colombia's banana industry, public revulsion over the killings in Ciénaga helped bring down the conservative regime that had been in power since 1904 and had provided tax waivers, cheap land, and other inducements to foreign investors. President Enrique Olaya, the center-left victor in the 1930 election, disappointed his radical supporters by not instituting a tax on banana exports and by extending United Fruit's lease on a railroad serving its zone of operations. However, President Alfonso López, who succeeded Olaya and was from the same political party, signed Colombia's first agrarian reform law, which among other things strengthened the property rights of peasants who had occupied the uncultivated fringes of large estates. Unions received support as well, including in the banana sector.[46]

After World War II, multinationals' prerogatives were even trimmed back in Central America, where national authorities formerly had spared no effort to propitiate foreign investors in the fruit industry. Costa Rica and Honduras modified old concession agreements, which had exempted foreign investors from taxes on their profits, in 1949. In 1943, Costa Rica instituted a labor code that established the rights of all workers, including in rural areas, to organize and strike; similar codes were adopted in Nicaragua in 1945 and in Guatemala in 1947.[47] Honduras did not follow suit immediately, although a strike in 1954 resulted in the recognition by United Fruit and Standard Fruit of a single union representing all the employees of the two multinationals.[48]

During the late 1940s and early 1950s, regimes preoccupied with communist influence, especially within the labor movement, came to power in most of Central America. The leading exception was Guatemala, where Jacobo Arbenz, a former army officer with leftist sympathies, was elected president in 1951. Not content with raising duties on fruit exports and introducing taxes on industry profits, as was happening in neighboring countries, Arbenz's government opted for "a head-on clash with [United Fruit] over land reform and financial compensation for expropriated land."[49] To be specific, an order was issued in 1952 that uncultivated areas in holdings larger than 269 hectares be redistributed to rural households with little or no land. The previous owners of confiscated properties, including United Fruit, were to be paid off with bonds valued according to those owners' tax declarations (which invariably amounted to a small fraction of the market value of real estate), paying annual interest of 3 percent, and maturing in twenty-five years.[50]

All told, Arbenz's agrarian reform redistributed 600,000 idle hectares to 100,000 rural families. Of those 600,000 hectares, 160,000 were taken from United Fruit, which formerly had possessed 220,000 hectares in Guatemala but kept 85 percent of its holdings in reserve. Even though the company insisted that its land was worth $185 per hectare or more, it only received bonds with a face value of approximately \$7.50 per hectare in compensation.[51] In response, The Octopus mounted an aggressive publicity campaign aimed at convincing U.S. leaders that Guatemala had become a hotbed of communist subversion.[52] Whether or not the campaign was as influential as some writers claim, the U.S. government grew much more antagonistic toward Arbenz after the inauguration of President Dwight Eisenhower in 1953. The following year, the Central Intelligence Agency (CIA) engineered a coup d'état that drove the Guatemalan leader into permanent exile.[53]

Enter the Ecuadorians

Despite close collaboration between United Fruit and the U.S. government before and during the Guatemalan coup, antitrust charges were filed against the company a few months after Arbenz's overthrow. Four years of litigation ensued, finally culminating in a consent decree signed in 1958 that obliged United Fruit to spin off railroads in Central America and marketing operations in the United States. The decree also required the divestiture of one-third of the industry leader's agricultural holdings.[54]

United Fruit had to deal with the antitrust lawsuit and other challenges without Samuel Zemurray. Seventy-seven years old and suffering from Parkinson's disease, the last of the banana industry's pioneers had no choice but to step down in 1954, this time never to resume the career he had embarked on at eighteen. McCann served under Sam the Banana Man, as he fondly refers to his former boss, and makes clear that Zemurray put his stamp on United Fruit: "His company and his character were almost exactly matched: . . . tough, no-nonsense, quick to act." McCann's employment continued after Zemurray's departure, which in his eyes diminished the company—causing it to become "forceful one minute, indecisive the next, living as much off its own past as for its future."[55]

The years following Zemurray's retirement were no time for indecisive management given the stiff competition The Octopus was encountering, from U.S. firms and South American entrepreneurs alike. Certainly, Noboa and other Ecuadorians were not to be taken lightly. Their environmental advantages were undeniable: a tropical setting ideally suited to tropical fruit production that admittedly was farther from leading markets in Europe and the eastern United States but that also was free of hurricanes, which were (and remain) a constant menace in the Caribbean Basin. The Ecuadorians had nonenvironmental advantages as well: being located in a port city with a long tradition of international commerce, complete with the business services needed to win over customers throughout the world. As is documented in the pages that follow, the skills and capacities of exporters based in Guayaquil exactly matched the entrepreneurial requirements for success in the international banana business.

Whether or not creative destruction has occurred in Ecuador can be debated. Defined narrowly, this process, which economist Joseph Schumpeter examined during the early 1900s,[56] involves major strides in productive technology, which Ecuadorians have never undertaken. However, entrepreneurs such as Noboa were creative in that they established something that did not exist before: a tropical fruit industry in Latin America that was not controlled by major corporations headquartered in the United States. This development was also destructive: the emergence after World War II of a large and independent source of bananas south of the Panama Canal directly undermined the monopoly The Octopus had enjoyed previously thanks to the control of agricultural resources farther north, in the Caribbean Basin. Thus, the commercial rivalry coming out of Ecuador did not confine itself to the remote margins of United Fruit's business. Rather, the country's entrepreneurs struck at the very core of that business. If this was not creative destruction in the strictest sense of the term, *El Pulpo* could be excused for not appreciating the difference.

CHAPTER 2

El Pulpo's South American Rivals

Latin American exporters and their contributions to trade and development are the subject of an incisive essay by Charles Sabel, a professor of law and social science at Columbia University. The essay draws directly on an insight about market prices from Friedrich Hayek, who along with Joseph Schumpeter was among the foremost economic thinkers of the twentieth century. These prices do not comprise a "detailed, reliable, and nearly exhaustive survey of current constraints and opportunities," as Sabel puts it. Rather, they are "statistical aggregates" that indicate the scarcity of "general classes of goods," which implies that entrepreneurship involves much more than a careful reading of market data. In Hayek's view, businessmen and women find opportunities by complementing the broad guidance encapsulated in prices with information about their respective enterprises that is of critical importance yet is not provided by markets—to be specific, "highly detailed, local, or idiosyncratic information regarding inputs, production processes, or products."[1]

This basic entrepreneurial task, which economists Ricardo Hausmann and Dani Rodrik characterize as "self-discovery," obviously requires time, effort, and thought. Additionally, problems of appropriation, or capture, frequently arise. For example, one firm might go to the trouble of designing a new product and introducing it to consumers, only to see profits slip away as competitors supply facsimiles. Likewise, the improvements one business makes in production processes thanks to its expenditures on research and development benefit other businesses insofar as those improvements are easy to copy—as is often, even typically, the case. Patent law and other arrangements for protecting the intellectual property of innovators exist for the sake of enhancing benefit capture. However, these arrangements are hardly a perfect solution, so entrepreneurial innovation is always discouraged to one degree or another because of imperfect appropriation.[2]

Imperfect appropriation has been an issue on occasion in the fruit business. For instance, the Chinese gooseberry was unknown outside Asia and the Pacific before the mid-1900s. At that time, New Zealanders developed a variety that could withstand the rigors of international shipping. They also mounted an advertising campaign to acquaint European and North American consumers with kiwifruit, as it is now known throughout the world. However, the benefits of New Zealand's investment in plant breeding and market development quickly spilled over to other countries—not least Italy and Chile, which are now the leading producers of kiwifruit.

Experiences of this sort have been irrelevant to entrepreneurial self-discovery in Ecuador's tropical fruit sector, mainly because consumers throughout the world were thoroughly familiar with bananas decades before the country became a major exporter. Also, multinational fruit companies headquartered in the United States determined long ago that their interests would be served by providing technology to Ecuadorian growers, who consequently have been spared the difficulties of appropriation faced by any country, firm, or individual that engages in research and development. Under these circumstances, entrepreneurs such as Luís Noboa have been able to specialize in winning customers for their countrymen's harvests. Their base of operations—the port city of Guayaquil—has been ideal for this endeavor.

Entrepreneurial Specialization in the Banana Industry

To understand the roles played by transnational firms, South American exporters, and other actors in the global banana business, it is useful to draw on a taxonomy of entrepreneurial innovations proposed by Joseph Schumpeter in the early 1900s. As he saw it, there are five ways that businessmen and women have an impact on the economy.

(1) The introduction of a new good—that is one with which consumers are not yet familiar—or of a new quality of a good. (2) The introduction of a new method of production, that is one not yet tested by experience in the branch of manufacture concerned, which need by no means be founded upon a discovery scientifically new, and can also exist in a new way of handling a commodity commercially. (3) The

opening of a new market, that is, a market into which the particular branch of manufacture of the country in question has not previously entered, whether or not this market has existed before. (4) The conquest of a new source of supply of raw materials or half-manufactured goods, again irrespective of whether this source already exists or whether it has first to be created. (5) The carrying out of the new organization of any industry, like the creation of a monopoly position (for example through trustification) or the breaking up of a monopoly position.[3]

Formulated well before Schumpeter´s migration to the United States, this five-part taxonomy was not illustrated with a case study about transnational fruit companies operating in the Western Hemisphere. Such a study would have been fitting, however. What those companies were doing more than one hundred years ago was, first, to acquaint U.S. consumers with bananas. Second, the vertically integrated firms founded by Lorenzo Baker, Minor Keith, Andrew Preston, Joseph Vaccaro, and Samuel Zemurray and much of the technology these firms pioneered represented a genuine departure from old methods of production in the banana business. Third, those same entrepreneurs, whose companies imported and distributed bananas in large quantities, created something that had never existed in the United States: a mass market for tropical fruit. Fourth, new sources of supply were developed, in Central America and elsewhere in the Caribbean Basin. Fifth, the banana business was reorganized, admittedly in a less competitive direction.

Once the tropical fruit industry had established itself, some of the five business innovations identified by Schumpeter figured much in its subsequent unfolding, although others did not. The first sort of innovation, for instance, was unimportant. True, the Gros Michel variety was replaced with Cavendish fruit, although the switch was prompted by the vulnerability of the former type of banana to Panama Disease and every effort was made to avoid changing either the appearance or the taste of the final product. Also, processing (aside from controlled ripening on board reefer ships and in storage facilities) has been a fairly unimportant part of the banana business, which is not the case with much of the food economy. Moreover, retail packaging today is indistinguishable from what it was in the past. Bananas have always been sold fresh and in the skins that nature provided them, adorned these days with nothing more than small stickers that advertise supplying firms and countries.

But while the introduction of novel goods ceased long ago for many intents and purposes in the tropical fruit industry, other innovations have been a recurring part of the business. Methods of production have changed substantially, largely because multinationals have supported much of the experimentation from which better agronomic practices and disease-resistant cultivars stem. For much of the twentieth century, the firms' willingness to finance research and development was a consequence of their dominance of leading markets, which enabled them to capture the benefits of technological advances not accruing to consumers.[4] In addition, Standard Fruit had a special motivation to improve technology. Opportunities for the company to establish new plantations after existing farms had been ravaged by Panama Disease were limited because so much territory had been snapped up previously by United Fruit. It is therefore unsurprising that Standard Fruit, not its larger rival, came up with the Cavendish variety, which could resist the soil-borne fungus.

To this day, U.S.-based multinationals invest in technological improvement, even though their standing in the banana industry is not what it used to be. One reason for this is that Chiquita Brands International (formerly United Fruit), the Dole Food Company (formerly Standard Fruit), as well as Del Monte Corporation (which has been in the banana business since its 1967 purchase of the West Indies Fruit Company) still handle a sizable share of the world's banana exports, and so can gain much from any supply-side advance. In particular, the adoption by independent planters of better cultivars and farming methods created by the multinationals still benefits Chiquita, Dole, and Del Monte, since these companies continue to deal regularly in fruit raised by those planters.

The ready availability of multinational technology in Ecuador, where independent growers predominate, reduces the need there for banana research and development. Spending on laboratories and test plots, salaries for scientists and technicians, and related expenditures are consequently avoided. In addition, "free-riding" growers, who hope to gain from the advances other farmers have paid for but whose reluctance to contribute financially can prevent those advances from materializing, would be a problem if foreign firms did not share their technology. Similarly, Ecuadorian exporters along with their counterparts in Colombia have been the long-term beneficiaries of United Fruit's popularization of bananas during the late 1800s and early 1900s—a marketing effort like New Zealand's popularization of kiwifruit and also involving appropriation issues.

Excused from having to undertake either the first or second business innovation identified by Schumpeter, Ecuadorian entrepreneurs have been able to concentrate on other innovations. Time and again, they have placed bananas in new markets. They also have entered a number of existing markets, thereby increasing competition. Exporters from the South American nation, which is smaller and poorer than Colombia to the north and Peru to the south, have been successful thanks largely to the business services and mutually-rewarding partnerships on offer in Guayaquil, which was a haven for international commerce generations before Noboa or any other Ecuadorian began selling bananas overseas. Since the mid-1900s, the country has maintained an edge over its competitors—including the Mesoamerican republics where United Fruit and Standard Fruit got their start.

Central Versus South America

Warm and humid, the Caribbean lowlands of Central America have always been an obvious place to grow tropical fruit for the United States, where demand was seemingly insatiable around the turn of the twentieth century and for many years afterward. Bananas from the region had been finding their way to New Orleans and other U.S. ports since the 1870s. Some of this fruit was harvested alongside the railroad Keith built in Costa Rica and more came from the Bay Islands of Honduras.[5] However, Central America's potential for banana production remained largely unexploited as the nineteenth century drew to a close, primarily because few rural laborers were willing to relocate from the temperate highland valleys where the region's population had long been concentrated to coastal settings that swarmed with disease-bearing insects.[6]

Multinationals dealt with labor shortages and other barriers to large-scale production as they established their own plantations, which were the core of company-controlled enclaves that had few linkages to the Central American economy. Some of the workers in northern Honduras, which during the early 1900s lacked a rail connection to the rest of the country, were from El Salvador, which was (and remains) more densely populated than its neighbors and is the only Mesoamerican nation with no Caribbean coastline. Also, many of Central America's bananas were harvested by West Indians who spoke English and were of African descent. Migration by this group into the highlands, which was proscribed by law in a number of countries,[7] was unappealing because the wages paid by foreign fruit companies far exceeded what other rural employers offered.

Sizable expenditures on the clearing and preparation of land and on infrastructure of every description were needed before tropical fruit could be produced and exported. Prior to these expenditures, investing firms demanded long-term concessions, which included grants of real estate as well as guarantees of minimal taxation. The handful of companies that received these concessions from public officials in San José, Tegucigalpa, and other capitals ended up with nearly all the best coastal land from Guatemala to Panama, which effectively preempted competition either on Central Americans' part or by outsiders.

Circumstances were not the same a century ago in South America. Whereas urban centers were lacking along the Caribbean coasts of Costa Rica, Nicaragua, Honduras, and Guatemala, there were cities of long standing in northern Colombia. Santa Marta, Ciénaga, and Barranquilla, within 100 kilometers of each other, were settled in the sixteenth century. Cartagena, a colonial stronghold built to prevent incursions by Spain's European adversaries and to discourage attacks by pirates, was a little farther down the coast, in the direction of Panama. In addition, sugar and other crops had been raised in northern Colombia for generations. In no sense, then, could the region be considered a *tabula rasa*, as Central America's eastern littoral was regarded in the late 1800s and early 1900s by the tropical fruit industry and even by national governments. Western Ecuador, which is bounded on the east by the Andes (the world's tallest mountains other than the Himalayas) and opens toward the Pacific Ocean, had agriculture and an urban population as well. Parts of the *costa*, as the area´s inhabitants and all their countrymen call it, have been farmed continuously for millennia. Also, Guayaquil, which was founded in 1538, was a commercial center decades before Baker, Preston, and Keith joined forces in 1899 to create United Fruit.

The *costa* was the first part of South America to export bananas, which had been brought to the New World by Spaniards following close on the heels of the conquistadors. However, Ecuadorian fruit traveled south, to Peru and Chile, instead of to the north. This trade, which was under way by 1877, grew modestly over the years and in 1908 a Chilean firm, the South American Fruit Company (SAFCO), opened an agency in Guayaquil to handle bananas and other tropical goods. None of the vessels plying the waters between Ecuador and Chile were refrigerated, so fruit was transported in small quantities as deck cargo. Banana exports amounted to $40,000 in 1915 and had risen to

$60,000 in 1933, with SAFCO consistently accounting for more of the busi-
ness than any other firm.[8] Tropical fruit comprised less than 1 percent of
Ecuador's total exports at the end of this period,[9] when United Fruit started
to invest in the country.

In Colombia, José Manuel González made an initial shipment of bananas
to the United States in 1889. However, this early venture failed because, as
Marcelo Bucheli notes, "the fruit rotted by the time it arrived in New York."
More rewarding was an enterprise launched shortly afterward by a pair of
Englishmen, Mansel Carr and Laurence Bradbury, who partnered with a
firm in New Orleans to deliver bananas regularly to the Crescent City. This
enterprise took off around the time Keith began buying farmland in South
America. His purchases were subsequently absorbed by United Fruit, as was
the Santa Marta Railway Company (originally a British-owned business and
Carr´s former employer). Like Keith's holdings in Central America, northeastern Colombia was thus drawn into the multinational´s orbit, where it
remained until World War II.[10]

Holland in the Tropics

With its fertile soils, abundant hydrologic resources, and direct access to
European ports and the southern and eastern coasts of the United States,
the Caribbean Basin has been the source of most of the bananas traded internationally since the late 1800s. But while Europe and the United States
are farther from the *costa*, the region is well suited to fruit production, more
so than many other parts of the Western Hemisphere. Northern Chile and
the entire Peruvian littoral, for example, are extremely dry. Arid conditions
result partly because the Andes impede the movement of moisture-laden
clouds out of the Amazon Basin, east of the mountains. Also, clouds that
form in and around the Humboldt Current, which has low temperatures
owing to its origins in the frigid seas near Tierra del Fuego and which flows
northward along the Pacific coast of South America, are thin as a rule and
therefore the source of little precipitation. For hundreds of kilometers along
the coast, the only green places are the narrow valleys of rivers careening
down from the nearby Andes.

A little north of Peru's boundary with Ecuador but still below the equator,
the Humboldt Current turns away from the continental mainland and heads
straight to the Galápagos Islands, 1,000 kilometers due west and the only

setting anywhere on the equator where the seawater is cool enough to suit penguins. The ocean is like a warm bath a little farther north and the resulting cloud formation is the source of torrential precipitation and lush vegetation in the surrounding region. In stark contrast to the deserts bordering the Pacific Ocean in Peru and northern Chile, rainforests formerly extended from northwestern Ecuador through western Colombia and into Central America. Patches of this ecosystem remain intact. Where Colombia and Panama meet, for example, impenetrable jungles and broken terrain combine to this day to block construction of the final segment of the Pan-American Highway, which otherwise runs the whole distance from Alaska to Patagonia.

Neither arid nor excessively wet, western Ecuador includes locations south of Guayaquil where precipitation falls short of bananas' water requirements, which are substantial. However, the southern *costa* is traversed by various rivers and streams flowing out of the Andes, so irrigation is fairly easy. Also, low clouds persist in the area during the dry season, which runs from May to December. As a result, solar radiation and the transpiration of moisture from plants are both limited, thereby reducing the need for irrigation. Geographer James J. Parsons highlighted these climatic advantages in an early description of Ecuador's tropical fruit industry.[11] A few years later, another geographer, David A. Preston, drew attention to an additional benefit of the dry conditions prevailing for half the year in the southern *costa*, which was that an airborne fungus called Yellow Sigatoka[12] (*Mycosphaerella musicola* Leach) moved slowly from field to field. Left unchecked, this pathogen manifests itself initially as spots on leaves, yet in short order reduces yields and causes the quality of fruit to deteriorate.[13]

According to Parsons, soils throughout western Ecuador are "good to excellent" and "perhaps as promising as any to be found within the rainy tropics of the New World."[14] Other observers provide more tempered assessments, emphasizing that soil properties vary. All experts agree that fertility levels are high on average, although problems such as excessive clay content and poor drainage are encountered in many settings.[15]

While the soils of western Ecuador may not be superior to soils in different parts of the Caribbean Basin, the *costa* enjoys geographic advantages of considerable importance. Since the region extends from one degree north of the equator to a few degrees south, bananas are harvested year round. Production peaks from September through March, which coincides with the time of year when demand is elevated in North America and Europe. This timing is advantageous for Ecuadorian growers because bananas cannot be warehoused for months on end, as is an option with apples, for instance.

The *costa* is also largely free of severe tropical storms, of the sort that hammer one part of the Caribbean Basin or another each and every year. Weather-related risks are correspondingly modest for the *costa*'s banana farmers. The significance of such risks in other places was put in sharp relief as growers in northeastern Colombia were making a sizable investment in order to convert from Gros Michel to Cavendish. In 1966, when this conversion was under way though not yet complete, a hurricane destroyed 45 percent of the banana crop. Another hurricane struck the following year, which reduced harvested area from 15,000 to 11,000 hectares.[16]

By no means are the *costa*'s environmental attributes valued only by Ecuadorian growers and exporters. So that Chiquita, Dole, and Del Monte can supply their customers with fresh produce regularly and without fail, the three companies purchase bananas in western Ecuador, especially when production falls short in other places. Doing business in the *costa* is a good way for any firm to cope with the disruptions in Central American and Caribbean supplies caused by hurricanes, which helps explain why multinationals have been willing to share technology with the region's growers.

While natural resources, the climate, and a location astride the equator all work in the *costa*'s favor, great obstacles formerly stood in the way of the region's agricultural development. Yellow fever, which is often fatal, was not brought under control until the second decade of the twentieth century, when critical assistance was provided by the Rockefeller Foundation and the U.S. Public Health Service.[17] Likewise, the Ecuadorian and U.S. governments launched an anti-malaria program in the late 1940s, which among other things involved disease monitoring and eradication of the anopheles mosquito.[18] As long as illnesses such as these were unchecked, there was untold human suffering. Also, agricultural activities that put large numbers of people in close proximity to one another, such as banana production, were impeded due to the risk of disease transmission.

Tropical illnesses were a problem that the *costa* shared with the Caribbean Basin. However, the region had an additional disadvantage owing to its location. Before the Panama Canal existed and especially before completion of the railroad traversing the Panamanian Isthmus, a long and arduous voyage was needed to reach New York, Hamburg, and other places where Ecuadorian goods could be sold. Setting out from Guayaquil, a ship would first beat its way south against the Humboldt Current. Once off the coast of southern

Chile, a sharp look-out had to be kept through the fog and mists that shroud the region's fjords and mountains for the Strait of Magellan, since missing this passage would necessitate a perilous detour around Cape Horn through heavy seas and gale-force winds. Leaving the Pacific Ocean in its wake and veering north, the ship then had to travel nearly the entire length of the Atlantic before reaching the world's leading markets.

In spite of mortal diseases and the great distances that separated western Ecuador from its most important customers, the agricultural potential of the region was extolled long before the turn of the twentieth century, including by foreign visitors. On taking up his post as French vice consul in Guayaquil, Charles Wiener was struck in 1879 by the commercial hustle and bustle of his new home as well as the flat, fertile ground surrounding the port city. Indeed, the diplomat was impressed enough to make comparisons with The Netherlands,[19] a nation that coincidentally is not much larger than the valley drained by the river emptying into the Pacific a little south of Guayaquil. Pleased with Wiener's description, the *costa*'s inhabitants have called the Río Guayas watershed *una Holanda tropical* ever since.

Tropical Burghers

While the comparison Charles Wiener made 135 years ago between the *costa* and The Netherlands had much to do with farmland and its productivity, Guayaquileños were particularly flattered by the suggestion that their city resembled a Dutch port, complete with its population of active merchants. It must be remembered, however, that economic progress does not result automatically whenever entrepreneurs—Dutch, Ecuadorian, or otherwise—exert themselves. As economist William J. Baumol stresses in what he modestly calls "a minor expansion of Schumpeter's theoretical model," business activities are often productive, in the specific sense of falling into one or more of Schumpeter's five categories. However, there are other activities that Schumpeter did not address and which Baumol characterizes as unproductive or, worse yet, destructive. Contributing nothing to overall growth and development, unproductive entrepreneurship is exemplified by the "discovery of a previously unused legal gambit" that only creates rents (as economists call the gains resulting from unproductive pursuits) for individuals and firms able to exploit the gambit. Destructive entrepreneurship, including organized crime, directly harms people and their legitimate livelihoods, so is nothing less than "parasitical."[20]

Baumol extends Schumpeter's analysis primarily with an eye toward addressing issues of public policy—for example, the ways taxes or legal rules strengthen or weaken incentives for businessmen and women to choose productive activities over unproductive or destructive alternatives. But as the same economist recognizes, these choices have multiple determinants, including geographic and historical realities of the kind that underlie the predominance of productive entrepreneurship in Guayaquil.

These realities are best understood by considering the long-term isolation of the port city from seats of governmental authority—isolation that did not truly end until many years after Vice Consul Wiener's arrival in western Ecuador. During the colonial era, the Spanish viceroy held court in Lima, far to the south. For nearly a century after Ecuador achieved independence, a grueling ascent into the Andes on foot or perhaps on horseback was required to reach the national capital. Before a rail line into the mountains was constructed, in the early 1900s, the authorities in Quito were unable to interfere much with foreign trade and other varieties of commerce in the *costa*. At the same time, the trouble and expense of reaching the capital city from Guayaquil limited the appeal of trying to win favors from representatives of government.

As unrewarding as unproductive (or destructive) pursuits were, the port city's entrepreneurs have been productively inclined, routinely putting their talents to use in the wider commercial world. They have sometimes introduced foreign buyers to Ecuadorian products previously unknown outside the country. Far more often, they have opened new markets for goods that Ecuador produces efficiently. Entrepreneurs from the western part of the country even have reorganized global markets in a few instances, always toward greater competition.

For nearly 300 years beginning in the sixteenth century, Guayaquil was the leading ship-building center on the Pacific coast, from Cape Horn to the Bering Strait, and vessels constructed in and around the city were reputed to be made of the "strongest and best" timber in the world.[21] In the mid-1800s, entrepreneurs from the *costa* organized the production of tightly woven straw hats, which they sold to gold miners crossing the Panamanian Isthmus on their way to California. These Forty-Niners, who risked exposure to tropical diseases to avoid trekking all the way across North America, mistook the origin of their purchases. Hence, the name they gave their new headgear, Panama hats, is still used today, more than 160 years later.[22] Guayaquil's merchants played a key role in the cacao boom of the late 1800s and early

1900s.[23] More recently, Ecuadorian entrepreneurs have exported shrimp and cut flowers. Local businessmen and women also have worked hard to make their country a favored destination for international tourists.

As one commercial opportunity overseas has been exploited, then another, and so on, business services that the *costa* formerly lacked have been introduced. For example, Juan F. Marcos built up a sizable enterprise around the turn of the twentieth century dedicated to the management of cacao estates. His approach to client recruitment was simple. An estate owner would be asked how much he or she expected to earn on his or her own, without any specialized assistance. Provided the response to this inquiry was realistic and less than 40,000 sucres per annum, which is worth about $300,000 in today's money, Marcos would then offer to administer the property, receiving half the income in excess of the figure the owner had named and nothing else.[24] This arrangement was accepted nearly every time it was proposed and, with the profits Marcos made, he founded the Sociedad General: a diversified firm that possessed a commercial bank, an insurance company (responding to a strong demand in Guayaquil, with its prevalence of flammable, wooden structures), as well as the huge El Guasmo hacienda on the outskirts of the city and several other rural properties.[25]

Marcos had a son, Juan X. Marcos, whose encounter with governmental authority at a tender age did little to encourage political engagement on his part, as would have been necessary for a career in rent-seeking. During violent clashes between opposing political parties in 1910, the privileged son of the founder of the Sociedad General had rushed outside the family home in central Guayaquil to investigate the commotion for himself. Nine years old at the time, he was punished for his curiosity with a sharp blow to the forehead, administered by a member of the armed forces. This left the younger Marcos with a permanent scar and, one must suppose, a lasting wariness of the rough and tumble of Ecuadorian politics. After expressing a desire at an early age to study medicine, he decided to join the family business instead.

As partners at the Sociedad General, the Marcoses offered business services in support of overseas trade, including export financing and insurance as well as the brokering of cargo space on oceangoing vessels. The Sociedad General also became the local agent for shipping companies such as Cunard White Star Line and Holland America. Simultaneously, the firm engaged in international trade on its own, exporting rice for example.

From Humble Beginnings

Many of Guayaquil's entrepreneurs were from the *costa*'s leading families. This was true of the Marcoses, for instance, who could trace their ancestry to colonial times. However, Noboa's employment at the Sociedad General and his subsequent rise into the commercial elite demonstrate that upward economic mobility was possible in the *costa*. The same can be said of northeastern Colombia. For example, Pepe Vives, a leading exporter of bananas from the region during the 1950s, was not "a member of any of the traditional, powerful families in the region and (was) without formal education." Regardless, he was able to amass "a fortune with his own commercial, financial, and manufacturing businesses."[26] In no sense is the *costa* or northeastern Colombia egalitarian. However, the barriers to advancement are much worse in places where a land-holding gentry is in complete control, as was true in highland Ecuador well into the twentieth century. Where commerce dominates, as it does in downtown Guayaquil, lofty material aspirations are not completely unrealistic for someone with talent who is willing to work hard.

Even in rural areas, the banana business has provided opportunities for individuals whose origins were modest. One such individual was Manuel Amable-Calle, who was born in 1893 to a rural washerwoman and began his business career when he was all of ten years old. Fashioning a raft by lashing together a few pieces of wood, Amable-Calle ferried people and their goods across the Río Jubones, south of Guayaquil and not too far from Ecuador's border with Peru. By 1920, he was able to purchase fertile land on the southern shore of the river, where he produced food for the Guayaquil market.[27] A decade later, Amable-Calle was a shopkeeper and the leading resident of El Pasaje, up the Río Jubones from the coastal city of Machala. Around that time, SAFCO representatives persuaded him to raise bananas for export. Soon afterward, he planted the Gros Michel variety on his farm and convinced other growers in the area to do the same. By the late 1930s, his own harvests combined with his purchases of neighbors' output were sizable enough for him to make weekly deliveries to the Chilean firm's ships anchored in the river by Guayaquil.[28]

In July 1941, the Peruvian army invaded southern Ecuador, doing much damage in El Pasaje and a number of other towns and cities. Amable-Calle and his family had no choice other than to abandon their farm and flee. Returning home in January 1942, Amable-Calle replanted and, because bananas from his farm could be floated down to Machala in small boats, he was producing fruit again for overseas markets within six months, at which time banana exports were grinding to a halt because of World War II.[29]

After the global conflict, few people in the Ecuadorian countryside seized opportunities in the banana business better than Esteban Quirola, who was born in 1924 and spent his early years on a small farm on the banks of the Río Jubones. After working part-time on the farm and in a local shop before he was a teenager, Quirola moved at fourteen to Guayaquil, where an older brother with a small grocery employed him. Every day before school, he rose early, went to the central market, bargained with farmers over the produce they had brought to the port city to sell, and took his purchases on the street-car to his brother's store. The commercial skills gained from this experience were further honed after Quirola joined the Ecuadorian army in 1944 and served his eighty-man detachment as a purchasing agent. After completing his military service in late 1945, Quirola rented a small cacao farm near his birthplace. He plowed all his earnings into real estate and, within a few years, started raising bananas. Totaling twenty-five to thirty hectares in 1950, Quirola's holdings dedicated to fruit production increased at a fast pace.[30] Ten years later, he was one of the leading landowners in the southern *costa*, with thousands of hectares planted to bananas.

Of all the South Americans who have prospered in the banana business, none had a more difficult start in life than Segundo Wong, who was born in Guayaquil in 1929 to an Ecuadorian woman who had married a Chinese immigrant. Wong's father disappeared when the future *bananero* was fifteen; the elder Wong either died or left the port city—no one seems to know for sure. Wong's mother passed away soon afterward, which left him to care for himself as well as several younger siblings. After scrambling for jobs in the port city, Wong found employment with a cattle rancher, which enabled him to learn about rural enterprises. He went on to trade bananas on a small scale, buying fruit from farmers and selling to exporters in Guayaquil. Wong subsequently found work with a banana planter in Quevedo who was also named Segundo Wong but was not a relative. Given the coincidence of a shared name, the planter delegated a number of business-related tasks to his employee, who not only gained knowledge about banana production but ended up buying his boss's entire operation.[31]

Wong would go on to become one of the *costa*'s leading growers, nearly on a par with Quirola. He also became a successful exporter, with accomplishments in overseas markets rivaling those of Noboa.

A Tycoon's Early Years

If Wong's beginnings in life were less auspicious than those of other leading *bananeros* in Latin America, Noboa took the longest path from humble
origins to success in the tropical fruit business. The future entrepreneur was
eight years old in 1924, when his father received a fatal kick from a horse. His
mother, Zoila Naranjo de Noboa, was pregnant at the time and living with her
three sons in northern Chile, where she had migrated with her husband a few
years earlier. Aside from three gold sovereigns, worth about $150 apiece, the
young widow had nothing to her name.[32]

Selling a few household effects, Noboa's mother scraped together passage
for her offspring and herself back to Guayaquil, where one of her husband's
elderly relatives provided modest quarters on the city's outskirts. Less than
four months after losing her husband, Zoila Naranjo de Noboa delivered her
last child and only daughter. She also sold one of her three gold coins and
used the proceeds to start a small business, thereby providing an early tuto-
rial in entrepreneurship to her sons. The business consisted of selling milk by
the serving throughout Guayaquil and required a modest investment in containers, purchases from neighboring dairies, and recruitment of local boys to
serve as a sales force. Any merchandise left at the end of the day was mixed
with eggs and rum to make *rompope*, which was hawked along with rolls
made from wheat and yucca flour.[33]

Out of a desire to help support his family, Noboa decided at eleven to leave
school after just three years with the Salesian Fathers. "One day," he vowed as
he presented his mother with the first sucres he had earned, "I will be a rich
man and will bring you lots of presents." After starting out selling magazines
on the streets of Guayaquil and even on trains running up to Quito, Noboa
consistently engaged in a diverse array of ventures. One was a sidewalk stand,
named "Basantes" after its former proprietor, where he and a partner named
Modesto Rivadeneira shined shoes and sold magazines and sundry items.
The two boys figured out that premium prices could be charged after six in
the evening, when other street vendors went home.[34] Learning the value of
long hours on the job, they each cleared 100 sucres (equivalent to $225 today)
a month at a time when the prevailing daily wage for adult laborers was little
more than one sucre. Noboa also sold cloths for polishing metal, which led to
his job at the Sociedad General as well as lifelong business associations and
personal friendships with Juan F. and Juan X. Marcos.[35]

Fully appreciative of Noboa's talents and capabilities, the Marcoses were wise enough to give him free rein. For example, Noboa was allowed to continue running his own businesses, including a small office in central Guayaquil where he traded currency and sold souvenirs and Parker Pens starting in 1933. Six months after joining the bank, the former street vendor asked the younger Marcos for a loan of 3,000 sucres ($6,750 in today's money), promising "you'll have your money back in three months and a profit of 3,000 sucres." The loan was made and Noboa delivered on his promise in full. He also asked for a follow-up loan under the same terms. When a third loan was requested—for 10,000 sucres ($22,500)—Marcos could no longer contain his curiosity and asked what was being done with the money. Only then did he find out that the thirteen-year-old had been trading in the auction room of the customs house.[36]

Just as the proprietors of the Sociedad General did not hold Noboa back from buying and selling on his own, the budding entrepreneur was not prevented from associating with other businessmen. His personal office was close to the Banco La Previsora, a leading financial institution managed by Victor Emilio Estrada. "This young man is worth his weight in gold," concluded the banker, who not only befriended the teenager but offered him a job as assistant manager. Noboa did not accept the position, although he became Estrada's partner in a company engaged in importing and in representing foreign firms, including Chrysler and Coca Cola. Before he turned eighteen, Noboa was managing the company, in which he held a one-third equity stake. Renamed Comandato S.A. after a few years, it is still in business.[37]

Aside from being a superb commercial operator in his own right, Noboa benefited substantially from his partnerships. In this, he had something in common with entrepreneurs who had preceded him in the banana business. Zemurray, for example, got an early boost thanks to associations with other merchants in Mobile as well as financial backing from United Fruit. By the same token, Latin American entrepreneurs who followed Noboa flourished in large part because of their partnerships. A case in point was Vives, who did well as an exporter by working with Francisco Dávila—someone who provided "a touch of sophistication" reflecting his undergraduate studies in France and the MBA he had earned at Stanford University.[38]

The Right Place, the Right Entrepreneurs

In a book about the Ecuadorian operations of United Fruit, Steve Striffler has little to say about the *costa*'s capitalists, other than to chronicle their disputes with *campesinos* and workers. He draws no distinctions between commercial farmers, some of whom operate on a large scale while others do not, and individuals engaged in overseas marketing and other non-agricultural pursuits. Nor is he concerned with entrepreneurial innovation and the various forms it takes. His commentary on capitalists largely echoes the convictions of a rural laborer named Patricio, whom Striffler quotes often. Firmly maintaining that workers such as he "produce the bananas," Patricio complains that farm owners, local intermediaries, and multinationals do little or nothing for the money coming their way.[39]

Alberto Acosta, author of a widely read economic history of Ecuador, does not endorse the view that capitalists merely appropriate the wealth their employees are solely responsible for creating, as adherents of an ideological perspective at least a quarter century past its expiration date would have it. Rather, he finds fault with the country's businessmen and women for lacking entrepreneurial verve. According to Acosta, this shortcoming has held Ecuador back—especially during the Great Depression, but also at other times.[40]

As a rule, the apparent defects of entrepreneurs are a weak explanation for disappointing economic performance, when and where it occurs. Along with other economists, Baumol emphasizes that firms and individuals can be counted on to seize opportunities for profit that come their way. If they are not venturing into new markets, for example, then the rewards for doing so must be weak.[41] Such has been the case at times in Ecuador, not to mention other Latin American nations, and Acosta undoubtedly would have arrived at better insights by examining economic incentives more and speculating less about the people responding to those incentives.

If businessmen and women in Ecuador really have been indolent and if the 1930s were an inauspicious time for entrepreneurship, no one seems to have told Marcos, Noboa, and others like them. Based in a port city that for centuries was remote both from its most important markets and from political capitals, these individuals never acquired the habits of rent-seeking and other unproductive pursuits. Instead, Guayaquil's entrepreneurs have specialized productively, seeking out and serving customers overseas.

Cities with a long tradition of productive entrepreneurship are rare in the banana-growing regions of the Western Hemisphere. There were no such settlements along the Caribbean coast of Central America when United Fruit and Standard Fruit started operating in the region. In addition, Guayaquil differed from cities along Colombia´s Caribbean coast. According to Bucheli, Cartagena, which well into the nineteenth century was a slave-importing terminal, was not a place to cut one's teeth in foreign trade. The area to the northeast, the same author adds, was "stagnant or decaying prior to the banana export industry," and Santa Marta languished between the wars of independence, during which it was a pro-Spanish bastion, and the turn of the twentieth century, when United Fruit´s arrival put an end to the city's "state of abandonment."[42]

One by one, the geographic and environmental impediments to economic progress have been overcome in western Ecuador. Yellow fever and other illnesses no longer prevent large numbers of workers from gathering in the same place, as happens routinely on banana farms. Notwithstanding the tolls charged for use of the Panama Canal, which producers in the Caribbean Basin need not reckon with, the waterway constructed under budget and ahead of schedule by the U.S. Army Corps of Engineers has been an enormous boon to Ecuador since it provides a direct route to markets bordering the Atlantic Ocean.

Once obstacles to development were removed, the commercial strengths and orientation of Guayaquil could be brought into play in the banana trade. Finance and other business services, which entrepreneurs in the port city began to provide during the cacao boom, did not disappear once the boom was over. To the contrary, "a financial infrastructure easily adapted to support banana exports as well as individuals with experience in the production and export of agricultural products" was in place,[43] which made international commerce much easier. Without local brokers adept at arranging transoceanic shipping, each and every aspiring banana exporter would have needed refrigerated vessels of his or her own. The expense of these vessels undoubtedly would have kept many out of the business.

Guayaquil's vocation for commerce has worked to the advantage of the surrounding region, the country as a whole, and even foreign customers of Ecuadorian products. Perhaps limited economic development during the centuries when the *costa* was remote and insalubrious was the price to be paid for the acquisition in the city of the habits of productive entrepreneurship. If so, sacrifices in the past have resulted in sizable dividends. Represented by individuals such as Noboa, Ecuador has been the world's leading exporter of tropical fruit since the 1950s, without ever being a corporate dependency.

CHAPTER 3

Never a Banana Republic

As large and as diverse as Colombia is, its candidacy for the ranks of banana republics was never promising. United Fruit might have been unrivaled in the northeastern part of the country during the first four decades of the twentieth century. However, the company exercised much less influence hundreds of kilometers away in Bogotá, especially compared to what it wielded in various Central American capitals. South of Colombia, Ecuador is smaller and less developed, a place where a foreign firm might seize and hold the commanding heights of the national economy and from time to time act as a political kingmaker. Yet the country never has experienced this kind of subservience, which has been examined from various scholarly perspectives.

Although he offers no specific observations about banana republics, economist Andrés Rodríguez-Clare has analyzed the multiple outcomes that can happen if an impoverished nation hosts a company from an affluent part of the world. Investment occurs and technology is introduced, to be sure. However, sizable gains for the host country are not guaranteed. It is possible, for instance, for the multinational to decide that its interests are best served by employing unskilled labor and little else from the local economy to produce "simple final goods," such as a number of farm products. Even if more complex ventures are undertaken, inexpensive communications with headquarters far away might deter the firm from building up factors of production that are locally scarce, including the human capital needed for management and marketing. If so, overall economic progress in the host country may well disappoint.[1]

Observations along these lines do not necessarily apply to the tropical fruit business. The operations Chiquita, Dole, and Del Monte have in Central America are intensively administered and most managerial jobs are held by local people. These people are as capable as their counterparts in places like the United States. Moreover, their familiarity with on-the-ground realities, commercial and otherwise, is often of great value and can be hard for foreigners to acquire. Transnational companies know that bringing in an expatriate usually makes less sense than recruiting a talented individual from the host country and training him or her as needed, which is why the local workforces of those companies do not consist only of unskilled laborers. Of course, local hiring is the norm for Latin American firms doing business in their respective nations.

Rodríguez-Clare's analysis, which does not address foreigners' possession of land, stands apart from the arguments of many authors who focus on the prolonged control of vital natural resources by multinationals in places like Central America. Writing about Honduras, for example, John Soluri contends that this control has had lasting and adverse effects.[2] Similar effects are possible today in Sub-Saharan Africa, where an indeterminate number of large rural holdings now belong to Middle Easterners and other outsiders.[3]

In the tropical fruit sector, resource ownership has been consequential not only for exporting nations such as Honduras. For decades, United Fruit safeguarded its control of the banana industry as a whole by locking up much of the best agricultural land in the Caribbean Basin. This dominant position traced back to Minor Keith's acquisitions of Central American real estate during the 1800s and lasted through the 1960s, when United Fruit still exported a large share of the region's bananas and grew much of the fruit it shipped overseas on its own plantations.[4] In northeastern Colombia, corporate control of farmland and its produce took a form other than outright ownership. As explained in this chapter, United Fruit monopolized exports from the region by the way it structured production contracts with local growers.

This monopoly broke down during World War II, when North America and Europe halted imports of tropical fruit, and could not be reestablished after hostilities ended and normal commerce resumed. In western Ecuador, no foreign company ever replicated either the huge plantations and land reserves of Central America or production contracts of the sort used to suppress competition in northeastern Colombia. Additionally, Ecuadorian entrepreneurs have engaged in international marketing since the early days of their country's banana boom, thereby preventing foreign monopolization of exports.

Making sure that their country would never become a banana republic, the authorities in Quito imposed restrictions on United Fruit in the late

1930s. However, it would be a mistake to infer from these restrictions that Ecuadorian opposition to foreign investment in the tropical fruit sector was ever categorical or unanimous. To the contrary, many national leaders pursued that investment assiduously, no less than foreign companies once tried hard for grants of land throughout the Caribbean Basin.

Ecuador Woos *El Pulpo*

The campaign to interest transnational fruit companies in Ecuador began in the early 1920s, when the cacao business was suffering a sharp decline. Output contracted because of a pair of fungal diseases: Witches' Broom, caused by *Crinipellis perniciosa*, and Frosty (or Monilia) Pod Rot, caused by *Moniliophthora roreri*.[5] Simultaneously, the prices Ecuadorian growers received for their diminished harvests fell because of increased cacao production elsewhere in the Western Hemisphere as well as in Africa.[6]

United Fruit would not have been able to establish new operations in Ecuador or anywhere else a few years earlier because a large segment of the company's maritime fleet (the most sizable collection of vessels at the time in the United States aside from the U.S. Navy) had been requisitioned during World War I to carry troops and supplies to Europe. But with its ships returned after the Armistice of November 1918, United Fruit could consider an expansion of its business—including south of the Panama Canal, which had been completed in 1914.

The company had ample motivation for such an expansion. Panama Disease, which was a constant menace in the Caribbean Basin, had yet to make an appearance in Ecuador during the 1920s and would not do so for several more years.[7] Also, the rarity of tropical storms in the *costa* was an important consideration because Gros Michel plants, which would not be replaced for another four decades, were tall with shallow roots and therefore were easily blown over—particularly right before stems of fruit weighing forty kilograms or more had been cut. Before the switch to the Cavendish variety in the Caribbean Basin, up to one-third of the banana harvest was destroyed every year because of hurricanes.[8] Yet another attraction of western Ecuador was that prevailing wages were low, no higher than compensation levels in other banana-growing regions.

One person who understood that United Fruit might be attracted to Ecuador and that this would be beneficial for the country was José Luís Tamayo, an attorney and self-made businessmen from Guayaquil whose most significant achievement in the private sector was to serve as legal counsel and a member of the board of directors for the Banco Comercial y Agrícola (BCA). Created to serve the cacao sector, the BCA played a pivotal role in the national economy—not least because it had been given the authority in 1915 to print the currency it lent to the national government, which lacked a monetary authority of its own and which became more indebted to the bank as the years passed.

Elected to a four-year presidential term in 1920, Tamayo assigned J. Cicerón Castillo, who at the time was managing an oil field west of Guayaquil, the task of convincing United Fruit to buy land in the *costa*, provide shipping, and introduce better technology for banana production. In February 1922, a letter written by Castillo reached Victor M. Cutter, the acting vice president of the multinational. In response to this letter, which stressed the advantages for United Fruit of growing bananas in Ecuador for shipment to California, Cutter provided a list of fifty-one questions for Castillo to answer so that the company could decide about sending down one of its technical specialists to carry out a definitive evaluation.[9]

Castillo responded in short order with a thorough report, one based on wide-ranging observations in the field and reaching the conclusion that western Ecuador was "ideal" for banana production. Guayaquil's deficiencies for modern shipping were acknowledged. For one thing, the Río Guayas was barely seven meters deep in front of the port city. For another, a sandbar between the river's mouth and Guayaquil blocked the passage at low tide of vessels displacing more than 4,000 tons. In contrast, Castillo sang the praises of Puerto Bolívar, farther south and in the vicinity of Machala. A natural harbor able to accommodate ships of any size, Puerto Bolívar also had road and rail linkages to inland areas well suited to agriculture.[10]

Castillo emphasized land quality—in particular, the depth and fertility of soils in the southern *costa* as well as their porosity, which facilitates the thorough drainage that banana plants require. Precipitation in the area was reported to be in line with the hydrologic requirements of fruit production for most of the year; at other times, water for irrigation was readily available from rivers and streams originating in the Andes, not too far from the coast. Finally, banana plants in Ecuador, which were used to shade cacao trees in addition to supplying food, exhibited no signs of wind damage, which was a normal feature of Central American and Caribbean plantations.[11]

Thanking Castillo for his "very excellent report," Cutter dispatched one

of United Fruit's ablest experts, Charles W. Sinners, to inspect land, irrigation possibilities, navigable rivers, and coastal harbors. Sinners was also in-
structed to determine needs for railroad construction and to gauge real estate
prices. Discretion was required since revealing the true purpose of this work
would have caused the owners of farmland, which had lost value because of
plant diseases and low cacao prices, to demand more for their properties.
So as long as he was able, Sinners let people think he was mainly interested
in untapped deposits of petroleum, which along with all other subsurface
resources would belong to the state and not to individuals with surface land
rights. This subterfuge was maintained for a while because he traveled with
Castillo, who was mainly known as a mining engineer and geologist.

The report Sinners submitted in 1922 was enthusiastic and United Fruit's
headquarters in Boston cabled him to remain in Guayaquil, to await orders
about how to proceed. After those orders arrived, Sinners journeyed to
Quito in August for a meeting with Tamayo.[12] During that meeting, Sinners
was shown a draft of a law authorizing creation of banana concessions. Steve
Striffler speculates that the law, enacted later in 1922, was perhaps "generated" by United Fruit, although he offers no evidence to support his suspicions.[13] In fact, the law was unexceptional in many respects. For example,
access was guaranteed to harbors suitable for oceangoing ships. Also, private
investors were authorized to construct railroads and other infrastructure.
In addition, the law included a two-year exemption from export duties,
which was not overly generous given the monetary outlay needed to ramp
up operations.

The duties to be applied after the exemption expired were not out of line
with export taxes during the 1920s in Central America, although Striffler's
characterization of those duties as "very low" is not off base. He also states
that "virtually unlimited quantities of land" were made available in Ecuador.[14] What Striffler does not mention, though, is that all the areas offered by
Tamayo were undeveloped and none were within reach of Guayaquil, Puerto
Bolívar, or any other seaport. Such areas appealed little to United Fruit, which
had its sights set on properties in accessible settings that had been cleared
during the cacao boom. That Tamayo's offer to the company did not extend
to these properties, more than four-fifths of which were in the hands of Ecuadorians,[15] revealed that national authorities actively pursuing foreign investment would only go so far, even as the country's leading export sector was
reeling. Since there would be no official intervention in real estate markets on
United Fruit's behalf, the banana sector would never develop in Ecuador as it

had earlier in Central America—in enclaves obtained for little or no money by foreign companies.

Denied in Ecuador the opportunities it had seized in countries such as Guatemala and Honduras, United Fruit maintained a presence in the South American nation by signing an agreement with the government in July 1923 to continue preparing for the production and export of tropical fruit.[16] This work went forward at a leisurely pace.

Prolonged Crisis

Had United Fruit moved quickly in Ecuador soon after the investigations and discussions of 1922, Tamayo might have been lauded as one of the country's greatest leaders: the head-of-state who spearheaded an expeditious and rewarding transition from the cacao era to the banana boom.

By no means was a transition along these lines beyond the realm of possibilities. U.S. imports of bananas, which were much higher after World War I than they had been at the turn of the twentieth century, continued to go up during the 1920s. At the same time, United Fruit and other producers were having difficulties in Central America, as already noted. Ecuador's currency was losing value; worth forty-four cents in 1920, the sucre was equivalent to twenty-three cents five years later.[17] However, this devaluation improved the country's competitiveness in international markets, to the benefit of the fruit industry and other sectors with tradable output. In addition, the need to purchase land, rather than receiving real estate free from the government, was not an insurmountable obstacle given that United Fruit would end up buying old cacao farms in the southern *costa* in 1934—a decade after Tamayo had left office and, more to the point, at a time when the U.S. market for bananas was weak due to the Great Depression.

The chances for what might have been Tamayo's crowning accomplishment, not to mention a watershed moment in the economic history of Ecuador, were not improved by the waning influence of the venturesome businessmen who had founded United Fruit. Neither Lorenzo Baker (born in 1840) nor Minor Keith (born in 1848) was as active in the company as he once had been, and Andrew Preston (born in 1846) passed away in September 1924. The following month, the same executive who had corresponded with Castillo and had sent Sinners to Ecuador became president of United Fruit, in spite of minimal time spent in the tropics. For the next several years, the firm was run out of its Boston headquarters by Cutter and other men whose understanding of the production end of the business was second-hand for the most part. Their lack of direct experience helps to explain why earnings stagnated and then declined after peaking at 44.6 million dollars in 1920,[18] and why opportunities in Ecuador were passed up when they first presented themselves.

Political tensions, which rendered Ecuador unattractive to investors and worsened as the national economy deteriorated, also undermined Tamayo's initiative. Tax receipts, which consisted primarily of tariffs on trade, diminished as cacao exports declined. Regardless, public expenditures were not cut significantly.[19] To cover the difference between spending and tax revenues, the government borrowed more from the BCA, which in turn issued more currency. This monetary expansion had the normal result, which was to accelerate inflation. Rising prices, especially for food, helped spark civil unrest, including a general strike in Guayaquil that the military suppressed in November 1922 with more than 300 lives lost.[20]

Tamayo was able to complete his four-year term. Forgoing the pension that he was entitled to, he returned to Guayaquil, where he was respected enough to win local office in 1940. Tamayo was honored two years later as the port city's outstanding citizen, thanks to his steadfast public service and his refusal to accept a salary. However, his successor as president, Gonzalo Córdova, fared poorly, holding onto office for less than a year. In July 1925, military officers with strong backing in Quito forced their way to power.[21] They blamed Ecuador's economic difficulties on the BCA, which soon went out of business because the government reneged on its debts and confiscated all banks' metallic reserves.[22] After a brief detention, the BCA's director fled to Chile. Other business leaders and a number of political figures also left Ecuador for a few years during this tumultuous period.

The closure of the BCA left Ecuador with no agency for administering the supply of money, which crippled the financial sector. In 1926, Edwin Kemmerer, an economics professor at Princeton University who previously had advised other Latin American governments on banking and monetary matters,[23] was brought to Quito together with a supporting group of experts. Based on the recommendations of Kemmerer and his colleagues, a central bank was established and the gold standard was adopted in 1927. Warning against expecting quick results from these and other measures, Kemmerer emphasized that they were really the first in a long series of reforms needed to revive the economy of Ecuador,[24] which during the 1920s had one of the worst credit ratings in the Western Hemisphere.

In fact, fiscal discipline was not maintained and the gold standard was honored in the breach. Reluctant to cut employment or levels of compensation in the public sector, Ecuador's new leaders also constructed roads and other infrastructure. Just as had happened in the past, spending consistently ran ahead of tax revenues. One effort to close the fiscal gap involved the appointment of William F. Roddy, who had been a member of Kemmerer's team, to administer the customs service. Given a mandate to reduce corruption and enhance government revenues, Roddy took his assignment seriously and was largely successful. Not coincidentally, he also became hugely unpopular, especially among importers and exporters, so his tenure was brief.[25] Once the meddlesome foreigner had been shown the door, business-as-usual returned in Guayaquil and other ports and tariff collections fell back to customary levels. Old habits of monetary management made a comeback as well, with the central bank printing money not in proportion to its metallic reserves, but rather on the basis of its holdings of government bonds—exactly as the BCA had done before the July 1925 coup d'état. The impact of monetary expansion was the same: ruinous inflation.[26]

Macroeconomic conditions in Ecuador worsened once the United States and other leading nations tightened monetary policy and raised barriers to trade after the October 1929 crash of the U.S. stock market. The collapse of international commerce brought on by protectionism largely explains why the Great Depression was so long and severe. As happened throughout the world, Ecuadorian exports declined precipitously, from fifteen million dollars in 1928 to a little over four million dollars in 1933, which among other things resulted in a dwindling of metallic reserves in the central bank.[27] The country went off the gold standard officially in 1931, by which time currency was being issued with abandon because of chronic fiscal deficits. The ensuing inflation and high unemployment fueled political instability, which manifested itself frequently as angry demonstrations and military takeovers. During the 1930s, the Ecuadorian presidency changed hands fourteen times, never because of an orderly succession from one elected head-of-state to another.

United Fruit Acquires Ecuadorian Real Estate

Even though United Fruit proceeded slowly after Tamayo left office and especially after the 1925 coup, Ecuador's capacity to supply the United States with bananas was not forgotten. Of particular interest to the company was

an old cacao estate named El Tenguel, which took in nearly 45,000 hectares a
little north of Machala. Rumors that Sinners might be negotiating on United
Fruit's behalf for the property had reached the U.S. consulate in Guayaquil
in December 1924. The company, however, was not yet ready to put money
down for farms in Ecuador, so El Tenguel, which had been mortgaged several
years earlier, was foreclosed in 1926.[28]

Three years later, in 1929, a U.S. businessman, Clarence L. Chester, began
pursuing an exclusive license to ship Ecuadorian bananas to the United States
for the Pacific Fruit Company, which he served as vice president. Chester
promised growers higher prices in order to win them away from SAFCO—
the Chilean company that had been the leading exporter of bananas harvested in the *costa* since the early 1900s. However, a bill in the Ecuadorian
Congress to grant Pacific Fruit a monopoly on exports to the United States
was defeated after the revelation that a legislator who had sponsored the bill
was also a member of the firm's board of directors. Chester left Ecuador for
good in 1933, when his employer went out of business.[29]

Just at this time, the country's banana sector was beginning to stir, in spite
of the Great Depression. The U.S. consul in Guayaquil, Harold B. Quarton,
reported in April 1933 that Ecuadorian merchants intended to sell 350,000
stems overseas in 1934—a projected increase of more than 50 percent in just
one year. Neither Quarton nor anyone else doubted that millions of stems
could be produced annually in the *costa*, although he was skeptical about the
projected increase in exports owing to the region's poor infrastructure.[30]

Roads, bridges, and rail lines did not get much better during the next few
years, although maritime linkages with North America improved markedly.
Grace Steamship Lines, which began transporting Ecuadorian cacao and coffee to New York in 1879, had offered the fastest service to the eastern United
States since 1893, when the company's fleet switched to steam power. Beginning in 1934, all the company's ships docking in Guayaquil had refrigerated
compartments, suitable for carrying bananas.[31] The response to this development was immediate. Ecuador exported 1,075,756 stems from January
through September of 1934, of which nearly three-quarters (745,450 stems)
went to New York. These shipments not only exceeded the aforementioned
goal of 350,000 exported stems for 1934, but also the 462,054 stems actually
sent overseas in 1933.[32]

With banana exports going up, United Fruit started at last to invest in
western Ecuador. Samuel Zemurray had taken over the company in January
1933 and one of his first acts was to send Francis V. Coleman to the *costa* with

instructions to acquire real estate. Coleman, who had worked in Ecuador more than a decade earlier for the West Indian Oil Company, knew the country well, including the places best suited to banana production for overseas markets. Mindful of the limitations of local infrastructure, he concentrated on properties close to existing railroads. One of the properties United Fruit purchased was El Tenguel. The company also bought the Taura-Vainillo plantation, with an area exceeding 30,000 hectares, and a dozen other holdings.[33]

Various legal conditions needed to be satisfied before United Fruit's rights in the land it was purchasing would be secure. Coleman established a residence in Quito, since Ecuadorian law required every foreign company active in the country to have a permanent representative in the capital city.[34] Also, great care had to be taken with national lawmakers. For example, the lower house of the Ecuadorian Congress passed a bill prohibiting foreigners from owning land within fifty kilometers of a national frontier in December 1934, a few months after United Fruit had bought El Tenguel. Legal squabbling followed, with the company's attorneys contending that the zone-of-exclusion should be measured from the limit of Ecuador's territorial waters; according to this interpretation, United Fruit's property rights in El Tenguel were not threatened. However, some congressional representatives insisted that the zone-of-exclusion should begin at the shoreline, which would have made practically all of the estate ineligible for foreign possession. This dispute was finally settled when United Fruit gave a large portion of El Tenguel—22,000 of 44,677 hectares, according to the U.S. consulate in Guayaquil—to the government. In June 1936, the "donation" was completed and the company's property rights in the land it had retained received official recognition.[35]

Political Ferment and Anti-Foreign Sentiment

"If there was ever a time and place when United Fruit could have dictated the terms of its presence," Striffler opines, "it was Ecuador during the 1930s and 1940s."[36] Certainly, the private sector realized at the time that Zemurray's company was in a unique position to help develop the *costa*'s huge capacity for banana production and exports, which was precisely the reason for President Tamayo's earlier pursuit of United Fruit. Yet the firm arrived as Ecuador was experiencing acute political instability. The victor in the presidential contest of 1934 was José María Velasco-Ibarra—a populist whose skill "as a campaigner was never equaled by his abilities as an administrator,"[37] yet who would go on to serve as chief-of-state on four other occasions.[38] In 1935, Velasco-Ibarra was replaced by Federico Páez, an engineer who was sympathetic to the private sector and also had the military's confidence.

Intending to promote the banana industry, Páez at one point authorized the creation of an office to oversee exports.[39] However, United Fruit opposed this move strenuously, ultimately convincing the president to relent. He decided instead to sign a concession contract with the multinational and its subsidiaries in April 1937, which contained a clause that permanently exempted exporters from control systems of any sort.[40] The contract stoked Ecuadorian fears of foreign corporations, so Páez directed his finance minister to publish a defense in *El Telégrafo*, Guayaquil's leading newspaper. In his article, the minister argued that taxes on United Fruit had to be fixed for an extended period in order to attract investment of the dimensions the company was contemplating. In addition, he emphasized the domestic benefits of that investment, including the guarantee that at least 40 percent of all fruit shipped abroad by the company would be purchased from Ecuadorian growers.[41]

The opposition was not mollified. After beating back an attempted coup d'état aimed at restoring Velasco-Ibarra to power, Páez had to hunker down most of the time in Quito. Marshaling his support, he appointed an all-military cabinet, although this measure and others he took did not suffice. In October 1937, the beleaguered head-of-state was overthrown by General Alberto Enríquez-Gallo, who governed from the left. A passionate nationalist who viewed every foreign business with suspicion, Enríquez-Gallo raised taxes on the mining industry and was convinced that all concession agreements were affronts to national sovereignty, and therefore were subject to unilateral revision or even cancellation.[42]

Within a year of seizing power, Páez's successor signed a decree that effectively invalidated the agreement with United Fruit. A supervisor of shipments was installed at the port of Guayaquil, both to approve the departure of every vessel carrying bananas and to settle disputes about exporters' payments to planters. The requirement that each exporter buy no less than 40 percent of its produce from Ecuadorian farmers, which had been specified in the April 1937 contract, was raised to 50 percent. In addition, Enríquez-Gallo's decree, which was soon followed by official nullification of the contract, stipulated that no foreign firm or individual could own more than 80,000 hectares— 30,000 less than United Fruit's holdings at the time. Yet another part of the 1938 decree was its fourth article, which authorized governmental review of the production accords that fruit exporters had signed with local growers.[43]

The purpose was to make sure that foreign companies would not take advantage of Ecuadorian planters, as had happened in other countries.

Production Contracts in Northeastern Colombia

Marcelo Bucheli concedes the possibility of exploitation in the banana business.[44] Since bananas cannot be warehoused for long and since there is a narrow time-window for harvesting if fruit is not to ripen before reaching retail outlets, growers are unable to withhold output out of dissatisfaction over prices or anything else. In addition, the shipping of bananas is characterized by economies of scale, mainly due to the sizable investment required in ocean-going vessels and land-based assets. Many local markets consequently are served by one exporter or a few such businesses, which may be tempted to pay low prices to farmers if the threat from potential competitors is reckoned to be slight.

Aside from having a monopoly in northeastern Colombia, United Fruit reinforced its advantages through a system of production contracts of the sort that Ecuador undoubtedly wanted to avoid. The company refused to buy bananas from planters without contracts and also forbade those with contracts to sell their produce to anyone else. However, growers had no guarantees that the company would take their fruit, as Bucheli makes clear:

> The contract established that the fruit belonged to United Fruit as soon as it was cut from the tree. If, however, the fruit happened to have any defect according to United Fruit's quality control officials, the property of the bananas reverted to the planter. Moreover, even if the company's officials approved the fruit and shipped it, but the bananas were later rejected by U.S. health authorities, the fruit again reverted to the . . . planter, who did not receive payment. The contract also specified that the local planters could not sell any of their fruit to another company, including the fruit United Fruit rejected.[45]

A production contract remained in force if the farm covered by the contract was sold. In addition, any new taxes that Colombia, the United States, or any other nation imposed on bananas would be paid by farmers, not United Fruit.[46]

Along with the obligations they took on and the risks they shouldered,

growers who signed production agreements gained indirect access to overseas markets, through United Fruit. They also received agricultural credit,
which banks in Santa Marta and other cities rarely provided. Available only
to farmers with contracts, the financing of production expenses by United
Fruit was a powerful reason to do business with the company—especially
because rates of interest on agricultural loans were "reasonable," as the multinational's critics admitted. Agricultural lending, however, was not the main
support for the system of production contracts and United Fruit's monopoly
in northeastern Colombia. Rather, the system was maintained by staggering
the expiration dates of production agreements. Due to this practice, only a
limited number of banana growers were free at any given time to consider
alternatives to doing business with *El Pulpo*. Also, the output of farms where
agreements had expired never reached the level needed to attract a competing
exporter. Under these circumstances, few planters decided against renewing
their contracts if the dominant multinational gave them the chance to do so.[47]

Over time, production agreements won ground at the expense of corporate agriculture in northeastern Colombia. Whereas 80 percent or more of
United Fruit's exports from the region came from the company's own holdings
in 1910, half its exports were bought from planters with agreements a decade
later. As overseas shipments continued to increase, so did United Fruit's purchases. As a result, contract farming accounted for four-fifths of total exports
in 1930, when United Fruit had yet to face significant competition.[48]

However, the company's monopoly in northeastern Colombia did not
last. A clause in the production agreements stipulating that all obligations
could be cancelled in the event of armed conflict was exercised in 1942,
when intercontinental shipments of tropical fruit ceased. Once World War
II ended, more than three years later, "a considerable number of (Colombians) were free from their contracts with United Fruit." For the first time
since the early 1900s, "they now could coordinate their actions and capture
scale economies" in overseas marketing and "were in a position to challenge
United Fruit directly."[49] They proceeded to do exactly that.

Ecuadorian Independence

Commenting on the restrictions that the authorities in Quito imposed on banana exporters little more than four years after United Fruit started purchasing farmland in the *costa*, Bucheli concludes that "Ecuador was unique in the

sense that its government helped keep the industry in the hands of domestic planters."[50] This conclusion merits close examination, not just to clarify the historical record in Ecuador but also for the sake of better understanding of the tropical fruit industry and its development.

Bucheli is correct that Ecuadorian farms were not displaced by estates belonging to multinational companies. As Parsons reported in the mid-1950s, foreign-owned plantations were the source of less than 15 percent of the country's banana exports.[51] Furthermore, multinational firms never imposed a system of exploitative production contracts. So it is accurate to say that most banana production has been and is still under Ecuadorian control.

Contrary to what some of the authors of the 1938 decree might have hoped for or expected, regulations applied to firms like United Fruit did not induce local entrepreneurs to get into the banana-exporting business immediately. However, this was because other commercial opportunities were more lucrative prior to and during the Second World War. In the same year when the decree was issued, for example, Juan X. Marcos and a pair of associates, Lorenzo Tous and Mariano González, paid off the mortgage on the Ingenio San Carlos, a sugar mill that had been in receivership for ten years, and then organized a stock sale to pay for the replacement of machinery and related updating. Shares worth 6,000,000 sucres (approximately $5,730,000 in today's money) were sold, including the stock that the Sociedad General purchased for 435,000 sucres ($415,000). The investment made possible by this equity issue was productive indeed; by 1950, the Ingenio San Carlos was the most valuable industrial property in Ecuador.[52]

Other effects of the 1938 decree were either negligible or turned out to be less important than what might be supposed. The stationing of a supervisor of shipments in the port of Guayaquil, for instance, had no noticeable influence on the banana trade. One can even argue that the requirement that every exporting firm purchase half or more of its bananas from national planters was inconsequential. Both before and after the decree's promulgation, United Fruit bought most of the produce it exported. As late as the mid-1950s, purchased fruit comprised two-thirds[53] to three-quarters[54] of what the company shipped out of Ecuador—well over the minimum threshold mandated by national law.

Authorizing public officials to review production agreements might have curbed the abuse of banana planters by fruit buyers and exporters. Regardless, a contracting system along the lines of what United Fruit established in northeastern Colombia in the early 1900s was never likely to be put in place in western Ecuador, with or without Enríquez-Gallo's decree. Neither United Fruit nor any other company ever controlled banana exports from the *costa* the way that the U.S.-based multinational once monopolized shipments from the Caribbean coast of Colombia. Hence, no firm was able to ensnare all growers in the region through contracts that effectively suppressed the operations of competing exporters.

Of all the elements of the 1938 decree, the restriction on land ownership by foreigners had the greatest impact. As already indicated, the maximum number of hectares allowed any non-Ecuadorian firm or individual was set below United Fruit's possessions at the time. In the absence of this limit, the company might have decided to divest some or all of its real estate in later years, for reasons made clear in the chapters that follow. Perhaps so, although the restriction on foreign ownership was seen seventy-five years ago for what it was meant to be: a clear signal from Ecuador about how United Fruit would be allowed to conduct itself in the country.

Not an aberration by any means, this signal was entirely consistent with broad political and economic currents in Ecuador, including before the administration of Enríquez-Gallo. It must not be forgotten that the restrictions of 1938 were preceded by United Fruit's donation of thousands of hectares for the sake of winning legal recognition of its ownership of El Tenguel. Of even greater significance was that the multinational had few opportunities in the *costa* to acquire real estate well suited to banana production and exports for free or nearly so—not even during the early 1920s, when Ecuadorian leaders were trying their level best to attract United Fruit to the country.

The simple fact that the best natural resources in the *costa* were already in private hands when United Fruit first showed an interest in Ecuador prevented the company from getting hold of sprawling tracts of land in the country, of the sort it had come by a few decades earlier in Central America. The unavailability of such tracts also jeopardized the company's dominance of the global banana business, based as this dominance had been on locking up environmental assets anywhere and everywhere in the Western Hemisphere tropical fruit was produced.

CHAPTER 4

Good Governance, for a Change

Even if its measurable impact on United Fruit's actual conduct was modest, the stance taken by the Ecuadorian government in 1938 toward foreign investment in the banana industry was remarkable in light of the economic difficulties that had beset the South American nation since the cacao boom ended, more than fifteen years earlier. That stance also contrasted sharply with the accommodations Central American governments made around the turn of the twentieth century. For foreign companies, however, other parts of the Western Hemisphere were harder to do business in before World War II. As indicated in Chapter 1, the liberals who governed Colombia during the 1930s initiated agrarian reform and backed the labor movement, including in the tropical fruit sector. Even less hospitable for multinational firms was Mexico—particularly from 1934 to 1940, during the presidency of Lázaro Cárdenas. More than his predecessors, Cárdenas made a serious attempt to prohibit the foreign ownership of rural land, as mandated in the constitution his country had adopted in 1917. Along with a number of state governments, the most leftwing president in Mexican history also favored the communal ownership of agricultural resources over private farming.[1]

After a few years of adapting to these changes in agrarian policy, Standard Fruit decided toward the end of Cárdenas's administration both to relinquish its Mexican properties and to curtail a nascent program to purchase bananas from local growers. The company's departure was followed by a sharp decline in fruit exports from Mexico, which had been the world's leading supplier of bananas in 1939 with total shipments of nearly fourteen million stems. Exports fell to seven million stems the following year and continued to deteriorate after World War II. By 1960, Mexico had ceased shipping bananas to the United States and other foreign countries.[2]

Tropical fruit production also went down in Cuba and Jamaica, which along with Mexico supplied nearly 30 percent of all bananas traded internationally from 1935 through 1939.[3] Always disputatious, the relationship between Standard Fruit and the government of Haiti became increasingly strained after World War II. The company halted new investment in the country in early 1947 and departed shortly afterward. Exports, which were just short of seven million stems in 1947, fell below three million stems the next year and two million stems in 1949. Three years later, Haiti shipped fewer than 500,000 stems overseas, marking its departure from the ranks of important banana suppliers.[4]

National authorities were not the only source of trouble in the Caribbean Basin for U.S.-based fruit companies. Panama Disease was a recurring problem in Central America and the toll taken by Yellow Sigatoka, which appeared in the region in the mid-1930s, mounted as the years passed. Output consequently went up haltingly through the late 1950s before declining for a few years.[5] Coinciding with supply-side difficulties after World War II was a recovery of demand. German submarines no longer prowled the seas, so shipments resumed to the United States. European imports rebounded as well—nearly tripling, for instance, during the 1950s, although Great Britain, France, and a few other countries steered as much trade as they could to current or former possessions in Africa and the Caribbean.[6] Economist David Schodt estimates that global banana consumption climbed by 35 percent between 1945 and 1955 while exports from the Caribbean Basin "remained relatively constant."[7] Prices shot up as a result, quadrupling between the mid-1940s and the early 1950s.[8]

The combination of rising global demand and level shipments from established suppliers created an opening for new banana exporters. The opportunity was understood full well by Galo Plaza—the son of a general who had been Ecuador's president from 1901 to 1905 and again from 1912 to 1916 but had departed the country following the coup d'état of July 1925. Having studied economics at the University of California (where he also played American football and helped support himself by selling apples on the streets of Berkeley), agronomy at the University of Maryland, and diplomacy at Georgetown University, Plaza served two years as Ecuador's ambassador to the United States beginning in 1944.[9] Among the prominent figures he met in Washington was Nelson Rockefeller, whose lifelong interest in Latin America had led President Franklin Roosevelt to appoint him coordinator of inter-American affairs in 1940 and assistant secretary of state four years later. Committed to hemispheric cooperation and development, Rockefeller found a willing ally in Plaza.

His time as a diplomat having come to an end, Plaza returned in 1946 to Ecuador, where the economic signs were encouraging. A positive balance of trade had been maintained for several years, in part because of the limited availability of many imports during World War II but also because of increased exports of rice and matériel such as kapok (used to stuff life vests) and cinchona bark (the source of quinine, which was used to treat malaria). Revenues from export duties had gone up as well, thereby shoring up public finances. Since fiscal deficits were modest, money creation and inflation were avoided. Under these favorable economic circumstances, Plaza ran for and won the presidency in 1948, benefiting from the record he had compiled as Quito's mayor prior to his ambassadorship.

Plaza consistently respected freedoms of speech, assembly, and the press while in office. He also made increased banana production and exports the centerpiece of his economic program. The thorny issue of foreign involvement in the tropical fruit sector had been resolved ten years before his inauguration, with limits placed on multinational investors that they could live with and therefore did not drive them away. Regardless of Alberto Enríquez-Gallo's antipathy toward foreign corporations, his 1938 decree proved at the end of the day to have been an exercise in economically judicious statecraft—something for which Ecuador is not renowned.

The same decree gave Plaza wide latitude during the late 1940s and early 1950s to pursue a strategy for development that made sense for the banana industry and for the country as a whole. Investment by companies such as United Fruit, which could provide the improved technology Ecuador needed, was a key element of this strategy. Other elements, including the construction of roads and bridges and making idle land available to large numbers of farmers, were entirely consistent with pro-growth economic management—management that benefited Plaza politically in the tangible sense that he was the first Ecuadorian president to complete a four-year term since José Luís Tamayo had done so more than a quarter century earlier.

Sound Macroeconomic Administration

Good economic governance during the Plaza administration included the avoidance of macroeconomic instability, of the kind that had gripped Ecuador during the 1920s and 1930s. In particular, inflation was kept in check, which was important because spiraling prices always create risks and costs that discourage private investment.

National macroeconomic management had been of little consequence during the early 1900s in many parts of Central America where tropical fruit was produced and exported—to be specific, in northern Honduras and other coastal settings where commerce was usually transacted in U.S. dollars.[10] However, a foreign enclave where money from another country circulated in place of the legal national tender was never going to be created in western Ecuador, certainly not as recently as sixty-five to seventy years ago. Hence, Ecuadorian inflation as well as the rate of exchange between sucres and dollars mattered a great deal in the middle of the twentieth century to any firm, be it foreign or domestic, considering the *costa* as a place to grow bananas for overseas markets. A particular concern was the possibility of the sucre's overvaluation.

Currency overvaluation always arises under a system of multiple exchange rates—one rate determined by market forces but also one or more official rates fixed by the central bank and designed for the de facto taxation of exports. To understand how this taxation occurs, consider a hypothetical country with banana exports and a national currency (called the peso) worth five cents in the free market. Let us say as well that exporters who have earned dollars by selling bananas in other countries are prohibited from exchanging those dollars at the unregulated rate of twenty pesos per dollar. Instead, they are compelled to hand over foreign currency to the central bank at the official rate, which the bank has set at fifteen pesos per dollar (roughly equivalent to $0.067 per peso). This confiscatory requirement has exactly the same impact on incentives to export bananas that a 25 percent tariff on exports would have if dollars were being converted into local currency at the free market rate.[11]

Widespread in Latin America as recently as the 1980s, multiple-exchange-rate regimes are less common in the region today. However, there is another way for currency overvaluation and the resulting penalization of exports to happen, which is the failure to match local inflation with commensurate adjustments in the exchange rate. Again, the problem can be illustrated with a hypothetical example involving a banana-exporting country. Suppose that a ton of fruit costs 6,000 pesos to produce and has an international value of $400. If a dollar can be converted into twenty pesos and vice versa, net earnings amount to 2,000 pesos per ton ($400 x 20 pesos per dollar – 6,000 pesos). Now suppose that a year has elapsed, during which inflation of 10 percent has occurred in the hypothetical country but the exchange rate has held steady—in all likelihood, by the way, because the central bank has periodically traded some of its holdings of U.S. currency for pesos in order to maintain the latter's "pegged" value. Due to this management of the exchange rate, exporters still receive 8,000 pesos for every ton of bananas they sell abroad at the end of the year, just as they did twelve months earlier, even though 10 percent more pesos must now be spent on farm labor and other local inputs because of inflation. With revenues unchanged but with production costs having risen to 6,600 pesos per ton, net earnings per ton equal 1,400 pesos, not 2,000 pesos.

This decline in profitability is part of an economy-wide distortion stemming from currency overvaluation. To provide a broader view of this distortion, which economists refer to as import bias, we now introduce a trading partner for the tropical exporter of bananas with annual inflation of 10 percent: the United States, to be precise, which exports apples and is free of inflation. At one point in time, bananas are being bought and sold for 8,000 pesos ($400) per ton and a ton of apples can be purchased for 16,000 pesos ($800); in other words, apples are twice as expensive as bananas, regardless whether those items change hands for pesos or for dollars. But during the next twelve months, inflation in the tropical country drives up the cost of producing bananas and therefore their price by 10 percent, to 8,800 pesos per ton. Meanwhile in the United States, where prices are entirely stable, apples are still being bought and sold for $800 per ton.

To avoid import bias, the peso must devalue, from an exchange rate of twenty per dollar ($0.050 per peso) to twenty-two per dollar (a little more than $0.045). This devaluation raises the prices of all imported goods in the tropical country by 10 percent, which is the same as the rate of inflation; since apples (now costing 17,600 pesos per ton) continue to be twice as expensive as bananas, imports of that fruit do not vary. The same devaluation prevents banana prices from changing in the United States, so the tropical nation's exports are unaffected. With an exchange rate of twenty-two pesos per dollar, a ton of bananas is still worth $400 (8,800 pesos divided by twenty-two pesos per dollar), exactly as it was at the beginning of the twelve-month period when inflation in the banana-exporting country drove up costs of production and therefore the price in pesos of tropical fruit.

Relative prices and trade patterns shift if there is no devaluation to correct for differences in inflation between the trading partners. No longer 50 percent cheaper than apples in the United States, bananas are now 45 percent less expensive: $440 per ton (8,800 pesos/20 pesos per dollar) versus $800 per ton. Banana exports to the United States consequently decline. At the same time, apples are still worth 16,000 pesos per ton in the tropical nation, even though the price of bananas has risen by one-tenth, so consumers there purchase more apples brought in from the United States.

To summarize, currency overvaluation, which results either if there are multiple exchange rates or if a country's central bank intervenes in currency markets to prevent the exchange rate from adjusting fully to differences in inflation, gives a boost to imports while reducing exports. This import bias, incidentally, is the mirror image of the export bias (i.e., diminished imports and greater exports) that comes about in a country where the currency is undervalued—as has been the case in China in recent years, according to many U.S. observers.

As already indicated, Ecuador had a trade surplus during World War II. With dollars received for rice and other exports exceeding the dollars spent on imports, foreign currency accumulated at the central bank and the sucre gained value, increasing from $0.064 in 1940 to $0.074 in 1945. After the global conflict, monetary authorities intent on defending the sucre's value gradually sold off the central bank's dollars. Thanks to this intervention, the exchange rate stayed the same from 1945 to 1948 even though inflation was consistently higher in Ecuador than in the United States, which has been the Andean nation's leading trading partner since the nineteenth century.

Immediately after Plaza was sworn in as president, the policy of pegging the sucre to the dollar was abandoned—as it had to be eventually since the central bank's holdings of foreign currency were dwindling—and the exchange rate went immediately from 13½ per dollar ($0.074 per sucre) to 18 per dollar ($0.056 per sucre). During the next four years, Ecuador's currency was allowed to "float," although variations in the exchange rate turned out to be modest. Since Ecuadorian inflation was generally in line with U.S. inflation, the problem of currency overvaluation, which had been dealt with effectively in 1948, did not arise again during Plaza's term as president.

Infrastructure Development

Aside from containing inflation, avoiding distortions in the rate of exchange between sucres and dollars, and otherwise maintaining macroeconomic conditions conducive to private investment, the Plaza administration went to great lengths to improve transportation infrastructure, especially in those parts of western Ecuador well suited to banana farming.

During the 1930s, when shipments of bananas to the United States began, much of the fruit harvested in the *costa* made its way to Guayaquil and other seaports exactly as all the region's products had done since colonial times. For the output of farms not adjacent to navigable waterways, the journey began on the back of a donkey or horse. After a few hours or perhaps a day, a transfer was made to a small boat headed for a port-of-call for ocean-going vessels. Once this destination had been reached, fruit was inspected by exporters' agents. Bananas that were not bruised and that showed no signs of incipient ripening were loaded in ships' holds. Rejected fruit, on the other hand, was "destroyed, consumed locally, or shipped illegally to Peru."[12]

The *costa*'s time-honored system of transportation had been fine for cacao—a dry seed with a hard exterior that could withstand up to three years of rough handling and storage in the Ecuadorian countryside, on inland waterways, and in a tropical seaport. That system was also adequate for Ecuador to gain a foothold in the international banana business, as the country did by exporting limited quantities of fruit harvested mainly on old cacao estates in the lower reaches of the Río Guayas watershed. In this setting, boats could circulate throughout the year—even from May to December, when stream flow ebbs because there is little precipitation.

However, major improvements in the transportation system would be needed if bananas were to be harvested in additional places, as Ecuador had to do in order to become a leading exporter of tropical fruit. Spoilage of fragile produce jostled on the backs of donkeys and horses was too great. So were the losses that occurred on boats, which had to proceed slowly and carefully in shallow rivers never disturbed by a dredge. Even truck transportation, which was an option in some places, was far from satisfactory. Paved roads were few and far between, so much of the fruit stacked on vehicles was rendered unfit for sale after being bounced around on rutted byways. Moreover, trucks stopped circulating whenever there were heavy rains, which turned rural lanes into quagmires. As noted in the preceding chapter, the U.S. consul in Guayaquil pointed to transportation bottlenecks when he expressed doubts about Ecuador's prospects as a banana exporter in 1933. Also keenly aware of the damage done as produce moved from inland farms to coastal parts were the business and banking leaders of Guayaquil, who formed a Comité Ejecutivo de Vialidad charged with elaborating a plan for improving the transportation system.

Implementation of the plan, which had a projected cost of 151 million dollars,[13] began in a limited way in 1946 with modest financing from local taxes, municipal funds, and road tolls. Tractors started cutting a path through tropical forests for a highway linking Quevedo (north of Guayaquil and a small settlement seventy years ago) to the port city. Work began two years later on a separate thoroughfare running east out of Guayaquil. Outside the Río Guayas valley, the national government initiated construction of a highway in 1946 from Quito down to Santo Domingo and, from there, out to the northwestern seaport of Esmeraldas.

The budgetary requirements of these projects and others envisioned by national authorities and regional bodies such as the Comité Ejecutivo de Vialidad exceeded Ecuador's financial resources, so support was sought from Washington. A precedent for U.S. assistance already existed. At Rockefeller's direction, U.S. teams had worked in the southern *costa* since 1942, helping with reconstruction following the Peruvian invasion of 1941. Roads and a narrow-gauge railway were built and harbor facilities at Puerto Bolívar, outside Machala, were improved.[14] Elsewhere, the U.S. government helped build a highway connecting Quevedo with Manta and its seaport. Both during World War II and for several years afterward, the U.S. Export-Import Bank lent more to Ecuador for infrastructure development than any other institution. For example, an initial disbursement of funds for the Quevedo-Manta highway occurred in 1947 and approximately eight million dollars were made available during the next nine years for the project, which on its completion in 1956 became a conduit for banana exports.[15]

Financing from other sources was impeded by Ecuador's poor standing with external creditors. Borrowing from the World Bank, in particular, was ruled out as long as the country made no payments to foreign bond-holders, as was the case from 1941 to 1954.[16] Furthermore, the chances that the same institution would lend money for roads and bridges serving Ecuador's tropical fruit sector were not improved by a report submitted in 1948 by one of the Bank's economists, who concluded that the best way to boost exports was to rehabilitate the cacao industry—mainly by providing technical assistance to farmers and not so much by investing in public works.[17]

Payments were renewed to foreign creditors in 1954. Soon afterward, the World Bank lent 8.5 million dollars for the construction and upgrading of infrastructure southeast of Guayaquil, in the same area where United Fruit's agricultural holdings were concentrated. Ecuador borrowed another 14.7 million dollars from the same source three years later. Thanks to loans from the U.S. Export-Import Bank and the World Bank as well as domestic funding, the overall linear distance of all-weather roads in the country increased by 136 percent between 1944 and 1958.[18] In 1959, the World Bank approved a loan of thirteen million dollars for a deep-water port in Guayaquil with berths for large reefer ships.

The improvement of transportation infrastructure never lacked for political support. It was also a recurring demand of the private sector. This does not mean, though, that governmental leaders always worked in concert with businessmen and women toward shared goals. In 1944, for example, José María Velasco-Ibarra became chief-of-state again after the overthrow of Carlos Arroyo del Río, who had been president during the war three years earlier with Peru and whom many Ecuadorians blamed for their country's defeat. Once Velasco-Ibarra was in office, Juan X. Marcos, who was a close associate of Arroyo del Río and for years led the effort to build Guayaquil's deep-water port, was briefly imprisoned. In light of Marcos's mistreatment, Luís Noboa chose to go into hiding.[19]

Coastal businessmen had much better entrée with the Plaza administration. The economics minister, for example, was a Guayaquileño named Clemente Yerovi who had worked for decades in agriculture, banking, and shipping. During the late 1920s, Yerovi piloted an old steamer on the inland waterways of the *costa*, which left him with a lasting impression of the region's system of transportation. He subsequently called for better roads, bridges, and ports while leading the chamber of agriculture for western Ecuador. As a member of Plaza's cabinet, Yerovi again championed infrastructure development, with the president's complete support.

Land Rush

Outside Ecuador, many of the railroads, seaports, and other public works needed for banana production and exports were put in place by vertically integrated firms with headquarters in the United States. Partly thanks to the many hectares of land received as a reward for infrastructure development, these firms ended up controlling a series of banana-producing areas. This control was reinforced wherever other growers relied on railroads belonging to U.S. based companies to take their harvests to market. In Guatemala, for example, United Fruit owned nearly the entire railroad system as well as the country's leading Caribbean seaport through the 1950s.[20]

Monopoly was the rule even in Honduras, where three multinational firms operated during the first three decades of the twentieth century. Samuel Zemurray's Cuyamel Fruit Company was unchallenged in the northwestern corner of the country, close to Guatemala, by virtue of its railroad connecting the seaside towns of Omoa and Cuyamel with inland farms. Just to the east, United Fruit controlled a larger territory served by an extensive rail network it had constructed, which ran dozens of kilometers south from the coastal settlements of Puerto Cortés and Tela. Standard Fruit was in complete charge farther east, where the company had port facilities in La Ceiba and Puerto Castilla as well as rail lines extending into the surrounding countryside.[21]

Discontinued in 1911, grants of land awarded for railroad construction were never as generous in northeastern Colombia as what foreign companies had received in Central America.[22] Nevertheless, United Fruit's monopolization of banana exports from the region was strengthened because the firm ran the area's only rail line. Many years later, during the 1970s, United Fruit tried to keep competing exporters out of the Urabá region in northwestern Colombia by denying them access to canals the company had built, which were the only viable mode of transportation. This attempt failed, but only because the Colombian president intervened on the competitors' side.[23]

Since the central government and regional authorities used foreign credits to improve highways, ports, and other infrastructure in western Ecuador, neither United Fruit nor any other company ever had the chance to translate ownership of the transportation system into a local banana empire. As James J. Parsons observed in 1957, the industry leader played "a much less conspicuous role" in the *costa* than it did in the Caribbean Basin.[24] Instead, more than half the area's exports during the 1950s were raised by independent farmers who owned fewer than 100 hectares,[25] many of whom had just settled alongside new highways constructed by the Ecuadorian state.

In addition to benefiting from infrastructure development, these farmers had access to subsidized credit from the public sector. At Yerovi's urging, fifteen million sucres (equivalent to $6,328,000 in today's money) had been allocated at the beginning of Plaza's administration to the government's agricultural development bank, the Banco Nacional de Fomento (BNF), to support banana production.[26] These funds were in turn lent to nearly a thousand growers.[27] To limit the rural elite's capture of BNF loans, which carried annual interest charges of 7 to 10 percent at a time when the annual interest rate on credit from commercial banks varied between 10 and 18 percent, no individual was allowed to borrow more than 50,000 sucres (worth a little more than $21,000 today).[28]

An excellent start in banana farming was certainly possible with a BNF loan. Clearing costs were modest, averaging $120 per hectare during the 1950s.[29] Hence, the owner of a forested parcel who had borrowed 50,000 sucres could rid up to twenty-two hectares of trees and other natural vegetation. Parsons estimated that the thousand or so banana farmers who received BNF credit ended up deforesting about 25,000 hectares,[30] which is a little greater than the figure of 22,000 hectares arrived at by supposing that 50,000 sucres were lent to each of those thousand farmers and that all funds were spent on land clearing. The discrepancy might actually have been wider because some borrowers received less than 50,000 sucres and because loans were sometimes taken out for other purposes, such as the purchase of fertilizer and other agricultural inputs. On the other side of the ledger, settlers who were clients of the BNF undoubtedly devoted some of their own money and sweat equity to deforestation, thereby augmenting their agricultural holdings. All in all, then, Parsons's rough estimate of 25,000 hectares deforested by farmers with BNF loans is credible.

Lending by the bank was concentrated in the vicinity of Santo Domingo and within reach of the highway running out to Esmeraldas. In these settings as well as in other sparsely populated areas with *tierras baldías* (idle lands) that public officials were eager to dispose of, agricultural settlement was also accelerated by policies administered by the government's Instituto Nacional de Colonización (INC). Formal property rights in a parcel of up to fifty forested hectares could be gained from that agency by occupying the parcel and then clearing at least a quarter of it for crop production during the next five years.[31] While waiting for an INC ruling, a homesteader could make a decent living. Fruit production began thirteen to fifteen months after a field had been cleared and planted to the Gros Michel variety—not after a few years, as would have been the case with cacao, coffee, or any other tree crop. Moreover, harvests continued throughout the year with modest seasonal variation, thereby generating steady earnings and reducing, or even eliminating, the need for agricultural credit.

Since bananas were uniquely profitable, many thousands of Ecuadorians took up tropical fruit farming. According to the country's first agricultural census, which was conducted in 1954, bananas were being raised on 25,319 holdings, almost entirely in the *costa*. The vast majority of these holdings were quite small, with limited sales of fruit by the holdings' owners complemented by subsistence production, counting the green plantains used for cooking. But there were 1,917 commercial planters as well, most of whom cultivated between 25 and 500 hectares and belonged to the Asociación Nacional de Bananeros Ecuatorianos (ANBE). By the early 1960s, members of this private, voluntary organization, which had been established by governmental decree in June 1955, were the source of all but 5 percent of the bananas shipped overseas from Ecuador.[32]

Few, if any, commercial growers had started life as *campesinos* (peasants) suffering quasi-feudal penury on haciendas in the Andes. Some might have been coastal *montuvios*, who were not socioeconomically privileged by any means yet had the advantage of knowing how to farm at or near sea level. *Montuvios* also were accustomed to functioning as independent economic actors—in part because forced-labor systems, which discouraged individual initiative and which survived well into the twentieth century in highland Ecuador, had not existed in the *costa* since the 1800s. However, many more of the people whose property rights were adjudicated by the INC and who received subsidized credit from the BNF had middle-class backgrounds, including in the urban professions and as military officers. This was reflected in the finding more than fifty years ago that forty out of the seventy-one landowners in one rural district near Santo Domingo had no agricultural experience prior to acquiring their respective farms.[33]

As Parsons, Schodt, and other scholars emphasize, middle-class homesteaders with medium-sized holdings of land—not impoverished peasants and also not large companies from other countries—were major beneficiaries of the geographic spread of banana farming in western Ecuador: an expansion directly facilitated by the Ecuadorian state, especially during the Plaza administration.

Farmland Consolidation

Following the resumption of normal commerce after World War II, Ecuador's rise in the global banana business was swift. Exports during the latter part of 1945 amounted to 693,551 stems—less than half the 1,874,595 stems dispatched abroad in 1940. However, shipments to other countries quickly shot past prewar levels, reaching 2,686,870 stems in 1947. With prices going up through the early 1950s, Ecuador was on the verge of becoming the world's leading supplier of tropical fruit in 1952, when 16,755,066 stems were exported. Five years later, exports reached 23,874,310 stems, far exceeding what any other country supplied.[34]

More than a few aspiring *bananeros* with little or no experience in agriculture had difficulties during this period. Parsons drew attention to businessmen and government officials from Quito for whom a banana farm had been "both a country home and a financial speculation, to be worked by wage labor and to be managed on weekends and vacations." These individuals often found out the hard way that "weeding, the determination of the stage of maturity of the fruit, and the dovetailing of harvesting and transportation . . . require constant, year-round attention."[35] Some absentee-landowners delegated managerial tasks to resident supervisors. However, some of these supervisors were less than capable, not conscientious, or dishonest. Farms left in the care of such people were subject to failure, even if fruit prices were high, labor was cheap, and plant diseases posed little threat.

After the early 1950s, when banana prices stopped rising, the exit of less-efficient growers accelerated, thereby hastening the transfer of agricultural real estate to planters who were more skilled, worked full-time at banana farming, or both. One sign of this transition was that the number of planters with multiple holdings rose. Another was that the average size of commercial farms increased. Both indicators of consolidating land ownership were easy to discern in settings with the longest history of tropical fruit production. One such setting was the southern *costa*. In 1962, for example, planters had two farms on average in the *costa*'s southernmost province while the average number in western Ecuador as a whole was 1.44 farms per owner and the mean figure for homesteaders around Santo Domingo was 1.10.[36] The southern *costa* also stood out in terms of the degree to which real estate was concentrated in a few hands, with half the land planted to bananas there having been acquired by four families or individuals by the early 1960s.[37] One of those four was Esteban Quirola.

Even though average farm size went up and the number of holdings per grower increased in the *costa* as the years passed, ownership of land planted to bananas was still much less concentrated than in Central America. United Fruit and Standard Fruit possessed more than 90 percent of the plantations in Panama, Costa Rica, Honduras, and Guatemala in 1963, with the remainder owned by local growers who had signed production contracts with one or the other of the two U.S. firms (Table 1). Ecuador had large estates as well: five with more than 1,000 hectares and eleven with 500 to 1,000 hectares. However, these estates were not at all typical in a country where the median size of a banana farm was barely 100 hectares and where there were hundreds of small holdings (Table 2).

Table 1: Ownership of Land Planted to Bananas in Central America, 1963

Owner	Panama	Costa Rica	Honduras	Guatemala
United Fruit	12,600 ha	11,275 ha	8,525 ha	8,435 ha
Standard Fruit	0	1,700	4,645	0
Growers with Contracts	710	630	2,955	60
Total	13,310 ha	13,605 ha	16,125 ha	8,495 ha

Arthur, Houck, and Beckford, 53.

Table 2: Size Categories of Ecuadorian Banana Farms, 1960–1961

Farm size (ha)	Number (percentage of total)	Area (percentage of total)
Less than 25	871 (47.9)	11,024 (10.9)
25 to 100	741 (40.7)	38,559 (38.1)
100 to 500	192 (10.5)	36,606 (36.2)
500 to 1,000	11 (0.6)	7,701 (7.6)
More than 1,000	5 (0.3)	7,313 (7.2)

Junta Nacional de Planificación y Coordinación Económica, 43, 48, cited by Arthur, Houck, and Beckford, 56.

Small and medium-sized growers survived in Ecuador and more than a few of them flourished for various reasons, such as a favorable climate, good soils, and the modest capital requirements of Gros Michel bananas. Yet another factor working in their favor was that the domestic marketing of tropical fruit was competitive, with thirty-three firms buying bananas from farmers in 1963 and with the two largest companies (one being a trading venture founded and led by Noboa) accounting for no more than a third of total purchases.[38] Marcelo Bucheli points to the "open market" for bananas that has existed for many years in western Ecuador,[39] which explains why no grower there has ever had to sell out to a larger operation solely because he or she was unable to get exportable produce to market.

Banana Development and the State in Ecuador

Much of what the government of Ecuador did for the tropical fruit sector after World War II was consistent with sound public policy, as understood by the economics profession. Especially during the Plaza administration, modest inflation and the avoidance of currency overvaluation encouraged investment throughout Ecuador's economy, including in banana farms. There was also unwavering support for the improvement of infrastructure. In addition, geographic expansion of the tropical fruit sector was promoted by the speedy recognition of farmers' property rights.

The government was not above meddling with market forces. For example, minimum prices were set for bananas while Plaza was president. However, these prices were tied directly to market values in New York,[40] so the policy's impact on production and exports was minimal. More consequential was the public sector's intervention in rural financial markets—to be specific, the low rates of interest paid by individuals who took out loans from the government's BNF so they could plant more land to bananas.

Low-interest lending to banana farmers dried up in the *costa* after 1956. However, this change in policy was not the result of public officials' embrace of free-market principles, of the sort most economists advocate. Rather, the cessation of credit subsidies for deforestation was a practical response to the mounting problem of placing Ecuadorian fruit in foreign markets. Moreover, national authorities interfered more with market forces during the years to come. This interference grew acute after Ecuador's adoption of import-substituting industrialization (ISI)—a development strategy featuring import tariffs and other protectionist measures to encourage the manufacturing of goods that otherwise would be purchased from foreigners.

Latin American governments that engaged in protectionism and departed in other ways from sound macroeconomic practice did not hesitate to intervene directly in individual sectors as well. The lengths that meddlesome governments went to was exemplified by events nearly five decades ago in northeastern Colombia, during the region's conversion from Gros Michel bananas to the Cavendish variety. As reported in Chapter 2, local planters made this conversion in the face of devastating hurricanes. They also had to accomplish the varietal shift on their own because United Fruit had wound down its operations in the region. In addition, these planters needed to overcome resistance from the central government. With the agriculture minister convinced that prices for the traditional variety would shoot up once Cavendish plantations had been established in other exporting nations, official approval was withheld for the import licenses needed to bring in foreign technology, which was essential for the new variety. Meanwhile, northeastern Colombia lost ground to its competitors.[41]

Rarely if ever do the results of governmental intrusion compare favorably with what is accomplished when the state sees to macroeconomic stability and invests in things like public works, but otherwise gives market forces free rein. Public policy in Ecuador was not entirely consistent with this ideal approach during the middle of the twentieth century. However, enough of the approach's elements were in place to foster entrepreneurship in the banana industry and otherwise further the industry's development.

CHAPTER 5

========

South American Entrepreneurs Go Global

For exporters accustomed to trading dry, nonperishable goods, such as cacao, grain, or any of a number of non-agricultural commodities, getting into the banana business requires quite a leap. A costly array of assets must be marshaled to move produce without delay from farm to port, then across the sea, and ultimately to retail outlets in importing nations. To use these assets thoroughly and effectively, as has to be done to earn a profit, fruit must be supplied regularly and in large quantities. In addition, quality control has to be exacting. All this is well beyond the normal competence of a solitary merchant—someone who makes a living, perhaps a comfortable one, buying low and selling high adroitly, with no one else's assistance and with little invested aside from the money fronted for whatever is being traded.

No homegrown entrepreneur could hope to export bananas where railroads, port facilities, and many thousands of hectares of farmland were in the hands of vertically integrated firms headquartered in the United States, as was the case in northern Honduras for most of the twentieth century. In northeastern Colombia, where foreign holdings were less extensive, a system of exclusionary production agreements between United Fruit and local planters discouraged competition prior to World War II. That system did not survive the global conflict, which gave Colombian exporters an opening. Opportunities arose as well for independent traders from Ecuador.

By the middle of the twentieth century, a few South Americans had taken a stab at exporting bananas. The results were often disappointing, particularly if an unassisted run was made at a market that United Fruit already had to itself. Superior opportunities beckoned outside the United States, in importing countries where the transnational firm lacked a significant presence. Wherever they might go, however, Latin American entrepreneurs would have to draw on lessons learned in previous ventures about the importance of a reputation for reliability as well as the value of partnerships, especially in new commercial undertakings. Luís Noboa and others like him applied lessons such as these and, as they did so, the global banana industry grew more competitive.

Taking on the Octopus

For decades after its founding in 1899, United Fruit jealously guarded the markets it had been able to monopolize. According to Colombian historians, the company thwarted an attempt in 1908 by a Santa Marta businessman, Ricardo Echeverría, to export bananas harvested in the surrounding area. Trains carrying fruit to port were delayed because of "damaged machines, sick machinists, (and) destroyed bridges" and the ship Echeverría had lined up to deliver bananas to a buyer in New Orleans took too long to load. By the time the ship reached its destination, most of its cargo was in no condition to be sold. *El Pulpo* preempted further activity by its would-be competitor by offering double the prevailing price for a while to farmers who previously had done business with him.[1]

The multinational's grip on the banana trade in northeastern Colombia went unchallenged for another dozen years. Then, in 1920, entrepreneur Juan B. Calderón, who served on Ciénaga's city council and was "a fierce long-time opponent of United Fruit's power in the region," brought together a group of local planters hoping for an alternative marketing channel. A deal was struck with a U.S. rival of The Octopus, the Atlantic Fruit Company, and an initial shipment occurred. However, that shipment was seized by customs officials in New York after United Fruit argued that its rights, as spelled out in production contracts, were being violated.[2]

Calderón tried again a decade later. After organizing the Cooperativa Bananera Colombiana, he reached an agreement on its behalf with the Robert Brinnings Company, an importer in Liverpool. Two shiploads were delivered in 1930 by the Leyland Line. But then, just as a third vessel was about to steam away from Santa Marta after filling its holds, United Fruit insisted on rigorous monitoring of the ownership of all traded produce. Hoping to avoid a dispute with a top-ranked U.S. corporation, Leyland left the entire matter to Calderón, who proposed that United Fruit place agents of its own in Colombian ports to verify that all the bananas the Cooperativa was shipping were its rightful property. The company refused to discuss this proposal or anything else with Calderón and recommended instead that the Colombian government inspect shipments. Declining to take on this responsibility, the government let United Fruit settle the dispute in Great Britain, where a court ended up embargoing all Colombian bananas imported by Robert Brinnings. Thus, Calderon's second, and final, attempt to compete against *El Pulpo* failed.[3]

Ecuadorians who tried to export bananas to the United States on their own fared little better. One of them was Simón Cañarte: the son of a coastal businessman who had started out as a shopkeeper's employee, invested his savings in a cacao farm, and went on to buy ships constructed in Guayaquil. When he was seventeen, Cañarte inherited the firm his father had created and, using the firm's vessels as well as chartered craft, exported rice and also sold bananas in Chile. During World War II, the company delivered matériel and labor to an airbase the United States had constructed in the Galápagos Islands to help guard the Panama Canal. According to his son, Cañarte's ships were the first to sail in international waters under the Ecuadorian flag.[4]

In 1944, Cañarte and a partner, Charles Fisher, formed the Tropical Fruit Company, with the intention of exporting bananas as soon as hostilities ceased. Several small vessels were purchased in the United States and refrigerated compartments were installed at a Guayaquil shipyard. Once an office, dock, and storage space had been leased in New Orleans, exports commenced. However, United Fruit and Standard Fruit found it easy to turn back the Ecuadorian upstart. Whenever one of Tropical Fruit's ships approached the Crescent City, a larger vessel belonging to one or the other of the two multinationals would pull in and start unloading bananas. Another such vessel would do the same immediately after the Ecuadorian ship's arrival, thereby saturating the market. Cañarte's firm responded by shifting its operations to Tampa, although United Fruit and Standard Fruit soon employed the same tactics in the Florida port that had been used in New Orleans.[5]

Between deliveries to Chile and sporadic sales in the United States and elsewhere, Tropical Fruit was the fifth largest exporter of Ecuadorian bananas in 1950. But by this time, barely five years after he started exporting bananas, Cañarte was diversifying into other businesses, including a couple of newspapers in which his U.S.-based rivals were regularly excoriated. Tropical Fruit folded in 1961, although none of the firm's ships were ever sold. Moored off an island in the Río Guayas fifty years ago, they remained there for decades:[6] oxidized monuments to the folly of solitary challenges directed at the titans of the global banana industry.

Scandinavia and West Germany, Scandinavians and Germans

South Americans daunted by the prospect of grappling with *El Pulpo* in its own lair had other options. In 1946, for example, Anacreonte González, a banana planter in northeastern Colombia, organized a growers' association for the purpose of exporting fruit to Sweden, where U.S. based multinationals were absent. Also, Pepe Vives and Francisco Dávila led a cooperative of Colombian planters, the Federación de Productores de Banano del Magdalena, which in 1952 started supplying a pair of German importers—Lutten and Sons and Afrikanische Frucht.[7]

West Germany was a particularly attractive market for independent exporters. Fruit companies headquartered in the United States were in no position to manipulate or interfere with banana sales in continental Europe. In addition, demand for tropical fruit was going up quickly as West Germany made a rapid economic recovery after the mid-1940s. The country was also more open to imports than its neighbors—either Great Britain or the five nations that joined West Germany in 1958 to launch the European Economic Community (EEC), which transformed itself into the European Union (EU) thirty-five years later. At 6 percent, the general tariff applied to bananas by the EEC's largest member was modest; also, it had no current or former colonies that might have been given favorable treatment (Table 3). Hence, Latin America benefited as West German imports surged, from 89,000 tons in 1950 to 576,000 tons fifteen years later.[8]

Table 3: Tariffs Levied on Banana Imports by Selected European Nations, 1964 (%)

Country	General rate	Favored rate
European Economic Community		
Belgium, Luxembourg, and The Netherlands	16.5	9.0^1 or 0.0^2
France	20.0	11.0^1 or 0.0^3
Italy	20.0	0.0^4
West Germany	6.0	0.0^1
United Kingdom	14.0	0.0^5

[1] Applied to future EEC members.
[2] Applied to former Belgian and Dutch colonies.
[3] Applied to former French colonies in Africa that continued to use the franc after achieving independence.
[4] Applied to Somalia as well as future EEC members.
[5] Applied to current and former British possessions in Africa and the Caribbean.
Source: Valles, 29.

An initial step toward exporting Ecuadorian fruit to Germany had been taken during the 1930s because of an unusual bid to save the Hacienda Clementina: a large estate 100 kilometers due north of Guayaquil on which cacao production had been devastated by Witches' Broom. The Ecuadorian owners, the Durán-Ballén family, registered a corporation in Hamburg dedicated to converting the estate to banana production. Capital was raised for the upgrading of infrastructure and other improvements. Also, agricultural specialists were sent out from Germany, although they were interned once Ecuador declared itself a wartime ally of the United States. During the early 1940s, the Hacienda Clementina passed to the Wallenbergs of Sweden, who for generations had been prominent in finance, industry, government, and philanthropy.[9]

Aside from compensating their Ecuadorian employees well, the new owners of the Hacienda Clementina made substantial investments. By 1963, bananas were being raised on 900 of the estate's 12,000 hectares, which were crisscrossed by 120 kilometers of high-quality roads and an internal railway.[10] However, the Wallenbergs' personal involvement in the Ecuadorian enterprise, which was a sideshow compared to their other businesses, was never significant. In contrast, Folke Anderson, who grew up poor in Sweden and who as a young man found employment in Gothenburg with a fruit-importing firm, played an important role in Ecuador's banana boom, both by facilitating exports to Scandinavia and by bringing new areas into production.

According to other Scandinavians who worked with or knew him, Anderson's international career began as World War II was drawing to a close, when he borrowed money to travel to Santa Marta after authorizing a friend who was a sea captain to help arrange for the chartering of reefer ships. In cooperation with Anacreonte González, Anderson lined up a supply of Colombian bananas. His next step was to return home, but only long enough to lock in sales to the largest supermarket chain in Scandinavia. Deliveries were made on vessels that Anderson chartered on credit. To handle shipments to Sweden and neighboring countries, which accounted for most of his business, Anderson founded Transfrukt, a company based in Gothenburg. A separate firm, the Estrella Fruit Shipping Corporation, was established to deal with exports to New Orleans. Even after port fees and other expenses, the first shipload of bananas delivered to the latter city generated enough revenues to make payments to the owners of chartered reefers and to settle all debts with González, at which point Anderson decided to develop an entirely new source of supply on his own in northwestern Ecuador.[11]

This part of the *costa*, which had exported balsa, leather, and quinine during World War II, had geographic advantages: a deep-water harbor at the
mouth of the Río Esmeraldas, near the city of Esmeraldas, as well as access
via the same river and its tributaries to thousands of hectares of fertile land.[12]
After two years dedicated to the acquisition of real estate, the construction of
a port and facilities for repairing ships and boats, and related preparations,
Anderson moved permanently to the region in 1948. Thanks to sustained
investment—in roads extending out from navigable waterways, aircraft used
to fumigate crops, river boats, etc.—his Astral Fruit Company was almost
entirely responsible for making the northern *costa* a mainstay of Ecuador's
tropical fruit sector. In 1953, more than one in every four bananas shipped
overseas from Ecuador moved through the port of Esmeraldas.[13] During the
next several years, production declined because of Panama Disease and Yellow Sigatoka, although as late as 1963 Astral's annual exports still exceeded
1,500,000 stems (Table 4). The company operated until 1968, when murder-
ers whose identities remain a mystery took Anderson's life in Guayaquil.

Along with Anderson, German investors had a major impact on the tropical fruit sector in Ecuador. Soon after World War II, Afrikanische Frucht
started buying bananas in the *costa* as a complement to its purchases in Colombia. Additionally, the company recruited German farmers to acquire and
clear land near Quevedo and plant their respective parcels to Gros Michel.

Table 4: Leading Exporters of Ecuadorian Bananas, Selected Years
(number of stems)

Company	1954	1959	1963
(ranked by 1963 exports)			
Exportadora Bananera Noboa*	3,212,000	3,215,000	7,292,000
UBESA	---	3,329,000	6,533,000
United Fruit subsidiary	3,959,000	7,067,000	5,888,000
Exportadora de Frutas Ecuatorianas	---	4,469,000	5,631,000
Standard Fruit	---	3,998,000	5,293,000
SAFCO	4,786,000	2,486,000	1,765,000
Astral Fruit Company	2,177,000	1,846,000	1,525,000
Others (number of firms)	4,700,000 (25)	8,351,000 (25)	8,331,000 (26)
Total	18,834,000	34,761,000	42,258,000

* Originally the Marcos-Noboa partnership, which through 1955 sold almost entirely to Stan-
dard Fruit and changed its name from Compañía de Comercio y Transporte to Exportadora
Bananera Noboa in 1964.
Source: Schodt 1995, 116.

Fruit was also purchased from Ecuadorian growers, thus guaranteeing compliance with the 1938 decree issued by Alberto Enríquez-Gallo. As a result, settlement and agricultural development took off in the vicinity of Quevedo.[14]

Afrikanische Frucht's enterprise in Ecuador did not become a durable fixture of the country's banana sector. Its exports only amounted to 432,705 stems in 1963, behind the overseas shipments of a dozen other firms,[15] and it pulled up stakes in the South American nation less than ten years later. Likewise, the Wallenbergs eventually decided against holding on to the Hacienda Clementina and in 1980 sold the estate to Noboa for four million dollars. Hiring away technical specialists from United Fruit, the new owner turned what originally had been the rural seat of an elite *costa* family into one of the most efficient farms in the country.[16]

In 1955, another German company, Exportadora de Frutas Ecuatorianas, started operating in Ecuador. Among its principals was Willy Bruns, who worked during the 1930s as an importer in Hamburg and after World War II purchased reefer ships and several plantations in the *costa*. In 1958, Bruns created his own firm, the Unión de Bananeros Ecuatorianos (UBESA), which brought in barges, production equipment, and skilled personnel from West Germany. Rural land belonging to UBESA and Exportadora de Frutas Ecuatorianas could supply only a portion of the companies' exports, so production agreements covering 80,000 to 120,000 hectares were signed with local farmers.[17] Along with financing, farmers who signed these agreements received technical assistance, so that their harvests would meet standards of quality on which West German customers insisted.[18]

By 1963, UBESA was the second leading exporter of Ecuadorian bananas—responsible for more overseas shipments than United Fruit's local subsidiary, which had been the top exporter a few years earlier, or Standard Fruit. Only the foreign sales of Exportadora Bananera Noboa were greater (Table 4). Looking outside the West German market, Bruns's company sought out customers east of the Iron Curtain. In addition, UBESA shipped Ecuadorian bananas to Japan on two occasions in 1961. This was accomplished without any losses due to spoilage, even though the refrigerated vessels used by the company needed nearly three weeks to traverse the Pacific Ocean.[19] Noboa, however, was already doing the same.

The Best of Partners

Like Cañarte and a few other South Americans, Noboa attempted at least once to enter a foreign market on his own, though without any positive result. In 1961, he dispatched a trio of ships packed with Ecuadorian bananas to California, where United Fruit still had a monopoly three years after signing a consent decree with the U.S. government to put an end to antitrust prosecution. Notwithstanding the decree, the industry-leader flooded the local market as Noboa's ships approached the Golden State—exactly as it had done a few years earlier to drive Cañarte's Tropical Fruit Company away from New Orleans and Tampa. With fruit prices reduced 50 percent or more, Noboa's entire cargo was dumped at sea,[20] and the former street vendor took care to steer clear of California for the next two decades.

This venture was exceptional given that partnerships had been a normal feature of Noboa's exporting activities since the 1930s, when he teamed up with Juan F. Marcos to ship rice grown in the *costa* to foreign customers—a business that expanded dramatically after supplies from low-cost producers in Asia were cut off at the beginning of World War II.[21] Acting as Marcos's main business agent and using funds provided by the Sociedad General, Noboa deployed the assets needed to move rice from areas upstream from Guayaquil where the grain was harvested and winnowed down to the port city, where storage and milling facilities were located. Even before the global conflict, these assets included tugboats as well as a number of barges. After the Japanese invaded French Indochina and other centers of rice production in the Far East, the fleet of river vessels acquired and managed by Noboa and Enrique Ponce-Luque (the husband of his sister) increased to sixty boats. The two brothers-in-law regularly outcompeted their rivals—in part by furnishing growers credit, which they needed to buy agricultural inputs and which was scarce due to the absence of banks in the Ecuadorian countryside. Foreign shipments multiplied, all on ocean-going vessels contracted by the Sociedad General.[22]

The association between Noboa and the Marcoses was symbiotic in various ways. Juan X. Marcos's long-time friend and former attorney, Carlos Arroyo del Río, was inaugurated as president in September 1940, which guaranteed an excellent relationship with the Ecuadorian state. Also, the proprietors of the Sociedad General were highly respected in the private sector. An assistant of the Marcoses to begin with, Noboa benefited greatly from their contacts and good names, although with time his personal standing went up among Ecuadorians and foreigners alike. To be sure, Noboa's profile was enhanced because many of the assets he acquired were named after him, alone. The Marcoses did not object, evidently appreciating that they would have their full share of the additional profits created as Noboa gained prominence and experienced success. By the same token, they understood what was to be gained by letting Noboa act on his own, so he was free to close deals without asking for advice or approval.

As Noboa's long-time attorney put it, the younger Marcos "inherited" the young entrepreneur as he took over the Sociedad General—which had impressive financial and physical assets, though none that yielded more dividends in later years than Noboa. The son of Juan F. Marcos is remembered in Guayaquil for his dedication to business: passing up morning rounds of golf and often working into the evening on weekdays.[23] Noboa was even more diligent, as revelers on late-night outings in downtown Guayaquil could affirm. Looking up and seeing the midnight oil burning in Noboa's office at the corner of the Malecón and Calle Pedro Icaza, they could tell that the young businessman was arranging for the sale of Ecuadorian rice to foreign buyers, placing the country's cacao and coffee overseas, or closing some other deal.[24]

Noboa's diligence paid off in various ways, including success in the delivery of rice even when supplies were short. Not long after he got into the rice business, for example, he encountered Juan F. Marcos, who mentioned that there was a ship near Guayaquil that could not depart because 1,000 tons of grain that another merchant had promised had not been delivered. Inquiries had been made throughout the port city, but no one had any rice to spare. Noboa assured his original mentor at the Sociedad General that he could fill the ship by bringing in grain from Colombia. This promise was audacious in light of the poor transport linkages with Ecuador's northern neighbor. Also, imports had been banned, in order to keep prices high for Ecuadorian rice producers. Nevertheless, Noboa made good on the promise, providing all 1,000 tons without delay.[25]

The experience, respect, and capital that Juan X. Marcos and Noboa gained in the rice trade made them attractive partners for Standard Fruit, which in the mid-1940s was intent on launching operations south of the Panama Canal—as United Fruit had done more than a decade earlier. Prospects for increased production were not good in the Caribbean Basin, so the company needed Ecuadorian produce if it was to maintain or increase its market share in the United States. In addition, the South American nation offered a trouble-free arrangement: relying on a pair of local businessmen to purchase bananas from independent growers. Taking it upon themselves to deal with fluctuations in local markets, outbreaks of plant diseases, and the like, Marcos and Noboa would be responsible for timely deliveries to Guayaquil and other ports, where fruit would be loaded on reefer ships belonging to Standard Fruit.

After Marcos paid several visits to Standard Fruit's headquarters in New Orleans, a partnership with a duration of five years was agreed to in 1945. This book's coauthor can attest personally to the company's wisdom in associating with the scion of one of the port city's most respected merchant-families and his former protégé, who was now a respected businessman in his own right. During her first trip to Ecuador, in 1950, she arrived from the United States as a passenger on one of Standard Fruit's ships: the *Gatún*, a reefer with a draft of less than 6.5 meters. A local pilot coaxed the vessel up the Río Guayas a little before high tide, avoiding rocks and sandbars and finally dropping anchor in front of Guayaquil. After the passengers disembarked and the cargo was unloaded, the captain waited until the tide was beginning to ebb, which was the best time to turn a ship around in the middle of the wide though shallow river. Thanks to the preparatory work done by Noboa and Marcos, stevedores spent the entire night filling the *Gatún* with bananas. The next morning, less than twenty-four hours after reaching Guayaquil, the reefer weighed anchor and headed back to New Orleans.

Standard Fruit's commercial undertaking with the Ecuadorian businessmen benefited all concerned. In particular, Noboa and Marcos, who previously had dealt only in dry agricultural commodities, learned about the speedy delivery of perishable fruit to overseas customers from their foreign partner—just as the former street-vendor had learned the ropes of exporting during the early 1940s thanks to his association with the proprietors of the Sociedad General. Being mutually advantageous, the venture, which originally was scheduled to run for five years, was renewed for another five years in 1950.

There was one difference between the Marcos-Noboa alliance and the partnership that the two Ecuadorians entered into with Standard Fruit. Even though Noboa could have discontinued the former alliance and prospered on his own, he never did so. Out of loyalty to the family that had taken him into the Sociedad General at age twelve, he maintained the relationship until Juan X. Marcos passed away in 1980. In contrast, ties with the foreign firm were strictly commercial, maintained only as long as there were tangible rewards— not least for the Ecuadorian businessmen.

A New York Debut

While they were still associates of Standard Fruit, Noboa and Marcos made commercial forays of their own in the United States. But before ties with the U.S. company were severed, sales to customers such as hospitals and military bases were modest. Significant exports to North America would have to wait until the two Ecuadorians went their own way, which they did in 1955.

Noboa and Marcos set their sights on New York, which was the leading entry point for U.S. fruit imports during the 1950s, though not the most welcoming place for foreign banana traders. With Standard Fruit's operations concentrated in New Orleans and other parts of the Gulf Coast, United Fruit dominated New York and the rest of the eastern seaboard. Furthermore, New York's harbor was thick with corrupt labor unions, of the sort depicted in *On the Waterfront*. The unions' capacity for intimidation was revealed when the producers of that motion picture, which won an Academy Award in 1954, were denied permission to film any scenes at United Fruit's dock in lower Manhattan—near the site where the twin towers of the World Trade Center would rise to the sky after the mid-1960s. Even The Octopus, it turned out, was careful to avoid needless provocation of wharf-side gangsters, of the sort portrayed by actor Lee J. Cobb.[26]

To break into the New York market, Noboa and Marcos chose to join forces with a local businessman, Shillo Adir. Born in Baltimore in 1927 and raised in that city as well as British Palestine, Adir had earned an undergraduate degree at the University of Miami following service with the U.S. Army. He then took a job with the Panama Line, which shipped meat and other perishable items to Central America. As a rule, the company's vessels returned to the United States with nothing in their refrigerated holds. This did not escape the attention of Adir, who arranged for the backhauling of bananas that were sold from Florida to New York.[27] The young businessman consequently learned a thing or two about competing against United Fruit.

Along with a Russian immigrant named Sol Palitz, Adir created a company, Banana Distributors, which obtained produce at low cost from SAFCO, which had a plantation adjacent to El Tenguel and also purchased the harvests of Ecuadorian growers. In addition, Adir had a profitable relationship with the Atlantic and Pacific (A&P) chain of supermarkets; "I had a special arrangement," he recalls, "to sell at a fixed price of fifty cents a pound."[28] However, Banana Distributors never rivaled United Fruit seriously as long as it depended on SAFCO, which had just two reefer ships of its own and also used Grace Lines to make deliveries to New York.[29]

Noboa and Marcos, who had been receiving thirty cents per pound for their bananas and had up to one million dollars to invest in a partnership, approached Adir in September 1956. Their proposal to supply fruit to Banana Distributors, which would be responsible for marketing in the United States,[30] was accepted. Adir and Palitz ceased dealing with their former supplier, which promptly went into decline. The leading exporter of Ecuadorian bananas through the mid-1950s—ahead of Standard Fruit, United Fruit's local subsidiary, and Astral—SAFCO had slipped to sixth place by the end of the decade. Its annual shipments continued to fall off during the 1960s, thus relegating the company, which had set up shop in Guayaquil not long after the turn of the twentieth century, to also-ran status in Ecuador's tropical fruit sector (Table 4).

Noboa never envisioned that Marcos and he would merely replace SAFCO as suppliers of Ecuadorian produce to Banana Distributors. His intention to be completely engaged in U.S. operations was made clear in November 1956, little more than two months after the initial approach to Adir, when he opened his own office at 911 Rector Street—an office that was dwarfed by United Fruit's center of operations in New York little more than a stone's throw to the north.[31] By 1958, Banana Distributors had been renamed Pacific Fruit and the Ecuadorian businessmen were Adir's equal partners, with Noboa "directly" involved in U.S. marketing.[32]

During their decade-long association with Standard Fruit, Noboa and Marcos had demonstrated a capacity for the consistent delivery, week in and week out, of tens of thousands of stems—all suitable for sale in the United States. Within a few years of gaining direct access to U.S. customers, thanks to the linkage with Banana Distributors, they were shipping 140,000 stems a week, on average (Table 4). For Adir, the gains of expansion justified taking on the Ecuadorians as full partners, which had never happened with SAFCO. As a result, Noboa learned how business was done in the North American metropolis. His attorney in Guayaquil recalls early brushes with the mafia, not to mention a special fund to cover undefined (yet unavoidable) expenses.[33] But according to Adir, Noboa ended up being on good terms with the stevedores' union.[34]

A deal was even struck with The Octopus. In the 1960s, U.S. authorities were investigating United Fruit for booking nearly all the refrigerated space on Grace Line vessels sailing to the United States from banana-producing regions in the Western Hemisphere. Meanwhile, Noboa was looking for different ways to ship tropical fruit—to complement the heavy use he was making of the Flota Mercante Gran Colombia, which was owned and operated by the Colombian and Ecuadorian governments. He went to United Fruit's offices in Boston and New York with a suggestion, that 5 to 10 percent of Grace's refrigerated space be reserved for the Ecuadorian bananas he was exporting. The deal was accepted,[35] so United Fruit executives got government regulators off their backs and Noboa gained an attractive shipping option.

With the tropical fruit Noboa and Marcos were able to supply, Adir envisioned a more prominent position in the global banana business. "We have enough to go around the world with bananas," he assured Noboa, "and we can go wherever Chiquita goes."[36] In interviews conducted by Noboa's daughter and this book's coauthor, Adir stressed the effort he dedicated to opening up markets outside the United States for his Ecuadorian partner. No doubt, Noboa made valuable contacts with European and Japanese buyers in meetings and lavish receptions that Adir arranged.[37] As a rule, however, the Ecuadorian businessman followed up on his own with these contacts, in effect using his association with the founder of Banana Distributors as a springboard for enterprises he controlled completely.

So the partnership between Adir and Noboa did not assume global dimensions. Nevertheless, the New York businessman expresses unqualified appreciation for his Ecuadorian colleague. "I really cannot remember ever having an argument with (Noboa), or any difference," he claims. The decision to work with Noboa was the best "I have ever made in my life."[38]

In Europe and on to Japan

During the years to come, Noboa consistently executed a regular sequence of moves as he entered a series of foreign markets. Initially, an established local importer, such as Adir, would be identified and recruited. The importer would be won over because teaming up with Noboa, who could supply tropical fruit cheaply and in large quantities, was an excellent way to expand one's business. If the Ecuadorian entrepreneur did not start out as the majority owner of an importing partnership, he would acquire at least a 51 percent stake as the enterprise prospered and grew. Noboa's ultimate aim was an operation under his sole control, one that was fully capable of competing with United Fruit or any other firm. Far more often than not, this aim was accomplished.

Trading partnerships were created elsewhere in the United States—in Charleston, South Carolina, for example, where Noboa worked with the Consolo family. Similar partnerships came into being in Europe, Japan, and other parts of the world. On multiple occasions, the reputation that Noboa gained in one setting for the dependable delivery of fruit and for honest and prompt payment facilitated the recruitment of associates elsewhere. Thus, a banana-trading network emerged, one based in Guayaquil but with worldwide reach.

Noboa got started in Europe during the 1950s. As in his early dealings with Adir in New York, he displaced SAFCO as the principal source of Ecuadorian bananas for shipping magnate Sven Salen, who supplied tropical fruit to his native Sweden. Noboa appears to have taken a cue about backhaul earnings from his Scandinavian colleague, who loaded automobiles to be sold in Guayaquil on every ship bound for that port after delivering its cargo of bananas to Europe. Within a few years, the Ecuadorian businessman was making a profit by ferrying German-made jeeps and other vehicles back to Ecuador on vessels he had chartered from Salen and other shippers. He also saved money on fertilizer, machinery, and other inputs used on his farms and non-agricultural enterprises by loading these items on ships that otherwise would have returned empty to South America.[39]

Salen introduced Noboa to Leon Van Parys, whose family had imported fruit in Antwerp since the 1920s and who helped finance and lead the Corporación Ecuatoriana Europea (COPORESA). The family also had banana plantations in the Belgian Congo and, with Congolese independence in 1960 and the warfare that erupted as the former colonial power withdrew from central Africa, Van Parys welcomed cooperation with Noboa. Within a couple of years, vessels belonging to COPORESA's Belgian Fruit Lines were delivering Ecuadorian bananas to Antwerp, which Van Parys marketed initially under the Sundrop brand name. By 1963, Noboa was also dispatching fruit to Hamburg, always taking care to supply the best bananas—his "pearls"—to customers in Western Europe. The reputation he consequently acquired for quality was worth millions of dollars in sales.[40]

More than a dozen years after he began working with Van Parys, Noboa began to secure a dominant position for himself in Belgium. The object of this maneuver was General Fruit, which was owned by four local importers. In 1973, the Ecuadorian businessman bought the 15 percent of General Fruit shares held by Bananen Import Maatschappy. Later the same year, he increased his ownership of General Fruit to 50 percent by buying Van Parys's stake, of 35 percent. Shortly afterward, the company was renamed Pacific Fruit Antwerpen. The remaining shares were acquired in the late 1970s: 15 percent from Gerald K. Freres and 35 percent from the Belgian Fruit Lines. Aside from buying out his former partners, Noboa recruited Belgians with experience in the tropical fruit trade—individuals such as Henri Van Weert, who formerly was in charge of Maatschappy and would go on to manage his Ecuadorian employer's activities throughout Europe.[41]

Noboa never tried to establish himself in France, which has always favored bananas from overseas departments in the Caribbean and from francophone Africa. Nor did he bother much with Great Britain, which imports most of its tropical fruit from Commonwealth members such as Jamaica and Saint Lucia, or with Spain, which produces bananas in the Canary Islands. Also, he consolidated his operations in and around Europe in a pair of hubs. Scandinavia, Germany, and the Low Countries were served from Antwerp. To handle sales in the Mediterranean Basin, an office was set up in Rome. One of the key people there was Hans Kreysing, a German who had been hired away from UBESA after working for several years as an agricultural specialist in the *costa*.

In his quest for customers, Noboa not only looked beyond the Panama Canal, to the eastern United States and Western Europe. He also moved into Japan, across the Pacific Ocean. The considerable advantage that Philippine growers enjoyed due to their closer proximity to the leading market in northeast Asia was overcome mainly thanks to Sven Salen. The Swedish shipper offered Noboa the services of his agent in Guayaquil, who in 1958 was transferred to Tokyo. That agent and one of Noboa's employees, who also journeyed to the Japanese capital, found an importing company willing to take Ecuadorian bananas. Beginning in 1959, deliveries were made to the company at minimal cost because of backhauling aboard Salen's ships, which were routed past Ecuador as they returned to Asia after dropping off Japanese exports in New Zealand.[42]

South Americans' penetration of overseas banana markets was comprehensive. By the mid-1960s, Colombia was selling no bananas in North America (Table 5) because United Fruit no longer operated in the northeastern part of the country after having shifted all its fruit production to corporate plantations in Central America. However, nearly half the bananas imported by The Netherlands were shipped out of Santa Marta and neighboring ports. The Colombians also had large segments of the Scandinavian and German markets (Table 5).

Table 5: Ecuadorian and Colombian Shares of Various Markets, 1964 (%)

Importing nation or region	Ecuadorian share	Colombian share
North America		
Canada	30	0
United States	46	0
European Economic Community		
Belgium and Luxembourg	47	33
France	7	2
Italy	0	0
The Netherlands	22	48
West Germany	57	21
Other European nations		
Austria	56	2
Denmark	16	0
Norway	41	26
Sweden	55	35
United Kingdom	0	1
Japan	46	0

Source: United Nations, 1009, 1173, 1857, 1224, 1422, 1618, 1941, 2034, 2395, 2669, 4971, and 5293.

In terms of tropical fruit exports, Ecuador was in a league of its own. In 1964, less than two decades after the postwar boom in fruit exports from the *costa* began, the country supplied nearly half the bananas consumed in the United States and Japan. Data presented in Table 5 indicate that discriminatory trade policies in France, Italy, and the United Kingdom truly had an impact. But elsewhere in Europe, Ecuadorian exporters were out-competing everyone else. Their biggest accomplishment on the other side of the Atlantic was to capture the lion's share of the German market, which fifty years ago had become the largest in Europe.[43]

Behind the Iron Curtain

Short of overcoming the protection enjoyed by current or former possessions of France, Italy, Spain, and the United Kingdom or taking additional market share from the Colombians in Germany, the Low Countries, and Scandinavia, Ecuador's prospects for additional sales were limited in Western Europe during the mid-1960s. Likewise, spectacular growth in sales was unlikely at that time either in the United States, where imports from the South American nation already had gone up significantly at the expense of shipments from the Caribbean Basin, or in Japan, where few additional inroads could be made into the Philippines' share of the market.

Ecuadorians would seek out and find new customers during the years to come—in the Middle East and North Africa, for example. A potential market also existed five decades ago in Eastern Europe and the Soviet Union. Communist governments could be talked into making an exception to their general policy of keeping out western goods since bananas were an inexpensive and tasty source of potassium and other essential nutrients. In addition, alternatives to straightforward commercial transactions could be found, which was imperative because national authorities hated to part with their holdings of hard currency.

In October 1960, little more than a month after the fourth presidential inauguration of José María Velasco-Ibarra, Ecuador's minister of education was in Prague and proposed to his hosts that bananas and other Ecuadorian products be bartered for Czechoslovak machinery worth $630,000. No specific commitments were made, however. The only tangible outcome of the ministerial visit was the assignment of three professors from the central European nation to the Escuela Politécnica Nacional, in Quito.[44]

Ecuadorians from the private sector had more success in the communist bloc. For example, Segundo Wong, the son of a Chinese migrant to South America, pioneered a countertrading scheme during the 1960s in which fruit from the *costa* was exchanged for vehicles, machinery, and other manufactured items—all at prices agreed to by the Guayaquil-based merchant and his communist customers. Acting on behalf of Comproba, a firm founded by Ecuadorians of Chinese descent, Wong, as the leading shareholder, exported Gros Michel bananas raised at low cost on small and medium-sized farms—bananas that had become difficult to sell elsewhere due to the switch that Standard Fruit and United Fruit had made to the Cavendish variety on their Central American plantations. Besides, much of the produce Comproba sent to the other side of the Iron Curtain was not good enough for customers in Western Europe and North America and therefore could be purchased cheaply in Ecuador.[45]

Wong and his associates kept transportation expenses to a minimum by using Soviet and Eastern European vessels. Also, money was made on imported goods. The tractors, trucks, and cars that Comproba bought from state-owned factories and delivered to Ecuador were inferior substitutes for

U.S., Western European, and Japanese products, so were generally sold at bargain-basement prices. Even at those prices, some of Comproba's imports had no takers, although Wong never came up empty-handed. He put unsold tractors to use on his own agricultural holdings, which extended across hundreds of hectares. Similarly, communist-manufactured trucks carried harvested fruit from his farms to export terminals.

Soviet and Eastern European markets gained importance over time for Ecuador's banana industry, accounting for example for 12 percent of total exports in 1974 versus 8 percent the preceding year.[46] By this time, Wong was no longer the only businessman from Guayaquil selling bananas in communist countries. Working initially with a local partner, just as he had done earlier in New York and Antwerp, Noboa delivered fruit to Yugoslavia, first in Zagreb but later in various Adriatic ports. True to form, Noboa eventually bought the partner out so that he could operate with complete independence.

Some of Noboa's dealings in Yugoslavia involved bartering: trading bananas either for agricultural chemicals used on Ecuadorian farms, for example, or for corrugated paper used to line cardboard boxes containing tropical fruit. But cash sales were more common. The payments received for Ecuadorian bananas were in Yugoslav dinars, which were not convertible. Noboa nevertheless accepted this currency, which he drew on to pay for reefers constructed in Yugoslav shipyards. No dinars were spared on those vessels, which included luxurious accommodations such as indoor swimming pools for Noboa and his guests. The accounts he set up in local banks also were a source of financing for a cold-storage warehouse and an adjoining office in Ploce, a Croatian seaport. In addition, the Ecuadorian businessman anticipated the day when the balances in those accounts could be exchanged for dollars and other hard currency.[47]

Aside from Yugoslavia, Noboa had a commercial presence in Czechoslovakia, countertrading top-quality bananas bearing his Bonita label for an array of manufactured goods beginning in 1974. The Ecuadorian businessman, who had no superiors to answer to, was a formidable rival for United Fruit, which had an office in Prague. It is hard to imagine that any representative of the U.S. company ever received strong encouragement to pursue deals like those routinely struck by Noboa: exchanging bananas for shiploads of farm inputs, for example. But since this was precisely the sort of deal that communist officials favored, United Fruit's share of the Czechoslovak market, which was approximately 70 percent in the mid-1970s, went down noticeably in later years as the share captured by the Ecuadorian businessman rose.[48]

Sales behind the Iron Curtain were less important for Noboa than for Wong, who specialized in supplying bananas to the Soviet Union—which did not buy bananas from any other noncommunist exporter—and various Eastern European nations. However, the Chinese-Ecuadorian businessman was careful to avoid serious rivalry with his compatriot, which could have ruined him.[49] Instead, Wong parlayed the commercial standing he had earned for himself in the Soviet Union and its satellites into flourishing businesses in other places. One such business was a partnership with Oscar Manrique and Tristan Elizalde (each from a prominent Guayaquil family) that won contracts to construct roads and other public works in Ecuador.[50]

What Makes for Success in the Banana Trade

Ecuadorian traders were no strangers to vigorous, one-on-one bargaining, of the sort nearly every merchant engages in regularly. Indeed, they seemed to relish dealings of this sort. A business colleague remembers Noboa as "a very tough negotiator," someone who "could spend the whole night in the office with packages of Marlboros" without missing a beat the next business day. "What Onassis was in the tanker business," he opined, "Noboa was in the banana trade."[51]

Recalling that Noboa "loved bargaining," another associate, Carlos Aguirre-Millet, shared an illustrative anecdote. Prior to the construction of a building for his Condor Insurance Company, the Guayaquil businessman "decided to negotiate himself over the cost of some steel girders." He traveled to Germany to meet with a pair of the manufacturer's representatives—a father and his son, as it turned out. Having invited the two salesmen to his hotel room for breakfast, Noboa demanded a lower price. "He was still bargaining when they brought in lunch," according to Aguirre-Millet. "When the waiters brought in dinner at seven that night, the son accepted the lower figure, exclaiming 'take the iron so I can go to my house and sleep.'"[52]

For many years, Noboa owned no reefer ships, so served his overseas customers with chartered vessels. Marcos, his old mentor and continuing partner, had been booking cargo space since the early 1920s. Nevertheless, Noboa insisted on handling this part of the business himself, evidently convinced that he could get lower rates than anyone else. Some negotiations could be done in Guayaquil. But before the 1970s, when Noboa acquired his first teletype machine, he dealt with shipping companies that lacked representation in Ecuador through Adir, who would be told what was to be shipped, the destination, and the charges Noboa was willing to pay. Marcos would stroll over every day or two from his office at the Sociedad General to stay abreast of developments.[53]

So Noboa was no slouch at one-on-one bargaining. Nor was Wong. However, the success of Ecuadorian exporters did not rest only on their knack for buying low and selling high. Identifying capable associates in New York, Antwerp, and other shipping hubs was essential. So was the care taken to develop and maintain a reputation for being a reliable supplier, which enticed businessmen such as Adir, Salen, and Van Parys into partnerships and enabled Noboa and Wong to flourish as competitors of United Fruit and Standard Fruit throughout the world.

CHAPTER 6

Keeping Up with Technological Advances

As a banana exporter, Ecuador always has had the disadvantage of being farther than its principal competitors from North American and European customers. Even when the country's banana boom was in full swing following World War II, moving produce from Guayaquil and other ports along the Pacific coast to major markets bordering the Atlantic Ocean was costly. Canal tolls and other shipping expenses for Ecuadorian exporters represented 27.5 percent of the cost-insurance-freight (CIF) price paid for bananas in New York, more than 4,500 kilometers away. In contrast, the same category of expenses comprised 23.5 percent of the CIF price for Central American exporters, who were nearly 1,400 kilometers closer to New York and who did not have to use the Panama Canal. The ratio of shipping charges to CIF values in Germany was 28 percent for fruit coming in from northern Colombia and 33 percent for Ecuadorian bananas.[1]

Through the 1950s, elevated transportation expenses were more than offset by low labor requirements, both for the initial clearing of land and afterward for banana production. Thousands of hectares were deforested, quickly and with relatively little effort, to accommodate geographic expansion of the tropical fruit sector. Once in operation, the *costa*'s banana farms out-competed their rivals in the Caribbean Basin, where banana production was more labor intensive.

This was not the first time that the South American nation enjoyed a comparative advantage in agriculture because of low labor requirements. During the cacao boom of the late 1800s and early 1900s, only one worker was employed for every five hectares planted to trees yielding the basic ingredient of chocolate, partly in pruning and related maintenance but mainly in the collection of seed-bearing pods. But even though labor intensities were higher in other parts of the world,[2] Ecuador did not remain competitive. Between low prices and production losses resulting from plant diseases, the cacao boom came to an end after World War I.

Tropical fruit development based in large measure on a favorable ratio of labor to land proved to be no more sustainable than the cacao boom had been. Exporting all the bananas harvested in the *costa* became more challenging with each passing year. As Americans increased their purchases of other fruit, including in a processed form, banana consumption per capita in the United States declined, from eleven kilograms per annum during the 1940s to 8.5 kilograms in the early 1960s.[3] With U.S. imports going up slowly, global demand growth slackened, even with shipments to Europe continuing to rise at a fast pace. Meanwhile, Ecuador's banana output continued to go up rapidly—so much so that the exported share of production fell. In 1955, for example, only 39 percent of the sixty-two million stems harvested in the country were shipped overseas.[4]

The Ecuadorian government responded to this difficulty by reducing its support for the creation of new banana farms. Property rights were still awarded to individuals who carved agricultural homesteads out of tropical forests. However, the government's purpose was to encourage farming and ranching of any and all sorts on unowned *tierras baldías*, not just geographic spread of the tropical fruit sector. A sharper policy pivot occurred at the agricultural development bank, the BNF. Having climbed steadily since 1951, the bank's lending to *bananeros* peaked in 1956 at thirty-two million sucres (approximately $11,600,000 in today's money). The following year, national leaders were "worried that the country was over-producing relative to world demand,"[5] and James J. Parsons reported that much less credit was being made available for banana farming.[6] Never again would low-interest loans be disbursed solely to encourage agricultural colonization and deforestation on the part of would-be fruit growers.

The exported portion of Ecuador's banana harvest recovered during the next few years, as Luís Noboa and other homegrown entrepreneurs found new customers overseas. However, other problems needed to be dealt with, including the containment of microbial infestations—something the cacao sector had not managed to do. If Ecuador was to stay atop the global banana business, it would have to switch from Gros Michel to the Cavendish variety and improve technology in other ways, as growers in competing nations were doing. Since the country's tropical fruit sector did not invest much in agricultural research and development or in agricultural education, technological improvement and human capital formation would depend on outside assistance, including what transnational firms provided.

Easy Harvests

The fertile prairies of the American Midwest are ideally suited to supplying the world with grain; the region's production of corn, more than anything else, is unrivaled. Likewise, Brazil has been the world's top coffee exporter since the nineteenth century and its leading position is unlikely to be ceded to another country any time soon. By the same token, there is no better place than western Ecuador to cultivate the most globalized of fruits.

As long as Big Mike was king, there was little to prevent any enterprising farmer in the *costa* from raising bananas as a cash crop. All one needed were several hectares within reach of a road or navigable waterway. In April or May, when the rainy season was over, the owners of undeveloped holdings would clear away trees and other vegetation; this was usually done with fire, for the sake of convenience and also because the ash that remained after burning enriched the soil. In many settings, such as the foothills of the Andes, the ground was gently sloped, so ditches did not have to be dug for drainage. Accordingly, land preparation was cheap, costing about $120 per hectare through the 1960s. Drainage ditches were required in Colombia, so the average expense of establishing a new plantation there was $600 per hectare. In Central America, the per-hectare cost was at least $2,000 and as much as $3,100, since additional effort was needed to clear thick forests, install drainage systems, and build roads and rail lines in areas lacking this infrastructure.[7]

With no further land preparation, Ecuadorian farmers would plant bulblike corms amid the charred stumps and underbrush. Weeding would follow every three months or so. Fertilizer might be applied, provided the necessary cash could be spared, and irrigation was rare.[8] The first sign of the harvest to come occurred nine to eleven months after Gros Michel corms had gone into the ground. A bud would appear at the center of a leaf cluster on each corm's pseudo-stem, which by this time had risen to a height of several meters after pushing up through the earth. The bud would gradually lengthen into a stem that would open to expose clusters of flowers. With time, each of these clusters would develop into a "hand" containing ten to twenty bananas (called "fingers"). The banana plant would be propped up as the stem, which bent downward under its burden of fruit, gained weight. Four months after the bud's appearance and thirteen to fifteen months after the corm had been planted, the stem would be severed from its pseudo-stem, which would be cut down as well. The harvest had to happen before there was any hint of bananas turning yellow, since fruit would continue to ripen as it made its way off the farm, to a coastal harbor, then on to customers across the sea.

Simple and inexpensive, raising bananas had considerable advantages over cacao production. An initial harvest happened fourteen months or so after planting, not after five years. Also, production and therefore earnings could be spread throughout the year, rather than being concentrated in a single annual harvest, by managing the pseudo-stems that would emerge regularly as long as corms remained in the ground. Cacao farming, it must be admitted, was less labor intensive, although the revenues generated by a hectare planted to bananas greatly exceeded per-hectare revenues for cacao. Indeed, no other crop provided landowners "a cash return with such ease."[9]

Just as raising Gros Michel bananas was more profitable than any other agricultural activity, tropical fruit production was less labor intensive and cheaper in western Ecuador than in other parts of the Western Hemisphere. Counting harvest-time effort, the ratio of labor to land on non-irrigated banana farms in the *costa* was 0.50 person-years of work per hectare. The same ratio was achieved on mechanized holdings in the French Antilles. But in Central America, the ratio of labor to land varied between 0.60 and 0.75 person-years per hectare. The average level of compensation in the Ecuadorian countryside was about $1.40 a day—little different from prevailing rural wages in Guatemala, Honduras, and neighboring countries.[10] Banana growers in the *costa* paid their employees above-average wages,[11] although compensation levels were much higher on corporate plantations in Central America. Under these circumstances, the estimated cost of harvested fruit was lower in Ecuador than in Central America—fifty-three cents per kilogram versus ninety cents per kilogram in 1958, for example—and overseas markets served by exporters from the latter region could be supplied more cheaply by their rivals south of the Panama Canal.[12]

Early Guidance from Foreigners

Another attribute of the *costa*'s banana farms was that the overall quality of output was satisfactory, as Richard Goodell observed in late 1934. But Goodell, the first manager of United Fruit's subsidiary in Ecuador, also drew attention to the damage done because post-harvest handling was poor. Much of the fruit offered to his company, which for nearly a year had been dispatching a shipload of Ecuadorian bananas north every fortnight, was not good enough for sale in the United States, so had to be rejected. United Fruit was willing to educate growers about proper handling techniques, but Goodell also warned that strict standards could not be relaxed.[13]

Buyers' rejections of Ecuadorian bananas, which along with losses between farms and ports amounted to 43 percent or more of what growers sent the buyers' way in the mid-1950s,[14] were sometimes criticized as excessive. In particular, some exporters were accused of not accepting fruit that was perfectly marketable after arranging beforehand to buy more produce than they could actually ship overseas—supposedly out of a desire to avoid the risk of not filling all available cargo space.[15] At the same time, exporters had their own complaints. Few of their agreements with planters were legally binding, complete with notarized signatures; most were sealed with nothing more than a handshake. Cash advances for future sales were common, though not an ironclad guarantee of fruit deliveries. A one-time buyer recalled that many growers were capable of reneging on their commitments to deliver bananas "without getting red in the face."[16]

As the years passed, United Fruit labored to convince Ecuadorian planters of the need to handle their perishable output with the utmost care. There was a redoubling of this effort as the firm increased its reliance on purchased bananas, as an alternative to the harvests of its own plantations. In 1956, for example, the company invited representatives of the growers' association, ANBE, to visit ports, wholesaling centers, and related facilities in New York and New Orleans. The tour convinced the Ecuadorians that, if their country acquired a reputation for inferior produce, exports would suffer, especially as competition intensified in the United States and elsewhere.[17]

While time spent at hubs for distributing and marketing bananas helped clarify the value of good post-harvest handling, a stop at United Fruit's research center in La Lima, Honduras, during the 1956 tour added to the Ecuadorians' appreciation of the company's farming practices. However, learning about those practices did not require foreign travel. Independent growers were "inspired by the technical cultivation" they viewed at El Tenguel, as a delegation from the French government's agricultural research agency, the Institut National de la Recherche Agronomique (INRA), reported after a 1959 visit to the *costa*.[18] Among other things, banana plants were spaced properly, with Gros Michel corms set out on a grid and with every corm and its pseudo-stem located about five meters from each of its four closest neighbors. Also, United Fruit's operations were exemplary in terms of fertilizer applications and hydrologic management. Having known since the 1920s that banana plants do poorly in soils that are too moist, the company complemented the estate's irrigation system with a network of drainage canals, which had to be cleaned frequently and which also were deeper than the ditches that had been dug in nearby fields of sugarcane for the evacuation of excess water.[19]

To this day, Ecuadorians familiar with the beginnings of their country's banana sector point to the contributions United Fruit made decades ago, including the demonstration of agricultural techniques at El Tenguel. Reflecting on the developments he witnessed at close range, a long-time aide of Juan X. Marcos characterized the U.S. company as a "pioneer . . . [that] brought in the technical culture necessary for world exports."[20] This judgment was shared by Sergio Seminario, whose career as a leading planter culminated in 2003 with his appointment as Ecuador's minister of agriculture. More than forty years after the transnational firm brought in its last harvest in the *costa*, Seminario declared that "El Tenguel and United Fruit were for me the banana industry." The company could take much of the credit, he maintained, for Ecuador's becoming a major exporter.[21]

Other foreign firms also shared technology with Ecuadorian planters, both before the end of United Fruit's agricultural operations southeast of Guayaquil and afterward. For example, Folke Anderson's company, Astral, was a consistent force in the northern *costa* for better standards of farming. Similarly, Roy Kerr, who was Standard Fruit's manager in Ecuador a half century ago, was widely appreciated for heading out regularly from his office in the port city to teach growers about pruning, fertilizing, and preventing the spread of plant diseases.

Assistance from the U.S. Government

Foreign companies were not the only driving force for technological improvement in Ecuador's banana industry. The public sector in the United States also provided assistance, especially as Yellow Sigatoka worked its way down the Pacific coast. By 1952, the airborne fungus "had reached epidemic proportions" in the vicinity of Esmeraldas; it was a serious threat four years later as far south as Quevedo.[22] To contain the disease, planters with large holdings had the option to undertake sizable investments of the sort made on multi-national estates in Central America—to be specific, in networks of elevated pipes used for the regular application of a fungicide called Bordeaux Spray (an aqueous solution containing copper sulfate and lime). However, this system was economically impractical for the owners of small and medium-sized farms. Moreover, ignoring this group would have resulted in speedy reinfection of treated areas.

In August 1954, not long after the disease began to reduce harvests in northwestern Ecuador, the Servicio Interamericano de Cooperación para la Agricultura (SICA), which in spite of its Spanish name was an agency of the U.S. government, responded to a request for assistance originating in Quito by dispatching a four-person team to the *costa*. The team was headed by Norman M. Ward and included his SICA colleague, Harold Hughes. Also included were two scientists from United Fruit, Russell Desrosiers and Robert Smith, whose participation in the initiative to safeguard harvests in western Ecuador met with their employer's approval.

Working at the Pichilingue agricultural research station, a little south of Quevedo, the SICA team investigated alternatives to Bordeaux Spray. French scientists in Guadeloupe and Martinique had recently discovered that coating banana plants with a mixture of oil, diesel fuel, and copper oxy-chloride protected the plants against Yellow Sigatoka. The chief advantage of this alternative was that the application rate was twenty-seven liters per hectare: 1 percent of the 2,700 liters per hectare of Bordeaux Spray that were applied annually at the time in Central America.[23] The four Americans and their Ecuadorian collaborators later achieved comparable results with twenty-three liters per hectare of oil, alone.[24] Additionally, Desrosiers and his colleagues designed a portable backpack applicator with small and medium-sized growers specifically in mind. With the operator working the applicator's hand-pump, spray oil came out as a mist through a super-fine mesh. This mist covered the entire banana plant, thereby protecting it from pathogens.

Putting the technological advances achieved at Pichilingue to use fell to ANBE. The association introduced the backpack applicator to the farmers for whom it was intended. This initiative had an impact for a number of years because the applicators (manufactured in Ecuador) and the spray oil needed to treat a single hectare were inexpensive. Of more lasting importance was the aerial spraying ANBE organized and administered, which was particularly effective if helicopters were used instead of fixed-wing aircraft because the turbulence created by spinning rotors resulted in better coverage of banana plants with sprayed oil. Helicopters were deployed in the campaign against Yellow Sigatoka after Marcos authorized his pilot—Harry Crawford, a veteran of the U.S. Army Air Corps as well as the first husband of this book's coauthor—to bring a fleet of those aircraft from California to Ecuador, hire and train pilots, hold demonstrations, and so on.

By all measures, the campaign against Yellow Sigatoka was successful. In 1964, for example, 115,000 of the 170,000 hectares used for commercial banana production were fumigated.[25] Preston credited ANBE for keeping the fungal disease in check at an affordable cost.[26] Another study reached a broader yet similar conclusion, that controlling Yellow Sigatoka by spraying oil diminished production costs as well as the capital requirements of banana farming; as a result, there was a "massive expansion" of Ecuadorian output.[27]

Agricultural Education

SICA's partnership with ANBE was essential for the dissemination of improved agricultural technology. Individual growers also served as conduits for technology transfer. For example, Noboa, who had no agricultural holdings for many years after getting into the tropical fruit business, bought the 785-hectare Martinica farm in 1964, not only so he could raise some of the bananas he exported but also so that improved practices could be demonstrated to other growers.[28] In later years, the Ecuadorian entrepreneur acquired equity positions in multinational fruit companies, which guaranteed him as well as his country uninterrupted access to the companies' technology.

Esteban Quirola, who formerly grew many of the bananas exported by SAFCO and became an important supplier for Standard Fruit after that company's partnership with Marcos and Noboa ended in 1955,[29] dedicated himself to the improvement of agriculture in the southern *costa*. More than fifty years ago, Quirola was one of the first farmers in the area to cover ripening banana stems with plastic bags, which provide protection against low temperatures during cool nights and limit insect damage.[30] In addition, he followed United Fruit's lead by digging deep ditches for the drainage of his rural properties in addition to pioneering the mechanized harvesting of bananas.[31] Efforts such as these brought Quirola to the attention of the INRA delegation that visited Ecuador in 1959. An invitation to go to Paris was soon extended, which Quirola accepted and which also gave him the opportunity to tour French plantations in Africa. The Ecuadorian grower returned to his homeland with new agricultural knowledge, including better measures for combating Yellow Sigatoka. This knowledge quickly found its way to other farmers.[32]

Valuable though their contributions were, even people as influential as Noboa and Quirola were in no position to raise standards of farming throughout Ecuador's tropical fruit sector on their own. To satisfy the demand for skilled planters, who would be aware of and adopt the latest advances, the sector came to rely on the Pan American Agricultural School, which owed its existence to Samuel Zemurray. In 1941, United Fruit's chief executive had asked Wilson Popenoe, an esteemed tropical botanist and horticulturalist, to create the postsecondary institution at a site of the scientist's choosing in Honduras. During the next few years, the company funded the educational project to the tune of six million dollars, although it did not hire any of the school's graduates so that no one could complain that the project actually served corporate interests.[33]

Known by the name of the property where the school is located, El Zamorano from the beginning offered a comprehensive education in tropical agriculture. Perhaps reflecting on his own origins, Zemurray insisted on the recruitment of low-income students. However, the offspring of prosperous landowners also applied and were admitted, though with the understanding that there would be no concessions at the school to socioeconomic privilege. This sharp break from the Latin American norm reflected Zemurray's values as well as those of Popenoe, who served as El Zamorano's founding director until 1957.

Ecuadorian Simón Malo has written a book about the school, including his own experiences there. Like other Zamoranos, as all students and alumni proudly call themselves, Malo was issued an army-style blanket for his bed (which consisted of a thin mat of woven reeds) on his arrival. Otherwise, he received two towels, a pair of slippers, and laundry soap. The young scholar was put to work right away, hoeing weeds until his blistered hands bled. A bell rang every morning at 5:30 a.m. sharp, although Malo rose a half hour earlier to join a group of students lifting weights to gain strength. These workouts paid off during his second year at El Zamorano, when he dug drainage ditches and irrigation canals through fields of corn, sugarcane, and rice.[34]

Every Zamorano attended classes four to five hours each weekday and there was a compulsory study hall lasting four hours every evening. Work obligations were also non-negotiable. If a pregnant sow was about to deliver, for instance, the student assigned to care for the animal had to remain on station in the barn—all night if necessary, regardless of any test or presentation scheduled for the following day.[35] Thus were lifelong habits of hard work and dedication forged.

The coauthor of this book saw those habits put to good use on a large banana plantation in the *costa* that was owned and operated by José Antonio González, an alumnus of El Zamorano as well as the grandson of one of the investors who had joined Marcos in restoring the Ingenio San Carlos after purchasing the sugar mill in 1938. González dressed like any other farmer and drove around his property in a flatbed truck. Arriving every morning before anyone else, he remained on site throughout the day and was never above demonstrating a task to an employee. The Zamorano had not learned how to raise bananas at his alma mater,[36] where instruction is offered on the production of a number of other crops. He nevertheless made it his business always to stay abreast of technological advances in the tropical fruit sector. González turned out to be a leading source of information for this book about how banana farming has changed over the years.

In keeping with Zemurray and Popenoe's original vision, more than a few Ecuadorian Zamoranos with humble backgrounds went on to distinguished careers. One was Marcel Laniado, who had to borrow money in order to travel home after his graduation in 1949. Soon after his return to Ecuador, he was hired by the BNF, which a few years later promoted him to its board of directors. During the 1960s and 1970s, Laniado helped run the agribusiness in which Quirola was a principal investor that was dedicated to banana production in the southern *costa*. León Febres-Cordero, the right-of-center winner of the presidential election of 1984, selected him as minister of agriculture, although the Zamorano never adapted to the public sector. As Laniado put it, he was only able to get results out of a tenth of his bureaucratic workforce.[37]

There have been other Ecuadorians who accomplished much after graduating from the Pan American Agricultural School. Mario Jalil, who attended El Zamorano on a scholarship, served his country as minister of agriculture after a long career at the UN Food and Agriculture Organization (FAO). Jorge Chang worked for Dole in Costa Rica and Ecuador and later managed a large sugar mill outside Guayaquil.[38] The total number of Ecuadorian alumni is greater than 1,500 and is exceeded only by the number of Honduran alumni; however, this ranking could change since Ecuadorian students have been the largest national cohort at the university in recent years (Table 6).

Table 6: National Origins of Students and Alumni at El Zamorano, Autumn 2013

Country	Alumni	Enrolled students
Ecuador	1,536	365
El Salvador	450	85
Guatemala	736	147
Honduras	1,878	299
Nicaragua	503	67
All Others	1,839	289
Total	6,942	1,252

Source: Dirección de Avance Institucional y Oficina de Registro y Asistencia Financiera, Universidad de Zamorano.

The practices of Ecuadorian Zamoranos employed in the tropical fruit sector differ markedly from the practices of many who raise bananas between the Andes and the Pacific Ocean—especially small growers, whose resources are scarce and who can be slow to change their ways. Speaking for many, Noboa complained about producers who "paid no attention to the rules and harvested fruit which foreign buyers would reject or pay very low prices for. It was a problem to convince them that the crop was part of an agribusiness."[39] In contrast, Zamoranos have always understood the commercial demands of their work, including varietal conversion when its time came.

Cavendish Comes to the *Costa*

In 1964, Ecuador had a dominating position in the global banana industry. The western part of the country boasted rich soils and a favorable climate. Plant pathogens did more damage in the Caribbean Basin. Also, labor requirements and wages were modest, so production costs were low—low enough to outweigh infrastructural deficiencies, Panama Canal tolls, and a location far from major markets.[40]

Western Ecuador's advantages were also durable, or so it was hoped even as Panama Disease showed up in farm after farm. First observed in the vicinity of Guayaquil in 1936, the soil-borne fungus was reducing harvests in the lower Río Guayas valley and the southern *costa* twenty years later, when little could be done about the problem other than to abandon infected fields. The expedient of shifting production to uninfected soils remained in some parts of the country, although this did not remove the microbial threat.

Growers and exporters in the *costa* knew full well that Gros Michel was giving way to the Cavendish in other areas hit hard by Panama Disease. The change was not instigated by United Fruit, which doubted that consumers would accept any substitute for the traditional variety. Sticking with Gros Michel cost the firm dearly through the 1950s in terms of the thousands of hectares taken out of production because of Panama Disease as well as reductions of 25 to 33 percent in the annual output of surviving plantations caused by tropical storms.[41] Standard Fruit, in contrast, staked its future on Cavendish bananas after 1954, when Joseph D'Antoni—a medical doctor and a son of one of the Italian-American immigrants who had founded the company— assumed leadership of the multinational firm. D'Antoni fully supported the agronomic research that preceded the planting of the disease-resistant variety on Standard Fruit's estates, beginning in 1957. An investment was also made during this period in factories for the manufacture of cardboard cartons and packing stations located among fields planted to bananas. These factories and stations were needed because Cavendish bananas, which have thin skins and bruise easily, must be transported in boxes instead of in the old way, on the stem. Changing varieties and revamping the shipping system were expensive, so the company earned just $233,969 in 1959 and posted a loss the following year of $7,750,477.[42]

Varietal transformation and the switch to boxed shipping soon paid off handsomely: "In 1962, Standard set new company records for production per acre, for total production from company-owned farms, and for net profit—an imposing $5,714,000 just two years after the company's worst year, in spite of prices that had been declining almost steadily for a decade."[43] United Fruit, meanwhile, was not standing still. The same year that its principal rival suffered record losses, the company initiated field-testing of a category of Cavendish called Valery bananas, with encouraging results.

[On] some farms where there was total destruction of Gros Michel plants during heavy winds, the Valery plant losses on adjoining plots were not more than 20%; on other farms where Gros Michel wind losses were up to 75% there were no significant losses of Valery plants. Valery fruit yields per acre promised to be as much as 2 to 2½ times what was then coming from the same acreage in Gros Michel.[44]

In light of these findings, United Fruit made the decision to plant Cavendish bananas on all its farms, which happened between 1962 and 1965.[45]

Ecuadorian *bananeros* did not follow suit immediately, mainly because they feared that switching varieties would drive up costs so much that their country would cease to be competitive. Since Cavendish bananas are fragile, funicular systems consisting of suspended cables had to be installed on farms so that stems could move with minimal bruising from the fields where they had been cut to local packing facilities. At the packing facilities, hands of fruit would be removed from the stem and then washed, dried, and placed in boxes with holes in the side for ventilation, ready for export. Another farm-level adjustment had to do with repeated spraying to control an airborne fungus (*Mycosphaerella fijiensis*) responsible for Black Sigatoka, which is referred to in the scientific literature as Black Leaf Streak Disease and which displaced Yellow Sigatoka and spread rapidly to banana-growing areas throughout the world after being detected in Fiji in 1964.[46] Worried about the combined expense of funicular systems, packing stations, and increased spraying, growers invented myths (as Jean Paul Valles described their beliefs in a 1968 study of the banana industry) that justified sticking with Gros Michel. One myth, that Cavendish bananas had an inferior taste and appearance, was contradicted by testing with consumers, few of whom truly were able to distinguish between the two varieties. Also not backed up by any evidence was the notion that the new variety would travel poorly, to the detriment of exporters in remote places like Ecuador.[47]

Beliefs such as these were clung to and the investment needed for varietal replacement was avoided long enough for Ecuador's standing in the global market to slip noticeably. Equal to 45 percent in 1964, the country's share of the worldwide banana trade was barely 30 percent two years later.[48] Some Ecuadorians might contend that Gros Michel fruit produced in the *costa* was peerless and that U.S. corporations were forcing the switch to Cavendish so that independent suppliers somehow would be weakened, if not destroyed. But the leaders of Ecuador's tropical fruit sector knew better. Due to the decline in production and exports resulting from the continued cultivation of Gros Michel, a shadow had been cast over the sector.

Valles was not optimistic in 1968 about the *costa*'s prospects, concluding that "there is little doubt that the banana boom in Ecuador is over."[49] However, this assessment was soon contradicted because the switch to the Cavendish variety, which began before Valles's study was published, shored up

Ecuador's competitive position in various ways. Shipping fruit in boxes rather than on the stem reduced the rate of rejection. This was because detection of a banana that was damaged or beginning to ripen resulted in the disposal of the hand containing that same banana, not the entire stem. Also, the cost of shipping a ton of fruit was reduced because more space in the holds of reefer ships could be filled with boxes. In contrast, vessels on which stevedores had hung as many stems as they could below deck typically set sail with a lot of empty cargo space. While lower shipping costs benefited all banana exporters, the impact was particularly important in western Ecuador and other places that were not close to major markets and where transportation expenditures consequently claimed a large share of gross revenues.

As growers had anticipated, the switch to boxes obliged them to install packing facilities and hire workers to destem and wash bananas and place produce in cardboard cartons. However, those cartons could be transported unopened from tropical plantations all the way to retail outlets, thereby eliminating all the destemming, cleaning, and packaging formerly carried out in importing nations before fruit was set out on grocery shelves. The overall impact, in other words, was to shift work to Central and South America from places like New York and Antwerp, where wages were much higher. No exporting nation benefited more from this shift than Ecuador, where thousands of people—mainly women—found jobs in box factories and packing stations.[50]

Varietal replacement also had impressive agronomic payoffs. Compared to Gros Michel plants, Cavendish plants are short, which explains why they are less susceptible to being blown over during storms. Smaller size also allows for greater planting densities; instead of 400 Gros Michel corms per hectare, 830 to 1,300 Cavendish corms per hectare were normal during the 1960s.[51] With Panama Disease no longer taking a toll, losses from strong winds largely eliminated, and fruit-bearing plants crowded closer together, output per hectare was much higher with the new variety.

Once they forgot their earlier reservations, Ecuadorian growers wasted no time switching varieties. Individuals who dealt regularly with Standard Fruit were the first to get the necessary root stock. Quirola received Cavendish corms thanks to personal connections with United Fruit.[52] There was no lack of takers for loans to facilitate varietal replacement offered by the Programa Nacional del Banano (PNB), a government agency that replaced ANBE in 1963.[53] Also, PNB technicians traveled to San Pedro Sula, where they bought approximately 2,000 Cavendish corms from a number of Honduran growers.

Late one night, the corms were put on a plane, which took off for Guayaquil a few hours later as dawn was breaking. Once the plane landed, the root stock for a revived Ecuadorian banana sector was distributed widely in the *costa*.[54]

Between 1965 and 1970, Gros Michel corms were uprooted in approximately 70,000 hectares; 50,000 hectares were planted meanwhile to the Cavendish variety, which comprised 7 percent of Ecuador's exports of bananas in 1967 but 70 percent three years later.[55] Once varietal transformation happened, the decline in output and foreign shipments registered immediately after 1964 was halted and Ecuador continued to be the world's leading exporter of tropical fruit.

Sustaining a Banana Exporting Powerhouse

Excelling at the task of selling their country's bananas around the world, Ecuadorian entrepreneurs never have taken it upon themselves to create new technology. Instead, research and development have been left to foreigners, above all multinational firms. This specialization has worked for Ecuadorian growers because U.S. corporations have regularly shared new varieties and farming practices. Those corporations also have been served well since they buy fruit regularly in the *costa* and so have an interest in avoiding supply interruptions there.

Both as individuals and collectively in groups such as ANBE, Ecuadorian *bananeros* have facilitated the transfer of technology. Furthermore, individuals such as Noboa and Wong have staked capital so that the latest advances could be applied in the *costa*, to the benefit of the entire tropical fruit sector. Illustrative in this regard is their investment in box manufacturing and packing facilities, which began a few years before the conversion from Gros Michel to the Cavendish variety. During the first four months of 1961, Ecuador's monetary authorities gave the shipping of bananas in cardboard containers a boost—in particular, by temporarily excusing those exporters who started using boxes from the requirement to convert all earnings from fruit shipments into Ecuadorian sucres at confiscatory official exchange rates.[56] Noboa responded to the permanent increase in box demand that this measure created by launching his own company, the Industria Cartonera Ecuatoriana, and drawing on his reserves of hard currency to import the necessary machinery. Corrugated material for lining cartons packed with bananas was obtained from a local sugar mill, which manufactured the material from cane byproducts. Noboa also traded bananas for the Kraft paper used to cover bunches of packed fruit and profited by backhauling the paper on reefer ships returning from the United States to Ecuador. Limited box production commenced in April 1961, although the capacity of the Industria Cartonera Ecuatoriana had to quintuple during the next few years to meet demand. With time, other entrepreneurs joined Noboa in the box business—including Segundo Wong, who founded Cartonera Andina during the 1980s.

At packing stations that Noboa, Quirola, Wong, and others established in the Ecuadorian countryside, labels recognized by consumers in importing nations were attached to fruit purchased from independent growers. Bananas were then placed in cartons that would not be opened until they reached retail outlets frequented by those same consumers. For example, stickers bearing Noboa's Bonita brand were fixed to the produce of independent farms; after being shipped to Antwerp, this produce was sold far and wide in Europe by Leon Van Parys, the Belgian associate of the Guayaquil businessmen. The entire process was indistinguishable from the distribution and marketing of bananas harvested on multinational plantations and farms covered by contracts with foreign firms—bananas bearing Chiquita and other corporate labels familiar to U.S. and European consumers.

In the absence of Ecuadorian investment in box factories and packing facilities, the only Ecuadorian growers with assured access to U.S. and European markets would have been those who had production agreements with foreign firms, such as Standard Fruit. But since the investment occurred, access was maintained for all growers, which among other consequences enabled the entire tropical fruit sector of Ecuador to meet the challenge of varietal conversion. The switch to Cavendish, once it occurred, resulted in some consolidation of banana farms. But with annual yields averaging 35 to 40 tons per hectare, many operators with relatively modest holdings of land found it worthwhile to make the investment required for production of the new variety. So in 1970, when all Guatemalan and Panamanian bananas were still exported by United Fruit and the bulk of Costa Rica's harvest came from large plantations, independent holdings of small and medium size remained the norm in western Ecuador.[57]

The *costa*'s experience with box manufacturing and packing plants also benefited Colombia's tropical fruit sector. In 1964, bananas from the northeastern part of the country were still being shipped abroad on the stem, although buyers in importing nations were insisting more and more on the use of cardboard cartons. Assistance with the switch to boxed exports was not furnished by United Fruit, which had departed from the region. Nor was help provided by Standard Fruit. Instead, a delegation of Colombian growers and exporters sought and received advice in western Ecuador. Applying what they learned from their South American neighbors, the Colombians were soon exporting tropical fruit in boxes,[58] thereby satisfying their customers and also maintaining a competitive presence in various markets.

CHAPTER 7

Agrarian Reform, Unionization, and a Policy Tilt Against Agriculture

After the switch to boxed shipments, for which homegrown entrepreneurs deserved much credit, Ecuador remained at the top of the global banana industry. Also, independent farms of twenty-five to a few hundred hectares still comprised the core of the country's tropical fruit sector, in marked contrast to the continuing importance in other nations of sprawling plantations owned by foreign corporations. The widespread presence of small and medium-sized farms in the *costa* had various consequences—not least putting a brake on the redistribution of agricultural land during and after the 1960s, when agrarian reform was undertaken in many parts of Latin America.

Breaking up large, underutilized holdings had been the main thrust of the agrarian reform championed by Guatemala's Jacobo Arbenz during the early 1950s. More than 150,000 hectares that United Fruit kept in reserve instead of exploiting immediately were confiscated, which influenced the U.S. government's decision to topple Arbenz in 1954.[1] But little more than a half decade later, the thinking in Washington was different. Intent on avoiding a repetition of the Cuban Revolution anywhere else in the Western Hemisphere, the administration of John F. Kennedy pushed throughout the region for agrarian reform, including the redistribution of idle land.

In Ecuador, social inequality and concentrated resource ownership were extreme in the Andes and José María Velasco-Ibarra, who became chief of state for a fourth time shortly before Kennedy's electoral victory in November 1960, appointed a Comisión Nacional de Reforma Agraria to draft legislation, although nothing came of this initiative. Four years later, the Agrarian Reform Law of 1964 abolished arrangements dating back to colonial times that bound highland *campesinos* to the rural estates where they lived and worked.

However, the law's limits on the size of rural properties were "so flexible as to be virtually meaningless" and were applied only to the most inefficient estates belonging to people with little political influence.[2]

In 1972, Velasco-Ibarra's fifth (and final) presidency was cut short by a coup d'état led by Guillermo Rodríguez-Lara. The general and his uniformed colleagues drafted an agrarian reform decree that derived from policies of the left-of-center military regime in Peru, where more than six million hectares were given to at least 265,000 households. But during the years preceding the coup, owners of Andean haciendas had sold tens of thousands of under-utilized hectares, which might have been seized and redistributed. They also joined with sympathetic officers in Rodríguez-Lara's government to block tighter ceilings on the size of landholdings.[3] The law actually enacted in October 1973 had little impact apart from the elimination of "precarious" forms of land tenure, defined to include the rental of agricultural real estate.[4] Between vague guidelines for land expropriation and delays in implementation of the 1973 law, barely 88,000 hectares were redistributed between 1973 and 1975.[5]

In January 1977, Rodríguez-Lara was replaced by a more conservative group of military officers who were unenthusiastic about land redistribution. A decree issued later the same year underscored the new regime's intention to increase the output of existing farms while accelerating the colonization of *tierras baldías* owned by no one.[6] Peasants in the Andes and settled parts of the *costa* who desired additional resources were not to expect the subdivision of nearby estates. As an alternative, they could stake claims along agricultural frontiers traversing northwestern Ecuador and Amazonian lowlands in the eastern part of the country.[7]

Contrasting with the agrarian reform and colonization initiatives of various military governments were the obstacles those governments and some civilian administrations put in the way of organized labor. Individual unions, most of which represented the employees of single businesses, received official recognition during Rodríguez-Lara's time as chief executive, though this process decelerated noticeably under the next military junta. The same junta also repressed a number of strikes. Unions received more backing after the return to civilian rule, in 1979. However, their effectiveness was undermined by the chronic rivalry of three national federations, each of which claimed to be the sole representative of all Ecuadorian workers.[8] From time to time, labor organizers targeted large agricultural enterprises, especially Astral but also major Ecuadorian *bananeros*. But smaller growers were left alone by and large.

All told, the tropical fruit sector was not greatly affected either by agrarian reform or by unionization. In contrast, the adoption of a development strategy that favored manufacturing enterprises directly undermined the sector. During the 1970s and early 1980s, Ecuador's leadership of the global banana industry was maintained in spite of, not thanks to, the government's economic policies.

A "Paradise" for Rural Workers

Steve Striffler's book about United Fruit's time in Ecuador, which does not address topics such as the technical assistance the company provided local planters, focuses on conflicts with peasants demanding land and with workers and the unions attempting to represent them. This emphasis is odd because United Fruit was by all accounts, including Striffler's, an exemplary employer. Aside from the Hacienda Clementina, which belonged to the Wallenbergs of Sweden for nearly four decades beginning in the early 1940s, no rural enterprise in the *costa* treated its workers as well.

As a rule, wages paid by banana growers were above the rural norm, which among other things resulted in substantial migration from the Andes to the *costa*.[9] Levels of compensation for United Fruit employees were even higher, as much as four times the prevailing agricultural wage. There were also benefits that were the envy of all but a few working Ecuadorians, such as paid vacation and sick leave.[10] Thousands of people consequently sought jobs at El Tenguel and other United Fruit properties, as one long-time employee witnessed:

> I came to Tenguel around 1940. My family had moved to Guayaquil in the 1930s because there was no work in (rural areas of) the coast. A friend told me there was this American company that was hiring workers. I got a job and the company took me and some others to Tenguel by boat. There wasn't much here when I arrived, and many people left right after they got here. We had to build everything. But later things improved and I brought my wife and we made a family here. After the Second World War, things really picked up and men would arrive with their families from Loja and Cuenca (in the southern highlands).[11]

The relocation of entire families to El Tenguel reveals much about its attractions. The estate's hospital was one of the best in the country—good enough to attract outsiders requiring medical attention and able to pay for same.[12] There were clubhouses and a swimming pool for employees as well as stores where food and other items could be purchased at below-market prices. Striffler, who peppers his writings with anti-corporate cant, characterizes the barracks for unmarried employees as "almost slave-like." However, most of the structures United Fruit put in place, including the bachelors' quarters, remain intact today, more than a half-century after the company's departure, since they were built of treated wood imported from the United States and were maintained well.[13]

According to Striffler, United Fruit wanted to avoid a repetition of the drunkenness and fighting among single male workers as well as the prostitution that had occurred on some Central American plantations. Intoxicated individuals were incarcerated and, to avoid having large groups of inebriates on its hands, the company "almost never directly sponsored fiestas." So that employees would have wholesome ways to pass their off-duty hours, United Fruit operated theaters and paid for sports teams. Additionally, families were a central feature of life at El Tenguel. During the 1950s, when overall employment peaked at more than 3,500 individuals, nearly 2,000 of the 2,500 laborers with permanent positions were married men with dependent relatives living on company property.[14]

"Virtually all" the individuals Striffler interviewed have fond memories of the time when United Fruit owned and operated El Tenguel. One former employee had this to say:

> There was plenty of work and we didn't lack anything. The food was extremely cheap and of good quality. The company sold us meat and rice at cost. We had pasteurized milk. . . . The houses were painted frequently, the streets were cleaned regularly, and we had light, good water, and entertainment. Tenguel was a paradise.[15]

Striffler does not dismiss these recollections, although he insists that benefits and services for workers and their dependents were part of a broader system of corporate control aimed at maximizing productivity and curbing labor strife. He also contends that families were an essential feature of this system. The hacienda's female residents, who were offered no jobs, "clearly benefited from the higher wages and benefits received by their male relatives." Since women relied entirely on the earnings of men, they could be counted on to admonish their husbands, fathers, and sons always to remain in good standing with the company.[16]

So for Striffler, El Tenguel was a paradise with a corporate purpose. To be sure, United Fruit exercised control in direct ways. Taking in more than 20,000 hectares, the hacienda had its own police force, which aside from keeping a tight lid on drinking, gambling, and other disruptive pursuits guarded carefully against trespassing. In particular, access to the estate was denied to the representatives of independent unions, whose contact with United Fruit employees (who were represented by a company union) was limited to occasional trips the employees made to Guayaquil. However, "high wages, well-maintained services, and a considerable range of benefits removed the need for more repressive forms of labor control."[17]

Historian Ronn Pineo has a more positive take on United Fruit's record in Ecuador. He agrees that the decision to "shower" El Tenguel's workforce with benefits reflected the "bad experiences with angry and organized workers" on corporate plantations in Central America. Regardless, Pineo concludes that the Ecuadorian estate represented "a remarkable, if singular, example of enlightened corporate generosity."[18] There is little doubt that Samuel Zemurray, who was an open-handed philanthropist in Latin America as well as the United States, and whose donations to the *Nation* rescued the leftwing periodical during the 1930s,[19] intended to demonstrate at El Tenguel the break United Fruit was making with old industry practices. Zemurray's commitment to change was expressed during an interview with *Life* magazine in 1951:

> I feel guilty about some of the things we did in the past (when) all we cared about was dividends. . . . You cannot do business that way today. We have learned that what is best for the countries where we operate in is also best for our company. Maybe we can't make people love us, but we can make ourselves so useful to them that they will want us to stay.[20]

U.S. Firms Leave Banana Farming to Others

Through its investments as well as the agricultural technology it shared, United Fruit served Ecuador well. Certainly, many of the country's citizens, not least *El Pulpo*'s employees, hoped the firm would never leave. But after the middle of the twentieth century, the company had embarked on a gradual transition—not just in Ecuador, but throughout the Western Hemisphere—from producing fruit on its own plantations to buying bananas from other growers.

By the late 1950s, the prospects for self-contained plantations, such as El Tenguel, were discouraging. Thomas Sutherland, who was recruited at this time to lead United Fruit, complained that independent growers in western Ecuador and other places "were not required to furnish housing, schools, hospitals, the necessary access roads, (and) port facilities," as his company did at its own cost in Central America.[21] In a study of the banana industry published in 1968 by the Harvard Business School, Henry Arthur, James Houck, and George Beckford characterized the agricultural operations of United Fruit and Standard Fruit as anachronistic. Aside from being expensive, self-contained plantations "could be characterized as industrial colonialism, with all its invidious images and vulnerability to the political sharp-shooting of local critics."[22]

There were other reasons to reorganize the agricultural side of the business. Per-capita consumption of bananas was going down in the United States even as Standard Fruit's experiments with Cavendish bananas were yielding promising results. In western Ecuador, annual production at El Tenguel and other United Fruit properties, which had climbed from 234,000 stems in 1945 to 1,284,000 stems a decade later, declined after the mid-1950s, mainly because of Panama Disease.[23] As harvests went down, holding on to agricultural real estate in the *costa* made less and less sense.

In other banana-producing nations, United Fruit was already transferring farmland to others. A case in point was the Associate Growers' Program (AGP), which was launched in Honduras in 1952 and to begin with involved one hundred former employees of United Fruit's subsidiary, the Tela Railroad Company. Each of these individuals was given twenty hectares planted to bananas and took charge of labor-intensive tasks such as weeding and harvesting. AGP participants agreed to sell all output to the company, which continued to be responsible for irrigation and drainage systems as well as access roads, and received titles to their respective parcels once the former owner had recovered the cost of farm improvements.[24]

Multinationals' motivations to divest Honduran real estate were reinforced in 1954, when an industry-wide strike forced the firms to recognize collective-bargaining rights and heavy rains led to widespread flooding. United Fruit, which the same year became the target of antimonopoly prosecution by the U.S. Department of Justice, slashed its payroll in Honduras, from 26,000 in 1953 to 13,000 in 1957. The company simultaneously reduced the area planted to bananas, from 16,000 to 11,300 hectares. Standard Fruit did not have to worry about antitrust litigation, yet joined United Fruit in cutting the number of corporate employees. Whereas 13,000 Hondurans worked for Standard Fruit in 1954, only 5,800 did so six years later.[25]

As divestiture proceeded, the AGP expanded. In 1958, the Tela Railroad Company leased 120 hectares apiece to four of its former agricultural supervisors; approximately 800 hectares were leased two years later to another ten ex-supervisors.[26] As of 1963, when United Fruit raised bananas on 8,525 hectares of its own land, 2,955 hectares were being cultivated by participants in the AGP.[27] The overall area, 11,480 hectares, was 28 percent smaller than the 16,000 hectares the company had used for banana production ten years earlier.

Aside from farmers given the chance to raise bananas on their own, few Hondurans expressed enthusiasm for the AGP. The national press and organized labor both interpreted the program as an attempt by United Fruit to shed responsibilities to its workforce. As company properties were spun off, these suspicions were confirmed. A retired associate grower interviewed by John Soluri conceded that laborers on farms such as his earned "about half" the wages and none of the fringe benefits they would have received on foreign-owned estates.[28] Sutherland and other representatives of United Fruit contended that the AGP would bolster the middle class and consequently alleviate political instability.[29] But Honduran authorities were skeptical. According to Soluri, they received the news that the company expected to sell all its plantations in the country and to become a banana buyer there instead like a "body blow." More such news soon followed from Standard Fruit. Established in 1966 and patterned on the AGP, that firm's divestiture initiative resulted in the transfer of 3,800 hectares to Honduran growers by the early 1970s.[30]

Honduras was by no means the only place where U.S.-based companies left banana production increasingly to local growers after the early 1950s. For example, United Fruit gradually sold all its assets in northeastern Colombia, leaving local growers in possession of the area's banana farms. When the same company chose during the 1960s to create a new source of fruit exports in the Urabá Valley, close to Panama, no corporate plantations were established. Instead, the plan was for all bananas to be purchased from farmers migrating into the region from other parts of Colombia.[31]

The End of United Fruit's Agricultural
Operations in the Costa

While United Fruit began a transition from growing to purchasing bananas in Honduras more than sixty years ago and in northeastern Colombia even earlier, the divestiture of company properties in Ecuador was little short of obligatory after 1958, when the consent decree reached with the Antitrust Division of the U.S. Department of Justice compelled the company to reduce its agricultural holdings in Latin America by one-third.[32] Two small farms, Pancho Negro and Tambo, were spun off to local growers.[33] However, plans for the divestiture of large properties—plans detailed in U.S. consular dispatches, though not mentioned in Striffler's book and other writings about the tropical fruit industry in Ecuador—were more complex. Coordinated by a local manager, Carlos Estrada, the plans for Taura-Vainillo and El Tenguel provided for the continued production of bananas and other crops while seeing to the interests of former employees, either as members of agricultural cooperatives or as individual farmers.

At the Taura-Vainillo plantation, 25,455 of 31,797 hectares were sold to private buyers. An agribusiness in which Esteban Quirola was the principal shareholder purchased 11,568 hectares.[34] The other 6,342 hectares were transferred to the Instituto Nacional de Colonización (INC) for the settlement of former employees, including approximately one hundred individuals who took advantage of the opportunity to buy fifteen-hectare parcels. Advocates of agrarian reform were disappointed that commercial planters received the lion's share of the estate. However, the parceling out of several thousand hectares by the INC represented the first instance in western Ecuador of land redistribution.[35]

At El Tenguel, outlying tracts with little agricultural potential were sold off for a few dollars per hectare. In addition, small cottages with electricity, running water, and ten hectares of land were made available to retirees for a token annual rent of thirty sucres ($10.75 in today's money); these parcels were snapped up quickly. Also consistent with the divestiture plans of 1959, employees who had worked with the multinational's livestock herds were organized into a cooperative that rented pastures belonging to El Tenguel and sold meat and milk in local markets. Reserve areas that could be cleared for banana production were leased to nearly a hundred neighboring growers. In addition, land infected by Panama Disease was subdivided and parcels were leased either to ex-foremen or to cooperatives made up of former employees, who took responsibility for planting crops other than bananas.[36]

In July 1961, Joseph Montgomery, another United Fruit manager responsible for the divestiture of real estate, provided an update to the U.S. ambassador in Quito. He described negotiations with prospective smallholders as
"difficult." On a more positive note, Montgomery reported on talks with Ecuadorian officials to transfer part of El Tenguel to the national government in
return for a payment of twenty-four million sucres (worth about $1,200,000
at the time and $7,270,000 today).[37] The purpose of this transfer was to give
the INC an additional opportunity to redistribute thousands of hectares to
former employees of United Fruit, just as the agency had done at Taura-
Vainillo. However, no money actually changed hands and negotiations were
curtailed when Velasco-Ibarra resigned the presidency in November 1961,
fourteen months after being inaugurated.[38]

Formulated barely five years after Arbenz's overthrow in Guatemala and
before the Kennedy administration made agrarian reform a key element of
its policy for Latin America, United Fruit's arrangements for El Tenguel were
visionary and the failure of implementation that occurred after Velasco-
Ibarra's resignation had disappointing consequences. The perennial standard
bearer of Ecuadorian populism was succeeded by his vice president, Carlos
Julio Arosemena, who was prickly, nationalistic, and a worry for the U.S. government because of his forthright affinity for Fidel Castro. In March 1962,
less than five months after the presidential transition, portions of El Tenguel
still in United Fruit's possession were taken over by the Cooperativa Juan
Quirumbay—the more radical of two groups of the company's former employees. The workers' invasion quickly received support from the government, in the form of a high-level commission which paid a visit to the estate
right after the invasion. Aside from jailing policemen who before the takeover
had arrested some of the cooperative's leaders, the commission announced
that the government would favor the Cooperativa Juan Quirumbay over the
Cooperativa Gala, which also comprised former employees of United Fruit
but had opposed the occupation.[39]

Two weeks after the invasion of El Tenguel, the Arosemena administration
expressed a willingness to buy United Fruit's remaining interest in the hacienda
and implement land redistribution little different from what the company had
proposed when Velasco-Ibarra was chief-of-state.[40] However, the Cooperativa
Juan Quirumbay was not dislodged and agricultural output soon collapsed.
Worse yet, vandalism and theft broke out, much of it perpetrated by individuals who had never worked for United Fruit but did not hesitate to take advantage of the chaos that followed the March 1962 invasion. Former neighbors of

El Tenguel witnessed the removal of company property, from tractors to baby incubators stolen from the estate's hospital, all destined for resale.[41]

In July 1963, Arosemena was overthrown by a military junta. Among the first initiatives of the new regime was to disband the Cooperativa Juan Quirumbay and take possession of the land it had occupied.[42] But by this time, United Fruit was gone, having completed the divestiture of Ecuadorian farmland prompted by the 1958 consent decree. The last several thousand hectares of what had been the company's flagship enterprise in the *costa* were reportedly sold for $200,000.[43]

Putting the Occupation of El Tenguel in Perspective

The 1962 invasion was not without precedent. In 1938—two years after United Fruit had donated nearly half of El Tenguel to the Ecuadorian government to defuse a controversy about foreign possession of land close to the country's borders—3,000 hectares had been occupied by tenants of the estate's former owner. The company, which according to Striffler had paid those tenants a "good price" for their holdings, promptly filed and won a trespassing lawsuit, although it allowed defendants who accepted the court's verdict to remain in place as renters. Advised by a Quito-based attorney associated with the Communist Party's labor union, the Confederación de Trabajadores Ecuatorianos (CTE), the same individuals spent the next several years pressing a collective claim to the 3,000 hectares. Frustrated by the government's failure to enforce the company's property rights in this particular instance, United Fruit gave in and recognized the claim in 1948.[44]

Another segment of El Tenguel was lost in much the same way more than ten years later. During the middle 1950s, former employees of United Fruit created the Colonia Agrícola Shumiral in the estate's northeastern sector: a stretch of hilly land with poor soils that had never been developed for agriculture. Not long afterward, in 1957, the company offered Shumiral's members leases on ten-hectare parcels for rent described by Striffler as "rather symbolic." This deal, which included technical assistance for banana farming as well as production contracts with the company, was accepted by the "overwhelming majority" of the squatters. However, there were a few holdouts—all advised by another CTE-affiliated attorney from Quito. He insisted on the donation of all 2,500 hectares occupied by the Colonia Agrícola Shumiral to the collective entity, including the ten-hectare parcels rented to individuals.

United Fruit accepted this settlement in April 1960, as the company was implementing the divestiture plans it had formulated the preceding year.[45]

Acknowledging that members of the Colonia Agrícola Shumiral were never able "to bring the land they won into production," Striffler nevertheless celebrates the settlement the community reached with United Fruit as a victory for workers and peasants, one that culminated "five years of struggle . . . against a major multinational."[46] He reads much more into the March 1962 takeover of El Tenguel. Just three years after the takeover, he states, all "foreign-owned plantations ceased to exist" in the *costa* and all "direct production was left in the hands of Ecuadorians." For Striffler, the 1962 invasion even had important repercussions outside the South American nation in that it "decisively shaped broader processes . . . within the global banana industry."[47]

Limited foreign land ownership in Ecuador indeed has had ramifications for the banana industry as a whole. But as documented in Chapter 3, the preponderance of locally owned farms in the *costa* traces back to the cacao boom of the late 1800s and early 1900s and was reinforced by Alberto Enríquez-Gallo's decree of 1938. Thus, the relative unimportance of foreign ownership was not the outcome of the hostile occupation of El Tenguel, as Striffler insists. Moreover, no other foreign company joined United Fruit in divesting farmland in Ecuador during the early and middle 1960s. Astral continued to produce and export bananas in the northern *costa* and, as noted in Chapter 5, its operations there ended in 1968 only because its proprietor, Folke Anderson, was murdered. UBESA was sold in 1978 because its German proprietor, Willy Bruns, wanted to retire in his homeland instead of in South America.[48] Two years later, the Wallenberg family sold the Hacienda Clementina for reasons of its own, not because El Tenguel had been taken over nearly two decades earlier.

Striffler's argument that the 1962 invasion drove United Fruit out of the Ecuadorian countryside might be more convincing had he analyzed all factors influencing the company's transactions of real estate in the *costa* more than fifty years ago. However, broader events and forces, such as declining per capita banana consumption in the United States and the 1958 consent decree, are barely mentioned in his book, which provides no real sense that the Cooperativa Juan Quirumbay occupied El Tenguel a few years after antitrust authorities in the United States compelled United Fruit to divest agricultural land throughout the Western Hemisphere. Also not taken into account is the decline in banana harvests the company suffered in Ecuador after the middle 1950s. In addition, Striffler, like others who have written about the country's banana industry, appears to be unaware of the divestiture plans of 1959, which United Fruit not only designed but made every effort to implement.

So the analysis Striffler offers of the driving forces behind the firm's actions during the late 1950s and early 1960s is less than comprehensive. However, the accounts he provides of specific conflicts over natural resources reveal something important about property rights in rural Ecuador: that groups such as the Cooperativa Juan Quirumbay with leftwing attorneys in their corner were not the only Ecuadorians capable of winning real estate that belonged to others. Commercial farmers also acquired resources through adverse possession, often by convincing officials responsible for implementing agrarian reform that current owners were underutilizing their holdings. At times, those farmers even prevailed in disputes with peasants and others whom agrarian reform was supposed to help.

Purposeful trespassing was rewarded at El Tenguel in the years following United Fruit's departure in spite of assistance for group farming furnished by the military government that enacted the Agrarian Reform Law of 1964. The Instituto Ecuatoriano de Reforma Agraria y Colonización (IERAC), the INC's successor, organized a dozen cooperatives with a combined membership of 580 individuals and 7,390 hectares of farmland.[49] In addition, some of the agency's best professional employees were assigned to furnish the cooperatives technical assistance. But levels of motivation and expertise among IERAC advisors soon deteriorated. Also, the expense of maintaining equipment, drainage canals, and other assets left behind by United Fruit was substantial and the Ecuadorian government never succeeded in winning financial support for its El Tenguel project from international sources. Perhaps the most serious impediment to group agriculture, though, was that rural people who were supposed to farm collectively never exhibited much enthusiasm for the undertaking.[50]

In 1967, three years after the passage of agrarian reform legislation, the armed forces had returned to their barracks and the civilian authorities who had replaced the military junta decided to try something different. The new approach was exemplified by a contract awarded to Carlos Cornejo, who owned a large estate south of El Tenguel, to plant 1,000 hectares of communal land to Cavendish bananas. Expenses, including salaries for Cornejo and other managers, were covered by a loan to be paid off by the cooperatives, which would take possession of the 1,000 hectares once normal operations began. However, more than 300 hectares were never put into production and the whole scheme broke down amidst charges of mismanagement by the contractors and lax supervision by IERAC and cooperative leaders. Cornejo fled to Canada in order to avoid a criminal trial, but his top associate was prosecuted, convicted, and jailed. Also, several agrarian reform officials were sacked. The cooperatives fared poorly as well. Fully responsible for the loan, their financial position was and remained severely compromised.[51]

In the wake of fiascos such as this, IERAC started turning a blind eye to sales of communal lands, which the 1964 law and other legislation forbade. A common ploy was to encroach gradually on a cooperative's land and, with time, invest in improvements. Once the trespass was discovered, the interloper would readily admit his "mistake" and volunteer to leave, provided only that he be paid for the improvements. However, few cooperatives could afford such reimbursement, so usually sold out—sometimes for very little money in order to appease trespassers threatening to sue in court for the value of their investments.[52]

Agrarian reform legislation could even be manipulated to relieve cooperatives of their resources. In one instance documented by Striffler, several members of the Córdova family, which was among the most affluent in the southern *costa*, formed their own cooperative in 1968 and immediately rented 400 of the 1,600 hectares that IERAC had given three years earlier to the Cooperativa San Rafael. In 1972, not long before the rental of farmland was outlawed because it supposedly was an inherently insecure form of land tenure, the Córdovas stopped making payments and also refused to vacate. In documents filed with IERAC, they emphasized that the 400 hectares they occupied had never been farmed by the Cooperativa San Rafael and that planting the land to Cavendish bananas, as they had done, served the national interest by increasing agricultural output and exports. Convinced by this argument, IERAC took all 400 hectares away from the original owner for redistribution to the Córdovas. Never compensated for this confiscation, the Cooperativa San Rafael limped along until 1985, when it was formally disbanded.[53]

Dealing with Labor Organizers

Just as local growers proved adept at forestalling land redistribution and using agrarian reform legislation for their own purposes, they were able to withstand challenges from the labor movement. This task was often accomplished by striking private deals with powerful actors within unions, not least the unions' own officials.

Rarely did unions in the tropical fruit sector represent the entire workforce even-handedly. One group in Central America that was poorly represented consisted of men who before the 1960s applied Bordeaux Spray manually to banana plants for protection against Yellow Sigatoka. Constantly exposed to the fungicide, spray-workers suffered eye inflammations, persistent coughing, and recurring headaches. Worst of all, the accumulation of copper sulfate (a key ingredient of Bordeaux Spray) in the lungs resulted in symptoms like those of tuberculosis[54]—which was widespread among banana workers,[55] not to mention poor people throughout the Western Hemisphere. In light of what they suffered, spray workers tended to be compensated relatively well. But at the same time, their status was inferior. One problem was that they were not equipped with machetes, unlike men who strode out into the fields only after girding themselves with that macho implement. They were also given a derogatory nickname—*pericos* (meaning parakeets in Spanish)—since constant exposure to Bordeaux Spray, which is blue, causes one's skin to acquire an aquamarine tint. In addition, *pericos* tended not to be union stalwarts, which cost them the support of other workers. The labor movement in places like Costa Rica even objected to the phase-out of manual fumigation because of reductions in the number of dues-paying members as well as the loss of bargaining power that unions possessed as long as they could interfere with the control of plant diseases.[56]

Whereas Central American *pericos* were poorly served by unions, some leaders of the labor movement in Ecuador did quite well for themselves, including in dealings with major *bananeros*. As was abundantly clear to all concerned, these leaders were in a position to inflict great economic pain at inopportune times on recalcitrant growers. This power was demonstrated during the late 1960s, when the agricultural workforce of Segundo Wong struck and took over his holdings. With fumigation suspended, there was a severe outbreak of Yellow Sigatoka. Also, farm implements and machinery were stolen during the occupation, which occurred as Wong was struggling to pay off loans he had taken out to buy land. Bankruptcy ensued and, many years later, Wong's son recalled that agricultural equipment was moved into the family's Guayaquil home, which was padlocked and chained to ward off creditors. Resolved never to repeat this experience, the Chinese-Ecuadorian businessman and farmer made sure afterward to stay on the good side of Jaime Hurtado, who during the 1960s and 1970s was in charge of unions representing field workers and stevedores and who subsequently ran for president as the candidate of Ecuador's most leftwing political party. Notwithstanding the direct hand Hurtado had in Wong's earlier bankruptcy, a cordial relationship of sorts developed between the two men. Even after the union boss retired, in some comfort, visits of a purely social nature continued.[57]

Noboa's response to labor militancy differed from Wong's. His acquisition of the Hacienda Clementina and other large estates, on which he constructed clinics, schools, and residences for employees and their families, put him in the crosshairs of union bosses. But rather than bargaining with them, Noboa negotiated directly with his employees. His secretary recalls the effort devoted to heading off potential strikes; talking and holding meetings with his labor force, Noboa always reached an agreement that kept farms running while satisfying workers.[58]

Noboa's approach of bypassing labor leaders and dealing directly with his permanent employees was not followed by many other large *bananeros*. Nor did many of them imitate Wong, who made it a point to maintain good relations with his unionized workforce and with organizers such as Hurtado. Instead, they eliminated the risk of strikes by trimming the number of permanent employees, who have always had the legal right to organize. One way to avoid a unionized workforce is to contract with intermediaries who see to hiring, firing, and making sure that laborers show up when and where they are needed. Another option is to take on employees "temporarily" on contracts that can be renewed indefinitely. Tens of thousands of banana workers are kept busy year round at pruning, harvesting, and other tasks under such contracts, which can be discontinued at any time and for any reason—including a worker's expression of a desire for union representation.[59] Among *bananeros* who have avoided hiring workers permanently was Quirola, who opined that "sometimes unions work well and sometimes not" and who never allowed labor organizers onto any of his properties.[60]

Adverse Public Policies

One way or another, Ecuadorian growers prevented unions from interfering seriously with production. Likewise, agrarian reform created few lasting difficulties for the tropical fruit sector. In contrast, economic policies designed to favor manufacturing over agriculture significantly harmed the banana industry.

Those policies were in place fifty years ago, when Ecuador fit the image of a banana republic—not in the political sense of being controlled and manipulated by The Octopus or some other foreign firm, but in economic and fiscal terms. Overseas banana sales comprised three-fifths of the country's exports; as indicated in Table 7, there was no other country in the world where the tropical fruit sector supplied as large a portion of total exports. Furthermore, customs duties levied on bananas shipped out of Guayaquil, Machala, and other port cities were a mainstay of public finances, accounting for half the national budget during the early 1960s.[61]

But the same year Ecuador's share of the global banana market peaked and the importance of the tropical fruit industry in the Ecuadorian economy was never greater, an initial step was taken toward the eventual overshadowing of the industry by the petroleum sector. Official authorization was given in 1964 to Texaco and its partner, Gulf, to search for energy resources in the northeastern part of the country. Three years later, large deposits were found near Lago Agrio, a settlement in the Amazon rainforest that U.S. oilmen named after Sour Lake—the small Texan town where oil was discovered in 1901 and where Texaco got its start two years later. Commercial production and exports began in 1972, following the construction of a pipeline over the Andes, a shipping terminal and refinery in Esmeraldas, and related infrastructure.[62]

One of the poorest places in the Western Hemisphere half a century ago, Ecuador experienced more economic expansion and improvement in living standards than any other Latin American nation during the oil boom. After increasing at an annual rate of 4 percent between 1965 and 1970, gross domestic product (GDP) rose nearly 11.5 percent per annum between 1970

Table 7: Value of Foreign Banana Shipments by Leading Exporters, 1963

Country	Banana exports (U.S.$ million)	Banana exports / total exports (%)
Ecuador	85.2	57.3
Somalia	14.2	44.7
Panama	25.1	42.4
Honduras	32.8	39.4
Martinique and Guadeloupe	23.9	32.3
Costa Rica	25.8	27.2
Guatemala	11.5	7.5
Jamaica	13.6	6.9
Ivory Coast	14.1	6.1
Dominican Republic	8.6	4.9

Source: Valles, 7.

and 1975, when 65 percent of Ecuador's exports comprised overseas sales of oil. The pace of expansion slowed to a little more than 6 percent after 1975, when the petroleum industry's share of total exports briefly slipped below 50 percent. However, Ecuador's GDP per capita in 1981 was $1,180, which was comparable to GDP per capita at the time in the country's larger and historically less impoverished neighbors—Colombia and Peru.[63]

Petroleum exports enriched the Ecuadorian government, far more than the banana boom had done. The military junta that seized power the same year that seagoing tankers started taking on crude oil in Esmeraldas wasted no time subjecting Texaco and Gulf to higher taxes. The royalty charged on the gross value of production was hiked and an income tax was phased in— from an initial rate of 44.40 percent in 1973, when the international price of crude oil was still under four dollars per barrel, to 87.31 percent four years later, when a barrel of oil changed hands for twelve dollars.[64] Decisive steps were also taken toward nationalization. A state-owned petroleum company was created in 1973, with a 25 percent equity stake in what had been a consortium of the two U.S. firms. Less than four years later, that stake rose to 62.5 percent when Gulf liquidated its Ecuadorian interests. According to a book published by the union representing the employees of the state-owned company, the national government captured $23.51 billion in income taxes, royalties, and dividends from 1972 to 1992, when Texaco relinquished its holdings in Ecuador. The U.S. firm's returns during the same period only came to 1.64 billion dollars.[65]

Corrected for inflation, public expenditures increased at an annual rate of 12 percent from 1973 through 1982, during which time the ratio of those expenditures to GDP rose from 22 percent to 33 percent.[66] In addition, the oil boom created a unique opportunity for the state to guide national economic development. Import-substituting industrialization (ISI) had been official policy since passage of the Law of Industrial Incentives in 1957, although actual implementation of the approach was halting for several years. One reason for the modest impact of ISI during the 1960s was that Ecuadorian consumers had little spending power, even though GDP per capita had grown steadily and an urban middle class had started to emerge during the banana boom. Another reason was that taxes levied on the tropical fruit sector and other parts of the economy did not permit generous subsidization of manufacturing enterprises,[67] many of which could not exist without public largesse. But once Ecuador became an oil exporter, the domestic market expanded rapidly, not least because increases in government employment and salaries claimed as much as 79 percent of the funds captured by taxing and national-izing Texaco and Gulf.[68] At the same time, public officials were in a much better position to provide subsidies.

Petroleum development created some benefits for Ecuador's banana in-dustry. The government spent tens of millions of dollars on irrigation works, including in those parts of the *costa* where fruit was harvested.[69] Tariffs on banana exports were eliminated. This was a welcome change because the duty had been as high as eleven cents on a forty-pound (eighteen-kilogram) box a few years earlier, when the tax in Costa Rica was only one and one-half cents per box.[70] Also, Ecuador refrained from becoming a member of the Unión de Países Exportadores de Banana (UPEB), which was created in the hope of restraining production and boosting fruit prices. Had the country joined the would-be cartel, chances would have been lost to recover market share from Central American rivals, where production costs had been brought down because of varietal transformation and other improvements on corporate plantations.[71] However, there were no sector-wide subsidies for *bananeros*, of the kind manufacturers received from the government along with protec-tion from foreign competition. Moreover, currency overvaluation grew acute, with the exchange rate in 1981 (25 sucres per dollar) identical to the rate ten years earlier even though inflation in Ecuador consistently exceeded inflation in the United States and other trading partners.

Barriers to industrial imports created monopolies within Ecuador for a number of local firms. They responded in the manner of all monopolists—by hiking the prices they charged their customers, whose incomes were rising due largely to increased employment and higher salaries in the public sector. In contrast, exporters of bananas and other agricultural commodities contin-ued to receive international prices determined by global market forces and not subject to manipulation by any national government. Also, the profit-ability of export crop production eroded because the exchange rate remained the same even as inflation drove up costs. Assessing the combined impact of an overvalued sucre, subsidies for manufacturing, and other government policies, Grant M. Scobie, Veronica Jardine, and Duty D. Greene highlighted the sharp distinction between economic trends prior to the initiation of pe-troleum exports and Ecuador's subsequent trajectory. Whereas there was comparable growth in agriculture and industry before the oil boom, manu-factured output expanded rapidly due to protectionism and public subsidies once the boom was under way. Meanwhile, farm output stagnated because of the "explicit" taxation of agriculture.[72]

Within the agricultural sector, traditional exports including bananas declined at an annual rate of 2.9 percent from 1972 through 1979.[73] Fruit harvests fell 20 percent and foreign sales were off 16 percent during this period. Nature dealt the fruit industry an additional blow in 1983, when prolonged storms during an El Niño event destroyed crops and washed out roads and bridges. In the southern *costa*, 198 farms with 2,252 hectares planted to bananas were completely destroyed and ditches and canals serving another 20,000 hectares were seriously damaged. A little farther north, including in the vicinity of Guayaquil, another 2,283 hectares of farmland dedicated to tropical fruit production were devastated. Even farms that withstood the wind and the rain suffered since deliveries of the oil spray and aviation fuel needed for fumigation broke down, which caused an outbreak of plant diseases, and because harvested fruit could not be transported.[74]

Banana production and exports in 1983 were 25 percent lower than in the preceding twelve months and shipments of crude oil as a share of total exports rose to 73 percent, the highest level ever registered in the country.[75] Ecuador even lost its position as the world's leading supplier of tropical fruit that year, when Costa Rica was the top exporter.

CHAPTER 8

Resurgence

Economist Sven Wunder describes the boom in tropical fruit harvests and exports that began in Ecuador during the mid-1940s and continued for nearly two decades as feverish.[1] This is no exaggeration. Between competitors' difficulties in the Caribbean Basin and its own environmental advantages, the South American nation needed only a few years to become the world's top supplier of bananas, shooting past several exporters of long standing. Growth was then sustained as entrepreneurs such as Luís Noboa excelled at finding customers for their country's produce.

The fever broke in the mid-1960s, when Ecuador lost its competitive edge due to the switch in Central America from Gros Michel to Cavendish bananas. After a few years' delay, growers in the *costa* changed varieties as well. No sooner had they accomplished this task, however, than they began to suffer the consequences of import-substituting industrialization (ISI). Oil exports, which began in 1972, provided national authorities the wherewithal to distort the exchange rate and interfere in other ways with market forces. The negative impact of those policies was enormous, swamping the benefits of irrigation investments and the lowering of tariffs on agricultural trade that occurred after oil exports began. Harvests and overseas shipments of bananas declined, although aside from 1983, when El Niño did its worst, Ecuador continued to ship more fruit abroad than any other country.

ISI was largely responsible for preventing the tropical fruit sector from taking advantage immediately when Colombia joined Costa Rica, Guatemala, Honduras, and Panama in 1974 to establish the Unión de Países Exportadores de Banano (UPEB). The organization's four Central American members promptly rendered themselves less competitive by instituting a sizable tax on banana exports. The same four countries also revoked the concessions held by United Fruit and Standard Fruit,[2] which encouraged the two firms to seek out supplies elsewhere. But for currency overvaluation and other policy-induced distortions, Ecuadorian planters and exporters would have pounced on the commercial opportunities that UPEB created for them—opportunities that were not diminished by the launching of a company owned by Central American governments that attempted to export bananas with no multinational involvement. After six years of supplying fruit to Yugoslavia (where Noboa also did business) and a few other places, the company folded in 1983.[3]

In spite of public policies that held back the agricultural sector, home-grown entrepreneurs persevered during the 1970s and early 1980s. A few foreign firms also remained active in the *costa*. As a result, much of the groundwork was laid for the banana industry's subsequent revival, which began once Ecuador moved away from ISI after the presidential election of 1984. This revival was needed if new difficulties were to be overcome in later years. Among those difficulties were restrictions that the European Union (EU) imposed on fruit imports from Latin America.

Ecuadorian Steadfastness

Just as José Luís Tamayo had hoped during the 1920s and Galo Plaza had expected after World War II, United Fruit made pivotal contributions to Ecuador's banana industry. But by 1970 the company had been largely absent from the country for several years. All the agricultural real estate it had bought and developed was in the hands of others. Its banana purchases from local planters were modest and variable.

Other foreign-owned firms still had a sizable presence in the *costa*. Acquired between 1964 and 1968 by Castle and Cooke,[4] Standard Fruit employed 2,500 laborers and 200 administrative specialists in and around Guayaquil and Machala in 1970.[5] Its portion of Ecuadorian banana exports, 25 percent, was greater than any other company's, including Exportadora Bananera Noboa's 22 percent share. UBESA, which accounted for 16 percent of the country's banana shipments, was in third place and the other 37 percent of the business was handled by more than three dozen other firms.[6]

Castle and Cooke, which had purchased the Dole Food Company in 1961 and which used the Dole label for all the fruit it marketed after 1972, expanded the operations of its Ecuadorian subsidiary in 1978 by purchasing Willy Bruns's controlling interest in UBESA. This transaction came about for two reasons. First, none of Bruns's close relatives were willing and able to make a success of the company he had founded two decades earlier. Second, the only offer he received before retiring to his native Germany was from Castle and Cooke. With the takeover of UBESA, the U.S. company received all Bruns's reefer ships and his 40 percent stake in a cardboard box factory, along with offices and facilities for loading and storage. Castle and Cooke also became the owner of the German businessman's plantations. In this way, Standard Fruit's policy never to possess any farmland in Ecuador was relaxed, but only for a few years. The policy was reinstated in 1984, when the plantations were sold to local growers.[7]

Regardless of all the dollars he had amassed, Noboa never contemplated retirement. No one could have blamed him had he followed Bruns's example, however. A chain smoker since his youth, the Ecuadorian businessman had suffered a heart attack in 1960, the same year he celebrated his forty-fourth birthday. He returned to his office as soon as he could do so, carried to and from his desk while seated in a chair. After an abbreviated convalescence, Noboa was working up to sixteen hours a day[8]—as he had done since his days as a preadolescent peddler in downtown Guayaquil, when he discovered how much could be earned by continuing to sell postage stamps and other sundries after other street vendors had called it a day.[9]

Four decades ago, Noboa's troubles were not limited to coronary disease and public policies that harmed Ecuadorian agriculture as a whole. His personal wealth and commercial prominence also made him a political target. Guillermo Rodríguez-Lara, the head of the military junta that had seized power in 1972 from José María Velasco-Ibarra and that was firmly committed to ISI, regarded Noboa as a monopolist who served his interests alone, not the country's. Accusations of tax evasion circulated as well. Whether there was something to the accusations or out of a well-founded lack of confidence in Ecuador's courts, Noboa decided to relocate to New York shortly after Rodríguez-Lara's coup d'état, slipping away during pre-Lenten *carnaval* festivities.[10]

This move did not mark a withdrawal from the banana trade. Nor did Noboa sever ties with his native country. Rather, he used his time in New York, which was closer to importers and associates in Europe not to mention the United States, to build up his core Ecuadorian business. During his self-imposed exile, the transplanted Guayaquileño bought out Leon Van Parys and the rest of his Belgian partners. He also installed four cranes, a refrigerated warehouse with space for more than 500 tons of boxed bananas, and related infrastructure at a site leased from the Port Authority of New York and New Jersey.[11]

Especially momentous was the decision Noboa made while residing in the North American metropolis to begin assembling his own reefer fleet, so that he would no longer run the risk of a contracted carrier's failure to deliver fruit promised to a foreign customer. Initially, all maritime assets of his shipping line, the Compañía Naviera del Pacífico, were registered in the Bahamas because of an ad valorem duty of 16 percent levied every time a vessel was registered in Ecuador. But after the late 1970s, when the duty was rescinded, the entire fleet—which in 1985 numbered sixteen ships, counting several acquired from the Flota Bananera Ecuatoriana and the Flota Mercante Gran Colombia after those two companies had ceased operating—flew the Ecuadorian flag.[12] These vessels along with various estates Noboa had purchased over the years, made his business conglomerate vertically integrated, just as United Fruit and Standard Fruit had been since the early 1900s.

No other Ecuadorian entrepreneur achieved complete vertical integration, even though several took steps in that direction during and immediately after the oil boom. Esteban Quirola, for example, complemented his agricultural operations with an exporting enterprise, which shipped fewer than 8,000 tons overseas in 1981 but more than 16,000 tons in 1990.[13] Segundo Wong accomplished much on his Ecuadorian farms and in the Soviet Union and Eastern Europe. He also took full advantage of the agreement that the government's Programa Nacional del Banano (PNB) struck with Del Monte in 1978 to supply 1,260 to 1,800 tons of fruit a week to the company, which previously had not done any business in Ecuador. This commitment was fulfilled largely by Wong's exporting firm, Reybanpac (the abbreviation of Rey Banano del Pacífico), which for several years was the source of many of the bananas Del Monte sold in the United States.[14]

A Second Banana Boom

Del Monte's purchases in Ecuador began before the resumption of civilian rule and signaled an improvement in relations between the country's uniformed leaders, on the one hand, and the banana industry and other agricultural interests in the *costa*, on the other. The military officers who pushed Rodríguez-Lara aside in early 1977 wasted little time eliminating the tax on fruit exports. Additionally, a rapprochement occurred with Noboa, who moved home from the United States. Accepting an invitation to help the government find ways to reduce the volume of un-exported bananas, the Guayaquil businessman served as an ambassador for Ecuador's tropical fruit sector. In that capacity, he made official visits as far away as Asia aimed at winning new customers.[15]

Noboa was not close to the center-left politicians who won office in 1979, when military rule ended. However, his influence waxed full after the 1984 election of León Febres-Cordero—formerly one of Noboa's top executives as well as a representative in the national legislature, where he was a reliable advocate of coastal agriculture and of his former employer. Trade restrictions were eased soon after the new president was inaugurated. The most important change in economic policy was to devalue the sucre, from one cent at the beginning of Febres-Cordero's four-year term to one-fifth of a cent when his elected successor took the oath of office. Grant M. Scobie, Veronica Jardine, and Duty D. Greene identify the establishment of a realistic exchange rate as the main reason for the recovery of traditional agricultural exports, which grew at an average annual rate of 6.2 percent in 1984, 1985, and 1986 after declining by 13.7 percent a year during the early 1980s.[16]

The tropical fruit sector led this recovery. During the Febres-Cordero administration, banana exports increased by 64 percent—from 924,000 tons in 1984, when production and exports were still depressed because of the previous year's El Niño storms, to 1,517,000 tons in 1988. Also, the sector's upward trajectory continued under later governments, especially after tropical fruit prices rose during the late 1980s. In 1991, less than four decades after Ecuador had reached the top of the global banana industry, the country was once again the world's dominant exporter; its foreign shipments were nearly 90 percent of the combined total for the second and third largest suppliers, which were Costa Rica and Colombia (Table 8).

Table 8: Major Banana-Exporting Nations, 1991

Country	Quantity exported (million metric tons)	Value of exports (U.S.$ million)
Ecuador	2.66	707.62
Costa Rica	1.54	381.84
Colombia	1.47	404.87
The Philippines	0.94	170.76
Honduras	0.71	314.40
Panama	0.71	196.25

Source: FAO, *FAOSTAT Online.*

This was also the time when the multinational enterprise that had led the banana industry for decades returned to the *costa*. Relaunched by Carl H. Lindner—the Cincinnati investor who had taken over Chiquita in 1984 and saved it from bankruptcy—the firm never regained the status it had enjoyed in Ecuador during the country's initial banana boom, however. Instead, the Dole Food Company, as Castle and Cooke renamed itself in 1989, had become the top foreign operator, not least because of Standard Fruit's abiding presence in the *costa* since the mid-1940s.

After the purchase of UBESA in 1978, Dole promoted Jürgen Schumacher, whose many years of effective work for Bruns's company had won him respect throughout the industry. Schumacher instituted the Grupo Básico program, which aimed to upgrade the farms supplying fruit to Dole. All participants in the program signed notarized production contracts with a duration of five years. The contracts spelled out the participants' obligations to deliver bananas that were at least twenty centimeters (eight inches) long and entirely free of stains, cuts, and other damage. Grupo Básico planters received advice and instructions about fungicide treatments, the wrapping of plastic bags around uncut stems of maturing fruit, and other agricultural practices from specialists recommended by the company and paid by the planters. Guidelines for the transportation of harvested bananas, in boxes supplied by Dole, had to be followed as well.[17]

Notwithstanding the production increases that Grupo Básico farmers achieved and the business Dole gained by absorbing UBESA, the U.S. company was not the leading exporter of bananas raised in the *costa* twenty-five years ago. Instead, the top firm was Exportadora Bananera Noboa, with nearly twice as many shipments out of Guayaquil, Machala, and other ports along the Pacific coast. Reybanpac was in third place (Table 9). So there is no factual basis for Steve Striffler's contention that multinational enterprises controlled exports and hence the tropical fruit sector during the 1990s.[18] Nor was the sector cartelized in any meaningful sense. With hundreds of growers dealing with dozens of firms engaged in foreign trade, not even Exportadora Bananera Noboa could dictate terms to independent growers with bananas to sell. Foreign companies routinely struck deals with Ecuadorian exporters to ship boxes of fruit bearing the companies' labels to North America and Europe, as illustrated by Del Monte's arrangement with Reybanpac. This sort of arrangement was neither exploitative nor permanent, but lasted as long as there were mutual benefits. For example, an Ecuadorian exporter who determined that doing business with a particular multinational was unprofitable

Table 9: Three Leading Exporters of Ecuadorian Bananas, 1989 and 2000

Company	Market share 1989 (%)	Market share 2000 (%)
Exportadora Bananera Noboa	30	32
Reybanpac	9	16
Dole Food Company	15	14

Sources: Spurrier-Baquerizo (1990) for 1989 shares; Brenes and Madrigal for 2000 shares.

would discontinue the association and find another client. Independent sales also occurred on a large scale.

Pressed to compete in a market with many commercial rivals, exporters lined up customers in a wide variety of destinations. Twenty-five years ago, a little more than half the bananas shipped out of Ecuador went to the United States and Canada and about a fifth were sold in Western Europe. The remaining 25 to 30 percent were delivered to Poland and Yugoslavia in Eastern Europe; Libya, Saudi Arabia, and Turkey in the Middle East and North Africa; New Zealand in the South Pacific; Argentina and Chile beyond the Tropic of Capricorn; and other places.[19] Exporters also figured out how to transport fruit at the lowest possible cost—by exploiting the occasional oversupply of reefer vessels more effectively than their counterparts in other nations usually did, for example. Thanks largely to nimble commercial dealing by Ecuador's entrepreneurs, who as a group supplied more than one in every five bananas bought and sold internationally, the country was consistently the source of 37 to 44 percent of the bananas Latin America shipped to the rest of the world during the 1990s.[20]

The Broader Economic Impact in Ecuador

Tropical fruit development has had far-reaching economic consequences for Ecuador. As David Schodt points out, the post-war banana boom left no part of the country untouched. With fruit exports skyrocketing, annual increases in gross domestic product (GDP) averaged nearly 7 percent between 1945 and 1950. Economic expansion decelerated during the next fifteen years, although GDP growth still averaged 4.8 percent per annum. Corrected for inflation, household expenditures went up at an annual rate of 5.3 percent during the 1950s, which had a direct impact on the demand for food. Since most of this food was produced in the Andes, economic opportunities arose there.[21] But clearly, the effects of the banana boom were greatest in areas where tropical fruit was harvested, packed, and shipped. Beginning in the 1940s, Ecuador became much less Andean and much more coastal. Schodt underscores demographic trends associated with this transformation, noting that the *costa*'s population doubled between 1942 and 1962 as the population of the country as a whole went up by 45 percent.[22] There was abundant evidence of the same transformation in Guayaquil, which overtook Quito to become Ecuador's largest city. High-rise buildings made of reinforced concrete replaced wooden structures downtown, migrants arriving from the interior found jobs, and moneyed families occupied a new suburb south of the port city. The middle class, which was small and not very prosperous in the late 1940s, grew as well.

Economic activity and employment have ramped up as inputs have been supplied for tropical fruit production. Jobs and GDP also have been created due to the transportation and marketing of bananas that take place beyond the farm gate. There have been few forward economic linkages similar to what often results from mineral extraction—nothing to compare, for example, to the smelting and fabricating ventures that spring up in the vicinity of many copper mines. This kind of impact has been unimportant because relatively few bananas are eaten in a processed form. In contrast, the tropical fruit sector has been a major source of backward economic linkages. The emergence of a cardboard box industry in Ecuador is one example. Another relates to the demand for plastic bags. To begin with, these bags were imported, although with time domestic supplies have been developed—by the Compañía Nacional de Plásticos, which Noboa founded in 1989, and by Wong's Exoplast company, among others.

Economic linkages also have to do with services. Urban incomes and employment have increased because the banana industry relies on banks, shipping agencies, insurance companies, and law offices in Guayaquil and other cities. Likewise, the domestic aviation sector—including Aerovic, which the Wong family owns—has expanded substantially to satisfy banana farms' demand for aerial fumigation. Some services have been supplied by government, albeit often with unsatisfactory results. Prior to Velasco-Ibarra's overthrow in 1972, for example, funds for pest control were not spent by the PNB, which had assumed this responsibility from the old growers' association, ANBE. A number of planters, including Quirola, consequently suffered interruptions in output.[23] The public sector also ran the Flota Mercante Gran

Colombia, which by 1965 possessed six reefer ships (three built in Germany and an equal number in Spain), and the Flota Bananera Ecuatoriana, which the Ecuadorian government launched in the early 1970s and which owned seven vessels by the end of the decade.[24] However, both these firms were eventually liquidated and many of their maritime assets were picked up by Noboa.

Backward and forward linkages are a major focus of impact assessments that use multiplier models to estimate three categories of economic activity and employment associated with a particular industry or sector. The first of these categories is direct, having to do with the industry or sector itself. The second is indirect, occurring in firms in the supply chain that provide services and other inputs to the industry or sector being studied. The third category is induced, resulting as households spend the wages and salaries earned in the industry or sector as well as its supply chain. One such assessment has been carried out for banana production and exports in Ecuador. Its principal finding was that direct employment on banana farms and elsewhere in the tropical fruit sector, indirect employment by box manufacturers and in other parts of the sector's supply chain, and induced employment added up to 1,915,000 jobs at the turn of the twenty-first century—equivalent to one-fourth of the national workforce at the time.[25] Like the results of other assessments based on multiplier models, this estimate requires careful interpretation. In particular, the vast majority of individuals holding these 1,915,000 jobs would have found work even if the banana industry did not exist, although many or most of them would have had other occupations and might have earned less money.

While multiplier models yield exaggerated estimates of direct, indirect, and induced employment, there have been other consequences of tropical fruit development that are difficult to factor into those models in spite of their importance. For instance, Ecuador's GDP has grown as earnings from the production and overseas sales of bananas have been invested in the country, though outside the tropical fruit sector and its supply chain. In 1959, Noboa initiated construction of a modern flour mill in Guayaquil. A few years later, he built an oat mill in the port city, to produce cereal that would compete with Quaker brand products imported from the United States.[26] Other leading banana entrepreneurs also have invested outside the tropical fruit sector. For example, Quirola added to his capacity for cattle, rice, and cacao production. In 1962, he led a group of investors who founded the Banco de Machala and oversaw its subsequent expansion, starting in the southern *costa* but later throughout the country.[27]

Another impact not captured in multiplier models has to do with the economic spillovers created as entrepreneurial talents are cultivated and the capabilities of Ecuadorian firms that provide business services to exporting industries are enhanced. For example, the expertise local entrepreneurs have gained with the delivery of perishable items thousands of kilometers away has translated directly to a number of other products and markets. Ecuadorian roses, which grow straight and tall in the Andes, are prized as far away as Moscow and national exporters have figured out how to supply these and other flowers just in time for Valentine's Day and Mothers' Day, when demand and prices peak. With overseas sales exceeding 700 million dollars per annum, Ecuador is the world's second-largest exporter of cut flowers.[28] The country has also been the leading exporter of farm-raised shrimp in the Western Hemisphere since the early 1980s.[29] There are obvious parallels here with the spillovers that occurred earlier in the twentieth century, when the boom in banana exports after World War II was greatly facilitated because entrepreneurial capabilities and resources had accumulated in Guayaquil during the years when Ecuador exported more cacao than any other country.

No one doubts that the employment created by banana production and exports in Ecuador is sizable, even though this impact has been over-estimated due to shortcomings in the available economic methodology. But at the same time, the national economy has benefited in other ways not addressed by that methodology, especially the strengthening of business services and entrepreneurial capabilities that has translated into export success in other sectors. Clearly, Ecuador's wellbeing is inextricably tied to its tropical fruit sector.

An Assault on Free Trade

Given this economic stake, national leaders must be vigilant about trade barriers in importing countries. Vigilance was certainly in order during the last decade of the twentieth century, owing to a turn toward protectionism in Europe.

Since the 1950s, Ecuadorian bananas had been shipped in large quantities to Scandinavia, the Low Countries, and West Germany. Importers such as Sven Salen in Sweden were active in this business. So was Bruns. Noboa worked closely with Salen in Scandinavia and also became the leading exporter to Belgium. Largely responsible for banana development in the northern *costa*, Folke Anderson sold many tons of fruit in his native Sweden and neighboring lands.

South American exports—from Colombia as well as Ecuador—flowed to Sweden, Norway, Denmark, and West Germany because of low trade barriers. Those nations had little reason to favor tropical fruit from some countries over other countries' bananas, since Denmark had sold its portion of the Virgin Islands to the United States in 1916 and Germany had been stripped of all its colonies at the end of World War I. Accordingly, the sole aim of public policy was to maintain unimpeded access to fruit imported from Latin America, where production costs have always been low. During negotiations that preceded the creation of the European Economic Community (EEC), for example, West Germany insisted on a special protocol in the Treaty of Rome, which came into force in 1958, that would excuse the country from taxing imports heavily, as the EEC's five other charter members planned to do. Fully aware of his countrymen's reluctance to pay too much for a product they loved, West German Chancellor Konrad Adenauer filibustered for three days to secure the protocol's inclusion in the EEC's founding document.[30]

The Treaty of Rome also allowed France to implement an entirely different policy, one meant to enhance rural incomes in Guadeloupe and Martinique—banana-exporting islands in the Caribbean that are neither colonies nor independent states, but rather are overseas departments with the same political status as, say, the Loire Valley or Provence. To shore up the earnings of fruit producers, the French government pegged banana prices well above the values at which Latin American exports were bought and sold. Even at those high prices, normal production in Guadeloupe and Martinique rarely exceeded two-thirds of French consumption. The remaining third was supplied duty-free by Cameroon, the Côte d'Ivoire, and Madagascar—each a former colony assigned a quota by the authorities in Paris. As a rule, imports allowed from Latin America were negligible.[31]

None of the four other charter members of the EEC had overseas provinces where tropical fruit might be produced. However, each used trade policy to benefit specific banana exporters. Since part of Somalia had been an Italian colony up until World War II, produce from that country could be shipped duty-free to Italy, which before the 1980s purchased few Latin American bananas. Likewise, current or former colonies of Belgium and The Netherlands had preferential access to the Low Countries, including Luxembourg, although Colombia and Ecuador supplied nearly all the bananas consumed in that corner of Europe (Tables 3 and 5).

The lack of a uniform policy on banana imports in the EEC created difficulties, not least for customs officials. They, after all, had to enforce the prohibition on shipping tropical fruit out of Germany, where prices were low because imports were unrestricted and lightly taxed, to France and other EEC members, where protectionism drove up prices. Such difficulties were compounded as other countries joined the EEC. Some of these countries wanted cheap imports as much as Germany did. But others sought to protect their own growers. Bananas were cultivated on the Greek island of Crete, for example. Portugal and Spain also had domestic production, in their insular provinces in the Atlantic Ocean. The UK had no counterparts to Guadeloupe and Martinique. However, officials in London were intent on favoring Jamaica, which had supplied British consumers with bananas since the 1890s, and other former colonies in the Caribbean.

If anything, German opposition to trade barriers intensified after the country reunified. Erich Honecker, the communist head of the German Democratic Republic up until a few weeks before the Berlin Wall fell in 1989, famously observed that the regime established by the Soviet Union after World War II collapsed in no small part because of its failure to maintain an adequate supply of tropical fruit[32]—an inexcusable failure given the eagerness and proven ability of entrepreneurs such as Noboa and Wong to provide such a supply. After reunification, Honecker's ex-subjects received all the bananas they could eat, mainly from Ecuador. From 3.1 kilograms in 1987 and 1988, their annual consumption per capita jumped to 22.5 kilograms in 1991, 50 percent greater than per capita consumption of tropical fruit in what had been West Germany. This and other material rewards of the collapse of communism benefited Chancellor Helmut Kohl politically since he had presided over reunification. When asked to explain Kohl's decisive victory in Germany's first nationwide election after the Berlin Wall was torn down, one of his opponents held up a banana in front of the television cameras.[33] There was no need for him to elaborate.

Not long after Germany reunified, the EEC began transforming itself into the EU, within which all commerce—including the buying and selling of tropical fruit—would be unrestricted. During the negotiations over Europe's Common Organization of the Market for Bananas (COMB), Denmark, the Low Countries, and a few other nations sided at times with Germany in opposing high tariffs and other import barriers. However, France and Great Britain never failed to assemble a winning coalition in support of their protectionist stance—including on the final and decisive vote shortly before the signing of the Maastricht Treaty in 1993, which brought the EU into being.[34]

Like previous French policy, the COMB was designed to safeguard the earnings of domestic producers. To be specific, deficiency payments, which covered gaps between target levels of income and actual earnings, were authorized for growers of so-called eurobananas in places such as Guadeloupe, Crete, and Spain's Canary Islands. Privileged status was also given to "traditional ACP bananas," up to 857,700 tons of which could be shipped duty-free to Europe every year from former colonies in Africa, the Caribbean, and the Pacific by virtue of the Lomé Convention and related international accords.[35]

Additional imports were subject to taxation. A duty of 100 euros per ton was assessed on imports of "dollar bananas" harvested in South America, Central America, and Mexico as long as the sum of those imports and purchases of "nontraditional ACP bananas" (produced in Africa, the Caribbean, and the Pacific, though not covered by favorable trading arrangements stipulated in treaties such as the Lomé Convention) did not exceed 2,000,000 tons per annum. But beyond this quantitative threshold, tariffs were prohibitive: 750 euros per ton for nontraditional ACP fruit and 850 euros per ton for dollar bananas. Moreover, there were import quotas. On the basis of historical trade patterns and other considerations, nontraditional ACP bananas were supposed to comprise approximately one-third of the 2,000,000 tons not subject to punitive taxation and the remaining two-thirds or so of those imports were supposed to come from Latin America.[36]

Even before European governments had finished debating the COMB, Latin Americans registered their dissatisfaction with the policy. Colombia, Costa Rica, Guatemala, Nicaragua, and Venezuela did so in January 1993, which did not interfere with the EU's adoption of the COMB the following month. No more than a year later, the same five nations issued an official complaint about the policy's inconsistency with the General Agreement on Tariffs and Trade (GATT). In response, the EU offered a new Banana Framework Agreement (BFA), which granted each of the five countries a quota. This addition to the COMB, which made the policy even more complex than it already was, did not mollify Guatemala. In contrast, Colombia, Costa Rica, Nicaragua, and Venezuela were satisfied enough with their respective quotas to sign the BFA.[37]

This agreement, which was to last eight years, took effect in January 1995—just days after the GATT as a multilateral agency was replaced by the World Trade Organization (WTO), which unlike its predecessor has the authority to rule on trade disputes. Aside from the BFA's four Latin American signatories, producers of dollar bananas got nothing out of the agreement. Nor did it alter the import licensing system. Quantitative restrictions on trade cannot be administered without licenses, although the EU's system was not evenhanded in that it rewarded European firms that specialized in the marketing of ACP bananas (traditional as well as non-traditional) and implicitly penalized companies from the Western Hemisphere that dealt in fruit produced in Central and South America and Mexico. Among the firms that benefited from the licensing system was Fyffes: a British subsidiary of Chiquita prior to its sale in 1986 to Irish investors.[38] Once the COMB was implemented, Fyffes and other enterprises with generous allotments of licenses could either use them in their own importing ventures or sell them—at prices that rose over time as trade was distorted more and more—to non-European businesses with dollar bananas to sell.[39]

Lobbied by Chiquita and other U.S.-based multinationals that objected to the import licensing system, the United States joined Guatemala, which had reserved its rights as a WTO member to protest European trade restrictions, in a complaint submitted in July 1995. Honduras and Mexico, which also belonged to the WTO and had not signed the BFA, participated in this complaint as well. The WTO responded nearly a year later, in May 1996, by setting up a panel charged with investigating alleged violations of GATT rules and proposing a settlement. The panel did not quarrel much with taxing Latin American bananas more than ACP fruit. In contrast, the EU's import quotas were found to be an unacceptable distortion of international trade. Also, the panel condemned the licensing system in no uncertain terms and recommended its replacement with a procedure for allocating licenses that would be transparent and would not discriminate among importers.[40]

After a WTO appellate body confirmed the panel's major findings, the EU announced its acquiescence in October 1997, although it stated "a reasonable period of time" would be needed to accomplish all necessary changes in policy. Among specific steps taken in the direction of compliance during the next couple of years were slight reductions in tariff rates. Also, the quantitative threshold at which the elevated duties designed to choke off imports became effective was raised, from 2,000,000 to 2,553,000 tons per annum.[41]

Ecuador Deals with the European Union

Never having signed on to the GATT, Ecuador did not combine forces with other Latin American nations that objected to the COMB in 1993. Likewise, it had yet to become a member of the WTO in July 1995, and so could not be a party to the complaint filed that month by Guatemala, Honduras, Mexico, and the United States. But no more than two weeks after becoming a member, in January 1996, the world's leading exporter of tropical fruit had joined in that complaint, which resulted in the WTO's rulings against the EU.[42]

Lack of official action on their government's part prior to 1996 did not prevent Ecuadorian exporters from dealing with trade barriers. With seasoned European representatives such as Henri van Weert and Hans Kreysing working out of his offices in Antwerp and Rome, Noboa was aware of the protectionist tide beyond the Atlantic Ocean as early as 1990 and wasted no time getting his hands on all the import licenses he needed—not just to maintain a commercial position in Europe, but to increase banana sales there. A significant number of these licenses were acquired at low cost in Malta, a tiny Mediterranean island between Italy and Libya with fewer than 500,000 inhabitants. Having met the Comb requirements, Noboa proceeded with an expansion of the Compañía Naviera del Pacífico, which was critical for export growth. Two reefer ships serving Antwerp and Hamburg were lengthened and, in June 1992, five new vessels were ordered from a Danish shipyard, at a combined cost of $245 million.[43]

Wong also adapted successfully to the COMB and BFA. A past master of entering new markets, he counseled fellow growers and exporters in Ecuador to respond to adverse developments in Europe by redirecting shipments elsewhere. Wong followed his own advice, announcing in 1993 that Reybanpac had locked in sales of 120,000 tons to Iran and more than four times that quantity to a trio of Arab nations: Lebanon, Libya, and Tunisia. Also, the company had just signed a contract to deliver 80,000 tons to Russia.[44] Four years later, banana shipments by Reybanpac and other Ecuadorian firms to Russia had reached 427,000 tons per annum, worth 10 percent of the value of all fruit exports from the *costa*.[45] Wong also made early visits to China and sold Latin American bananas there before anyone else; from 10,000 tons in 1993, fruit deliveries from Ecuador to the East Asian nation rose to nearly 300,000 tons three years later.[46] In addition, Reybanpac prevailed over Central American and Mexican rivals in South Korea after that country reduced its tariff on imported bananas from 100 to 30 percent.[47]

Few firms weathered European protectionism as well as Ecuador's two largest exporters. Their respective shares of the country's overseas banana shipments consequently increased during the 1990s, even as those shipments were going up at a fast clip. At the turn of the twenty-first century, nearly one in every three bananas sent overseas from the *costa* was transported by

Exportadora Bananera Noboa. From 9 percent in 1989, Reybanpac's exports shot up to 16 percent of the national total in 2000. Meanwhile, Dole's share of Ecuadorian exports slipped a little, from 15 percent to 14 percent (Table 9). The commercial achievements of Noboa, Wong, and their companies in the face of European protectionism probably explain why they do not figure prominently in writings about the trade dispute surrounding the COMB. They certainly have received much less attention in those writings than Chiquita, Dole, Del Monte, and even Fyffes.[48]

The successes of Exportadora Bananera Noboa, Reybanpac, and affiliated firms were not shared by other growers and exporters in western Ecuador. Chiquita, for example, suffered major setbacks because of the COMB. The company previously had made sizable investments in response to higher banana prices and an expected surge of demand in Europe once the old Iron Curtain was gone. New reefer ships were constructed and additional land was acquired in Central America. An expansion also occurred in the *costa*, where Chiquita had been exporting 100,000 to 130,000 tons per annum in partnership with César Malnati of Guayaquil. To manage this expansion, the company brought in Luís Felipe Duchicela from Costa Rica. Under Duchicela, an Ecuadorian who had grown up in El Tenguel and who was a direct descendant of the last Incan Emperor,[49] production contracts were signed with growers, agricultural credit was extended, and real estate that might be purchased was identified. But after 1993, his primary task was to wind down most operations, reducing the company's professional staff and workforce from approximately 400 individuals to twenty-one. This retreat was the direct result of European import barriers, which countries such as the Czech Republic and Poland had to adopt as soon as they joined the EU.[50]

Ecuador attacked those import barriers vigorously once it was in the WTO. Alliances were made at times with the United States and other hemispheric opponents of EU policies. In addition, Ecuador did not shrink from "forging its own path," as economist Tim Josling observes. In November 1998, for example, Ecuador requested separate consultations with the EU out of dissatisfaction with the pace at which the COMB was being brought into compliance with WTO rulings. Mexico was the only other participant in these consultations.[51]

Meanwhile, the United States was pursuing a separate case against the EU at the WTO. The case culminated in April 1999 with a ruling that inadequate reform of the COMB could be sanctioned by levying tariffs on imports from Europe. Similarly, the WTO authorized retaliatory tariffs in November 1999 on up to $450 million in EU trade with Ecuador. However, this created a quandary for the country since its purchases of consumer goods from Europe were modest: barely $17 million per annum. Imports of heavy machinery and other capital goods might have been taxed instead. However, Ecuador itself would have paid a far higher price than any European exporter, in terms of reduced investment and diminished GDP.[52]

Ecuadorian leaders resolved the quandary by proposing something unprecedented, which was to hike tariffs on services provided by European firms and to weaken the protection of European intellectual property (e.g., recordings and industrial designs) within the country's borders. A WTO arbitrator ruled in March 2000 that European trade subject to retaliatory measures amounted to $202 million, not $450 million. But of greater significance is that the arbitrator permitted Ecuador to apply the novel sanctions it had devised.[53]

A little more than a year after this development at the WTO, the dispute over tariffs and quotas on EU banana imports was defused. On 11 April 2001, U.S. and European trade negotiators suddenly announced that they had arrived at a solution. For its part, the EU agreed to phase out all quotas and licenses and eventually rely solely on tariffs, though with lower rates for favored ACP suppliers. In return, the United States refrained from imposing retaliatory duties.[54] Policy reform, which originally was supposed to happen by 2006, is still incomplete. However, a renewal of the dispute between Europe and the United States has been avoided.

Ecuador did not embrace the US-EU compromise at once. To the contrary, a governmental spokesman denounced it as a ploy to "override the principles of the multilateral trading system." But on 30 April 2001, the country announced its own agreement with the EU, which guaranteed that there would be no discrimination either against its fruit exports or against Ecuadorian exporters.[55] With this agreement, the last WTO member with formal objections to the COMB had been placated, with due consideration for the country's tropical fruit sector and the sector's entrepreneurial leaders.

Trading Fairly Too?

The debate surrounding EU tariffs and quotas on banana imports was, as economist Stefan Tangermann put it, "so complex, in terms of the facts, the economics, the politics, the legal implications, and the policy instruments involved, that it tends to impose a heavy tax on the knowledge and intellectual capacity of even the analyst with the best intentions."[56] Of the many countries involved in WTO proceedings, few played a more important role than Ecuador. The measures it devised to combat trade barriers, which one legal scholar characterizes as "revolutionary and groundbreaking,"[57] may not have moved the EU very far toward trade liberalization. Still, they accomplished what they were supposed to accomplish for Ecuador's banana industry.

The industry would be put much more to the test if a serious attempt were made to apply fair-trade principles, including the elimination of child labor, guarantees that all workers can unionize, and the curtailment of chemical inputs that threaten human health. If a report issued by Human Rights Watch in 2002 is any guide, much of the sector's workforce is under the age of eighteen, presumably including farmers' offspring who toil on their families' holdings. Children employed in fields and packing facilities are exposed to hazardous chemicals, routinely work with machetes and other dangerous tools, often haul heavy loads, and are vulnerable to sexual harassment. The author of the Human Rights Watch report, Carol Pier, also criticizes the suppression of labor organizing, pointing not only to the tiny segment of the banana industry's labor force that is unionized but also to the firing of workers suspected of union involvement of any sort.[58]

Pier concedes that leading growers and exporters have fairly good labor and environmental records. For example, Wong's rural holdings have received "ECO-OK" certification from the Conservation Agriculture Network (CAN). This certification focuses mainly on pesticide use and other environmental matters, although it also forbids under-age labor as well as practices that frustrate union organizing—for example, the hiring of temporary laborers, who can be fired in an instant for any reason, rather than permanent workers with legal protections.[59] Dole's farmland, which included 800 hectares in the *costa* at the turn of the twenty-first century, is similarly certified. Additionally, the U.S.-based multinational is a signatory of SA8000, which has to do with labor rights as well as environmental practices; when the Human Rights Watch report was published, Dole was working to achieve full compliance with all standards of this accreditation system. Chiquita had not signed SA8000, although it had developed an equivalent code of conduct for itself.[60]

The operations of firms such as Dole and the Favorita Fruit Company (a conglomerate that Wong established in 1998 to consolidate all his farms, exporting ventures, and so on) are not paragons of fair agricultural trade, as Pier emphasizes. But as she takes pains to point out, the real problem in

Ecuador's tropical fruit sector is found in major exporters' supply chains. There is under-age employment, for example, on the holdings of growers who have signed multi-year production contracts either with Dole, Chiquita, or Del Monte or with enterprises belonging to Noboa or Wong and few of those growers' operations are unionized. Then there are other producers, who have not signed contracts but are still part of the supply chain because they provide bananas occasionally or even on a regular basis. Pier singles out these producers as the worst violators of labor rights set forth in national legislation and in treaties Ecuador has ratified.[61]

As acknowledged in the Human Rights Watch report, no such violator has much to fear from the Ecuadorian government, which does a poor job of enforcing its own laws and treaty commitments. Under-age employment, for example, is widespread, with three of every five rural children above age nine holding some sort of job. Many of these children work shoulder to shoulder with their parents on family properties; others find jobs elsewhere, often because there is no other way to meet school expenses. Pier also recognizes, with regret, that the WTO cannot be counted on to impose fair-trade principles since its fundamental mission is to reduce barriers to international commerce, not to protect minors, adult workers, and the environment. Instead, her hopes for bringing the tropical fruit sector into compliance with the labor and environmental standards favored by Human Rights Watch are pinned on the influence that major exporters wield with the farms that supply them bananas.[62]

Confidence in major exporters' influence would be well placed if Ecuador were more like Costa Rica, where Chiquita, Dole, and Del Monte still dominate the tropical fruit sector and where most bananas are raised on large plantations. Since those three firms are reluctant to offend consumers and activists in North America and Western Europe, under-age employment is rare, both on company-owned estates and on the holdings of contracted suppliers. Likewise, union representation is the rule, not the exception. Of course, unionization has economic consequences, such as the additional cost of producing bananas in Costa Rica.[63]

Ecuador is not Costa Rica. For one thing, banana exporting is highly competitive, with the *costa*'s growers free to sell their harvests to the Grupo Noboa conglomerate, Wong's Favorita Fruit, the local affiliates of U.S.-based multinationals, and a number of other buyers. As a result, no single exporter can order around its supplying growers. Consider what might happen, for instance, if a foreign company followed Pier's guidance and insisted that its independent suppliers adhere to fair-trade principles. Some of them would refuse, knowing that their bananas can be marketed easily in China, Russia, the Middle East, and other places where customers exhibit little concern about Ecuadorian workers or the country's natural environment. Other growers would agree to produce fair-trade bananas. However, there would have to be monitoring, almost surely paid for by the foreign company, since individual suppliers would be tempted to cut costs by employing laborers under the age of eighteen or by keeping union organizers off their properties—exactly as many of their neighbors would continue to do.

Another fundamental difference between Ecuador and Costa Rica has to do with banana farming. A pair of Costa Rican economists, Esteban Brenes and Kryssia Madrigal, point out that only 25 percent of the area dedicated to tropical fruit production in the *costa* is in the hands of large *bananeros* such as Quirola and Wong. Farms between thirty and one hundred hectares account for 35 percent of that area and, at the turn of the twenty-first century, holdings smaller than thirty hectares were the source of two-fifths of Ecuador's banana exports.[64] Like small and intermediate-sized farms throughout the world, including in wealthy nations such as the United States, none of these holdings are unionized. Nor will they ever be.

Advocates of fair agricultural trade like to imagine universal unionization and the elimination of under-age employment on family farms, which are also supposed to conserve natural resources as they deliver produce inexpensively to consumers. However, this is an ambitious vision, even an impractical one. In Costa Rica, large plantations could be broken up and redistributed, although child labor would probably make a comeback and few banana workers would continue to enjoy union representation. Conversely, tropical fruit could be produced by a unionized, adult workforce in Ecuador, though no longer at low cost on farms of modest size. The unlikeliest outcome, in either country, would be a combination of cheap bananas, small family farms, and fair trade.[65]

CHAPTER 9

The Environmental Impact

The ways agricultural products are raised in the *costa* and elsewhere in the developing world do not only preoccupy organizations such as Human Rights Watch. Ecuadorian consciences are troubled that rural poverty drives so many of the country's children to toil on farms when they should be in school. Many Ecuadorians object as well to the lack of union representation for agricultural laborers.

They are also bothered by the adverse environmental consequences of tropical fruit production. One such consequence is on display in coastal waterways during the dry season—when rivers become streams, creeks disappear, and it is easy to see what happens to plastic bags that have been thrown away after having covered maturing stems of bananas. One might think, and many accept, that the unsightly aquatic mess is part of the environmental price Ecuador has to pay for exporting more tropical fruit than any other nation. However, a relaxed attitude is hard to justify since there are banana growers, including many in Costa Rica, who recycle wastes, reforest riverbanks, and otherwise protect natural resources.[1] Ecuadorian farmers feel the pressure to do likewise, and not just to please activists and eco-conscious consumers in affluent parts of the world.

Farmers' struggle with Black Sigatoka is a particular concern. The *Mycosphaerella fijensis* fungus, which overpowers the closely related organism (*Mycosphaerella musicola* Leach) responsible for Yellow Sigatoka and is capable of devastating fruit yields, can spread like wildfire and develops pesticide resistance quickly. John Soluri describes the banana industry as "running to stand still" wherever Black Sigatoka has struck, "on a treadmill driven by expensive agrochemical inputs and ever-evolving populations of fungi."[2] As a result, the risks that pesticides create for human health and natural ecosystems have come to outweigh what for many years was the principal environmental downside of tropical fruit development, which was the leveling of forests and other habitats that occurred as agriculture spread across the landscape.

From Forests to Farms

At first glance, tropical fruit production does not appear to have had an overwhelming effect on land use in western Ecuador. Sven Wunder, a leading authority on the causes of deforestation in Latin America and other developing regions, points out that the total area planted to bananas in the *costa* has never exceeded 250,000 hectares. This area is no larger than the annual rate of land use change registered at times for the country as a whole and small relative to cumulative forest loss since the mid-1940s. With millions of hectares having been cleared to make way for crop and livestock production of all kinds, trees and other natural vegetation covered no more than one-third of the *costa* at the turn of the twenty-first century—down from two-thirds fifty years earlier and nearly 100 percent prior to human habitation.[3]

To understand why this environmental change has had much to do with tropical fruit development, one must bear in mind that there are two categories of banana-related deforestation. One category is direct and obvious: the displacement of natural habitats by new banana farms. The other is indirect: the loss of forests due to demographic and economic changes triggered in one way or another by increased fruit production and exports. The relative importance of each of the two categories of land use change has varied over time and from place to place. Wunder finds, however, that the indirect consequences of several decades of growth in the banana industry have far exceeded the industry's direct deforestation. Moreover, indirect deforestation represents a large portion of the overall loss of natural habitats west of the Andes.

To be sure, the direct category of land use change was important during Ecuador's post-war banana boom. Some of the most fertile parts of the *costa*—on the lower slopes of the Andes, for example—were classified by the government as unowned *tierras baldías* and therefore free for the taking. At the same time, raising the Gros Michel variety required neither advanced technology nor a sizable investment. Additionally, the government provided low-interest loans to banana farmers settling around Santo Domingo and in other forested settings.[4] Under these circumstances, fruit growers cleared tens of thousands of hectares. According to Ecuador's first agricultural census, which was carried out five years or so after the banana boom began, 500,000 hectares were being cultivated in the western part of the country in 1951, of which 100,000 to 150,000 hectares were planted to Ecuador's principal export.[5] So in the narrowest possible sense, tropical fruit development was responsible for 20 to 30 percent of the land clearing required for crop production in the *costa*. Direct deforestation was actually greater if the many hectares abandoned because of plant diseases or soil exhaustion after a few years of banana farming are counted, as they ought to be.

But without a doubt, land use change during the banana boom was primarily an indirect result of tropical fruit development. Some of the indirect deforestation was unmistakably tied to expansion of the tropical fruit sector. For example, meat, milk, cassava, and other edible goods produced at El Tenguel comprised most of the food supply for United Fruit's employees and their families, so pastures and the area on the estate sown in crops other than bananas far exceeded the hectares planted to bananas. More broadly, tropical fruit development caused the population to grow in the *costa*—almost entirely due to migration out of the Andes, where rural wages were appreciably lower. The economy was also stimulated. In turn, burgeoning human numbers and improved living standards enhanced the demand for food. Since this demand was not satisfied completely by increasing imports from other countries and harvests in the rest of Ecuador, coastal farmers and ranchers produced more as well, almost always by putting more land to work.

Wunder points out that deforestation was an indirect outcome of the banana boom for another reason. As detailed in Chapter 4, a major investment in transportation infrastructure was made in the *costa* after the mid-1940s. Some of this investment was paid for with taxes levied on fruit exports. Much more was financed with loans provided by institutions such as the U.S. Export-Import Bank and World Bank once they determined that Ecuador was creditworthy, owing to the upward trajectory in the country's exports and gross domestic production (GDP) that derived mostly from tropical fruit development. Either way, the construction of additional roads and bridges allowed more agricultural colonists to settle in previously undeveloped areas.[6]

Two decades after it started, the post-war banana boom was over, as was practically all direct deforestation originating in the tropical fruit sector. As growers switched from Gros Michel to the Cavendish variety, the area planted to bananas stopped increasing. That area occasionally rose above 200,000 hectares during the 1960s.[7] But with the yield gains that accompanied

varietal conversion, the sector's land requirements declined. In 1974, for example, those requirements were 10 percent lower than what they had been
twenty years earlier, when the banana boom was in full swing (Table 10). This
geographic contraction was not evenly distributed. Since Cavendish bananas
were harder to transport than the Gros Michel fruit they had replaced, agricultural operations far from coastal harbors were at a disadvantage. Accordingly, landowners switched from bananas to other crops and even to livestock
around Santo Domingo and in other settings well to the north of Guayaquil.
Hectares dedicated to tropical fruit production were also lower in 1974 than
in previous years in the province where the port city is located. In contrast,
there was no geographic retreat in the southern *costa*, where bananas were
shipped out through Puerto Bolívar, near Machala. In that part of Ecuador,
the boom continued, as measured in terms of production as well as land use
(Table 10).

While there was no direct deforestation to speak of outside the southern
costa during the 1970s and early 1980s, Wunder contends that tropical fruit
development in earlier years had a lagged indirect effect on land use. For example, people who had migrated from the Andes to western Ecuador during
the banana boom continued to have children after the boom ended. Thus, demographic change catalyzed by expansion of the tropical fruit sector between
the mid-1940s and mid-1960s resulted in forest loss in later years.[8] Wunder
offers no estimate of this lagged impact, highlighting instead the difficulty of
apportioning land use change among its various drivers—including drivers
stemming from the discovery of oil in northeastern Ecuador in 1967.

Increased production and exports of fossil fuels usually cause deforestation to slow down, not accelerate. This deceleration has to do with strengthening of the national currency—caused by the dollars and other foreign
exchange that oil exports bring in and resulting in import bias, with non-oil

Table 10: Spatial Distribution of Ecuadorian Banana Farms, Selected Years

	1954	1974	1996
Total area (ha)	147,270	132,441	120,984
Total share (%) in:			
southern *costa*	9	19	35
same province as Guayaquil	23	19	32
rest of western Ecuador	68	62	33

Source: Wunder 2001, 177.

exports going down and goods purchased from other countries displacing more domestic output in national markets. As a rule, agriculture suffers as the currency grows more valuable, so farmers and ranchers encroach less on forested habitats.[9]

Wunder, who has examined energy booms and agriculture's geographic expansion throughout the tropics and subtropics, emphasizes that Ecuador after the 1960s was an exceptional case. True, the country experienced currency overvaluation since monetary authorities drew on the foreign money received for oil exports to maintain a fixed rate of exchange between the sucre and the dollar in spite of much lower inflation in the United States. However, the livestock industry did not suffer the consequences of import bias because the government placed tight restrictions on beef, pork, chicken, and dairy products coming in from other countries. With living standards rising at a fast clip during the oil boom, demand increased rapidly for these goods.[10] Protected from external competition, Ecuador's ranchers, more than anyone else, ramped up production, mainly by carving new grazing land out of forests.[11] Another factor contributing to deforestation was the subsidization of gasoline and diesel fuel, which lowered transportation costs throughout the agricultural sector but was particularly important for crop and livestock producers in remote locations undergoing agricultural settlement.[12] Infrastructure development in those same locations likewise caused settlement and forest loss to accelerate during the 1970s and early 1980s, in spite of currency overvaluation.

Devaluation of the sucre and other changes in economic policy during the administration of León Febres-Cordero reinforced the comparative advantage of Ecuadorian agriculture, so the tropical fruit sector rebounded. Output climbed dramatically, mainly thanks to the sector's geographic expansion around Guayaquil and in the southern *costa*. Meanwhile, banana farming continued to decline farther north, in settings poorly suited to production of the Cavendish variety because of their distance from coastal ports. The net result was a reduction in harvested area for Ecuador as a whole (Table 10).

During the past twenty to twenty-five years, banana farming has become more technologically demanding, with greater capital requirements and higher yields. With yields going up, output growth has been achieved without much geographic expansion of the tropical fruit sector. Also, indirect deforestation has dwindled to negligible levels.[13] Banana production remains labor intensive, though not as much as it used to be. With overall employment stabilized, the sector's continuing expansion is no longer a reason for migration from other parts of Ecuador to the *costa*. Likewise, roads and bridges are not being built either to serve the banana industry or because fruit exports are financing improvements in infrastructure. The rural landscape is still changing, though for unrelated reasons.

Black Sigatoka

Deforestation has environmental tradeoffs, such as diminished biodiversity, although agriculture's geographic expansion also creates benefits. But regardless of whether or not the economic gains have exceeded the costs in western Ecuador, land use change that can be attributed directly or indirectly to the area's banana industry has ceased. In contrast, growers' use of agricultural chemicals has reached major proportions, certainly compared to levels of use when the banana boom was getting underway seventy years ago.

During the late 1940s and for many years afterward, fertilization was modest since soil fertility was high where banana production was concentrated. Pesticide use was limited as well. No chemical countermeasures existed for Panama Disease. Also, combating Yellow Sigatoka with yearly applications of 2,700 liters per hectare of Bordeaux Spray was impractical for all but the largest planters, who could afford the necessary pumps, pipes, hoses, and nozzles. However, comparable results were achieved after the mid-1950s through the aerial spraying of oil, at an annual rate of just twenty-three liters per hectare.[14] Thus, the fungal disease could be controlled at a reasonable cost and with minimal consequences for the environment and human health.

Fifty years ago, a new pathogenic threat to the tropical fruit industry was detected in the same Fijian valley where Yellow Sigatoka had been identified in the early 1900s. The first visible sign of Black Sigatoka consists of small spots on leaves, which quickly become long, dark streaks. These streaks diminish photosynthetic capacity and therefore production. The fungal disease also accelerates the ripening of harvested fruit, which leads to sizable economic losses. Left unchecked, Black Sigatoka reduces marketable yields by 20 percent, at a minimum, and sometimes by as much as 80 percent.[15]

The fungus responsible for the disease is carried by winds across great distances and can infect plants quickly, especially if leaf surfaces are moist and temperatures are high (27 degrees Celsius or more). In settings with abundant rainfall, frequent applications of fungicides are the only remedy. Some chemical treatments are not absorbed by vegetative tissue although they prevent *Mycosphaerella fijensis* spores from penetrating banana plants. Other fungicides attack pathogens directly after entering the vascular systems of diseased plants. In places such as Costa Rica, where bananas are raised in areas with elevated humidity, multiple fungicides are used because *Mycosphaerella fijensis* can develop resistance to an individual chemical treatment and weekly fumigation is becoming the norm.[16]

Less than a decade after its discovery in the South Pacific, Black Sigatoka had shown up in Central America. Treatments that had successfully contained Yellow Sigatoka proved ineffective against the new disease, which struck northern Honduras in 1973 and affected 1,200 hectares. One of those treatments was Dithane, a fungicide manufactured by Dow Chemical that Standard Fruit had adopted in 1968. Benlate, introduced that same year by Dupont Corporation, had better results, although strains of *Mycosphaerella fijensis* that can withstand the fungicide developed quickly. After a few years' experimentation, agricultural specialists employed by multinational fruit companies figured out that Black Sigatoka could be controlled with regular applications of Dithane, Benlate, and oil, albeit at a large cost. Whereas combating Yellow Sigatoka with Bordeaux Spray accounted for 6 to 7 percent of United Fruit's operating costs in Honduras during the mid-1950s, approximately 26 percent of those costs twenty years later had to do with the chemicals and labor employed in the fight against Black Sigatoka.[17]

By the early 1980s, the disease was taking a toll on Colombian production. Then, after unusually humid conditions during the El Niño of 1983, Black Sigatoka arrived in northwestern Ecuador. The Programa Nacional del Banano (PNB), the government agency that had assumed overall responsibility for the management of plant diseases twenty years earlier, was slow to acknowledge the problem. An ad hoc Frente Unido de Bananeros Ecuatorianos demanded in January 1987 that a national emergency be declared and PNB monies be allocated for pest control, including the construction of additional airstrips in affected areas. However, there were divisions within the industry, with many planters in the southern *costa* and close to Guayaquil in favor of razing every banana farm in the province where Esmeraldas is located. Rejecting this proposal, the authorities in Quito instead imposed a quarantine, prohibiting the transportation of bananas out of that province to the rest of the country. Subsequent investigation revealed that Black Sigatoka only infects leaves, never fruit, so the quarantine did not slow disease transmission at all. However, restricting the movement of bananas compounded the economic losses growers in the northern part of the *costa* suffered because of *Mycosphaerella fijensis*, since large reefer ships rarely called at Esmeraldas and since the quarantine put Manta, Guayaquil, and other seaports beyond the growers' reach.[18]

With Black Sigatoka spreading quickly in western Ecuador, the Febres-Cordero administration levied a temporary tax on banana exports in late 1987 to pay for fumigation.[19] The tax was extended by the next president, Rodrigo Borja, after his inauguration in August 1988. However, funds for the maintenance of airstrips and the purchase of fungicides were released sparingly and exporters argued that the government's efforts were ineffective. Borja responded by cancelling the tax and distributing unspent monies—not to the exporters who had complained after making obligatory payments, but instead to growers. Aside from continuing spray oil treatments for Yellow Sigatoka and contributing $50,000 to the Fundación Hondureña de Investigación Agrícola (FHIA) in return for access to its findings on disease control and other matters, the PNB accomplished little.[20]

Leading *bananeros* took action on their own. Esteban Quirola, for instance, hired a couple of pilots to fly him above his plantations so that he could scout for signs of *Mycosphaerella fijensis* and assess the effectiveness of aerial fumigation. Luís Noboa bought a dozen helicopters outfitted for spraying operations and Segundo Wong acquired one such aircraft. Also, several pages of the notarized contract signed by participants in Dole's Grupo Básico program have to do with plant diseases, including protections for workers who handle fungicides or who should be out of the way when chemicals are being sprayed by helicopters or fixed-wing planes.[21]

Outside the northern *costa*, where there is a lot of precipitation and which is no longer an important source of bananas, Ecuadorian growers have the advantage of a fairly dry climate in their struggle against Black Sigatoka. For many of them, disease control involves monitoring the tender, new leaves *Mycosphaerella fijensis* favors for spots and incipient streaks and then removing infected leaves.[22] Even if these measures prove inadequate, fungicides need not be applied weekly, as is routine in Costa Rica and other rainy parts of Central America. Fifteen treatments over twelve months suffice in western Ecuador if annual precipitation is close to average, although the number can be as low as seven in a year with little or no rain and as high as twenty if precipitation and humidity are well above the norm. In a few settings, it is possible to curtail fungicide use entirely, which explains why most of the *costa*'s organic bananas are raised on irrigated farms in dry areas—including many of the rural properties Dole started acquiring in the late 1990s to satisfy consumers who demand fruit produced without resort to agricultural chemicals.[23]

In spite of the climatic advantages of western Ecuador, Black Sigatoka adds significantly to production expenses. One Grupo Básico participant estimates that fighting the disease costs between $450 and $480 per hectare.[24] Another participant with eighty hectares planted to bananas reports that the bill for each application is $4,000, which implies that the per-hectare expense of fungicide treatments averages $750 per annum and varies between $350 and $1,000 per annum. There are also payments to workers who monitor plants for fungal infestations and prune away diseased leaves.[25]

Disease control is particularly burdensome for small operations. The hand pumps used to good effect against Yellow Sigatoka between the 1950s and 1980s proved to be a poor substitute for aerial spraying aimed at the newer and more destructive plant pathogen. For a short while during the late 1990s, the national government provided five free cycles of aerial fumigation every year to properties no larger than thirty hectares. Otherwise, the expense of chemical treatments has been prohibitive for the owners of many of these properties, especially on a per-hectare basis, so fumigation has been discouraged. Yields suffer, in a quantitative sense and qualitatively, which explains why banana production has been abandoned on a number of holdings with five, ten, or even twenty hectares.[26]

One of Ecuador's leading agricultural scientists, Dr. Jorge Chang, remembers working in the southern *costa* three decades ago, when Black Sigatoka had yet to strike and the region boasted many well-kept farms—large, small, and in between. But just a few years later, idle fields were common, once banana plants had been consumed entirely by the *Mycosphaerella fijensis* fungus. Unable to survive several months with no money coming in as healthy replacements for diseased plants matured, many small growers, in particular, had no choice other than to find different ways to support themselves and their families.[27]

External Costs

Growers can sometimes avoid the depredations of pests with minimal use of chemical inputs. More than forty years ago, for example, United Fruit determined that the best way to contain the damage done to the roots of banana plants by parasitic nematodes (*Radopholus simlis*) was to prop up plants with

wooden stakes and sow corms that had been treated in nurseries with dibromochloropropane (DBCP), a nematicide manufactured by Shell Oil Company; the alternative, which was to apply DBCP in infected fields, was found
to be more expensive.[28] Along with biological measures, the same approach
is employed to this day in Ecuador to keep nematodes in check.[29] But where
Black Sigatoka is concerned, aerial fumigation is hard for banana producers
around the world to avoid, as reflected in the 500 million dollars or more they
spend every year on fungicides.[30]

The constant effort to stay ahead of fungi, nematodes, and other pests
boosts employment, due to the labor required for plant monitoring, leaf removal, staking of banana plants, and other tasks.[31] In effect, farmworkers have
organisms such as *Mycosphaerella fijensis* and *Radopholus simlis* to thank for
staying busy year round. However, job security can come at a steep price if
workers' health is endangered. Following the discovery in 1977 that some
of the men employed at a factory where DBCP was produced were sexually
sterile, tight restrictions on use of the nematicide were put in place in the
United States. Similar restrictions were adopted in banana exporting countries, though not immediately. Due to the severity of nematode infestations,
Costa Rica waited two years before following the lead of U.S. regulators and
Standard Fruit continued to rely heavily on DBCP, which extended the exposure of some of its employees to the nematicide.[32]

In an analysis of nematode control in Costa Rica's banana industry, economist Lori Ann Thrupp found that Standard Fruit opted for repeated field applications of DBCP during the late 1960s because doing so was cheaper than
alternative treatments, some of which were less hazardous.[33] Thrupp's finding
is in line with Soluri's general conclusion, based on his review of corporate
documents and correspondence from the same period, that decisions about
whether and how to use pesticides hinged on the expected impact on production and costs. Workers' health was a consideration, especially if irritated
eyes, vomiting, and other symptoms impaired labor productivity.[34] Otherwise, health effects amounted to an "externality," which is how economists
refer to costs not factored into any company's bottom line.

With few exceptions, externalities are difficult to evaluate. This is certainly true of environmental externalities, such as the ecological disruptions
that can result if pesticides intended for harmful insects and nematodes also
kill other organisms. With respect to pesticide poisoning, reliable estima-
tion of sterility, cancer, and other illnesses and conditions requires systematic
monitoring and data collection over many years as well as epidemiological

investigation that takes into account all relevant causes of morbidity. Research
efforts of this sort are rare in Latin America, which means that the number
of people whose health has suffered due to exposure to harmful substances
is difficult to gauge. As many as 10,000 Costa Ricans and 2,500 Hondurans
were affected by DBCP, yet as Soluri points out "a precise figure will never
be known."[35] In the report about Ecuador she prepared for Human Rights
Watch, Carol Pier identified various organophosphates and other chemical
inputs to banana production that are categorized as "moderately hazardous"
by the World Health Organization (WHO). Also, the forty-five adolescent
workers she interviewed recalled various instances when they had handled
plastic bags treated with pesticides, sprayed fungicides on harvested fruit, or
been in or near fields during aerial fumigation. However, Pier made no attempt to quantify health risks, for the simple reason that the data needed to
do so were lacking.[36]

The absence of reliable estimates of non-internalized environmental costs,
the incidence of morbidity related to pesticide poisoning, and other externalities has not impeded civil litigation. For example, lawsuits have been filed
in the United States on behalf of Ecuadorian shrimp producers for losses they
allegedly suffered due to the runoff of Benlate from banana farms. The losses
were real enough: a spike in shellfish mortality that caused annual exports
to decline by approximately 10 percent between 1992 and 1993.[37] However,
elevated mortality happened several years after a surge in fungicide applications upstream from artificial ponds along the coast where shrimp are raised
and harvested. Also, the claims of some plaintiffs, such as shrimp producers
at the mouth of the Río Guayas many kilometers downstream from the closest banana farms, were far-fetched. Furthermore, scientific investigation had
established by the mid-1990s that Benlate and other fungicides were not the
source of lesions and other symptoms exhibited by diseased shellfish. Instead,
mortality was caused by a virus that thrived in Ecuador's shrimp ponds.[38] In
spite of this finding, however, lawsuits targeting Dupont Corporation, which
stopped producing Benlate in 2001, have been winding their way through
courtrooms in the United States for a number of years.

DBCP has been the subject of civil litigation as well. After financial settlements had been reached with thousands of men claiming to be sterile after
being exposed to the nematicide on corporate plantations in Central America, Dole was sued by forty-seven Nicaraguan plaintiffs in California in 2007.
Most of the individual cases were dismissed because evidence was lacking
or for other reasons. However, five million dollars in damages were awarded

to a half dozen plaintiffs, although the company decided to appeal because of its suspicions about much of the evidence presented in court.[39] Dole was vindicated three years later, in July 2010, when the presiding judge threw out three of the six cases after finding that plaintiffs' attorneys had perpetrated "massive fraud," including recruitment of clients who had never worked for Dole and submission of misleading medical testimony.[40] The company settled a little more than a year later with the three other plaintiffs for an undisclosed sum.[41]

There is an alternative to legal contests that pit plaintiffs' attorneys, who discount causes of human illness and environmental pollution for which the parties they are suing are not responsible, against defendants' counsel, who make every attempt to portray their clients as blameless. Indeed, scientific effort in laboratories and experimental fields is much more likely to bring down the external costs of banana production. Hopes have been raised for the biological control of Black Sigatoka by studies of bacteria that prey on *Mycosphaerella fijensis*.[42] However, none of these studies' findings have passed through peer review, as is required for publication in a scholarly journal. Bio-technological advances are considerably more promising, particularly since there are wild banana varieties with some innate resistance to Black Siga-toka.[43] Introducing the gene or genes responsible for this resistance into the Cavendish and other vulnerable varieties would safeguard food production while sharply reducing, or maybe even eliminating, pesticide use.

The future of the tropical fruit industry and perhaps its very survival might well depend on advances of this sort.

CHAPTER 10

====

Continuing Challenges, New Risks

Multinational agribusiness comes in for stern criticism in writings about the banana industry. But in books and articles focused on Ecuador, the power and abuses of foreign companies are not so much proved as vehemently asserted. Was SAFCO, for instance, a bad actor? More than eighty years ago, the Chilean firm talked Manuel Amable-Calle into planting the Gros Michel variety in the southern *costa*. The firm profited, no doubt, but so did Amable-Calle. Moreover, SAFCO's leadership of Ecuador's banana industry was far from permanent. In the late 1950s, half a century after the company had set up shop in Guayaquil, its business was disappearing—mainly because Luís Noboa and Juan X. Marcos had just won over a pair of key customers: Shillo Adir in New York City and Sven Salen in Sweden.

Or take United Fruit. Most of the *costa*'s best resources were in local hands long before banana development began, so the multinational corporation was never going to dominate Ecuador the way it used to control the fortunes of Central America. Its first purchases of agricultural real estate during the mid-1930s, a dozen years after the firm was courted by President José Luís Tamayo, were followed immediately by a forced donation of several thousand hectares to the government, to soothe nationalistic lawmakers decrying foreign land ownership. Soon afterward, *campesinos* advised by leftwing attorneys invaded company farms and a military strongman issued a regulatory decree targeting United Fruit. Still, the firm persevered. At El Tenguel, it converted a bankrupt cacao plantation into a showplace where well-paid workers were provided a modern hospital, schools for their children, stores offering cheap food, and recreational facilities. Two generations after El Tenguel's divestiture, resulting primarily from an antitrust settlement in the United States, Ecuadorians who once worked on the estate remember it as a "paradise."[1] The *costa*'s *bananeros* do not liken United Fruit in retrospect to a marine monster; to the contrary, they hold it in high esteem for its pivotal contributions during the formative years of their industry.[2]

How about Standard Fruit? It arrived in Ecuador right after World War II, a little more than a decade after its principal competitor purchased El Tenguel. Rather than harvesting bananas on its own plantations or buying directly from local growers, the company opted to delegate all purchasing to Marcos and Noboa, who had traded rice and other commodities successfully for many years. The mutual benefits of the decade-long association persisted long after the two Guayaquileños started selling fruit to overseas importers of their own choosing. The U.S.-based multinational has never lacked for willing associates in western Ecuador. For Marcos and Noboa, the partnership with Standard Fruit was a crucial first step toward worldwide prominence as banana suppliers.

So the claim that Ecuador's tropical fruit industry is a mere subsidiary of exploitative corporations headquartered in the United States is inaccurate and misleading. Instead, the industry's salient feature is a free market, one in which enterprising growers and exporters with national origins are rewarded. Teaming up when it has suited them and operating independently on other occasions, these local businessmen and women have excelled time after time at finding and serving customers, which explains their country's sustained export leadership.

Previous commercial accomplishments are no guarantee of future success, of course, and the question of whether or not Ecuador and its entrepreneurs will remain at the top of the banana business is obviously of national significance. The same question is important for the country's competitors and for its customers throughout the world.

Ever Entrepreneurial

If Ecuador's tropical fruit sector falters during the years to come, a contributing factor might be the absence of individuals of the sort who seized opportunities during the midcentury banana boom and subsequently dealt with a series of domestic and international obstacles. Marcos's passing in 1980 was not disruptive given his close relationship with Noboa, who remained active until his death fourteen years later. But replacing either Noboa or Segundo Wong (who lived until 2002) was never going to be a trivial matter, at least as far as their respective businesses were concerned. Also, the two entrepreneurs made essential contributions to banana development in the *costa* by placing as much Ecuadorian produce as possible in each and every overseas market they could reach. Foreign companies that grew or purchased bananas throughout the Western Hemisphere would never have done likewise.

The challenge of transition is illustrated by the experience of United Fruit after the departure of Samuel Zemurray. Due to his father's untimely death, Zemurray had been obliged at a young age to shoulder adult responsibilities and providing for his mother and younger siblings left him with a deeply ingrained work ethic. He worked intelligently as well, as demonstrated by the scheme he came up with at the age of eighteen to market ripe bananas that everyone else was discarding. Working intelligently certainly involved establishing profitable associations: early on, for example, with Ashbell Hubbard, who participated in the acquisition of the Cuyamel Fruit Company.[3] With these personal antecedents, Zemurray fashioned a multinational enterprise that was "tough, no-nonsense, quick to act." But after his retirement in 1954, United Fruit was often "indecisive" and tended to live "off its own past."[4]

Not unlike Zemurray, Wong became the main source of support for his brothers and sisters as an adolescent after the death of his mother, who was either widowed or abandoned. Scrambling for whatever employment he could find on the streets and docks of Guayaquil made him into a tireless worker. Another characteristic he shared with Zemurray was a knack for mutually rewarding partnerships, initially with other Ecuadorians whose forebears had migrated from China. However, there was no succession crisis at the Favorita Fruit Company after Wong's demise. Now in the hands of his offspring, the vertically integrated business continues to prosper. Favorita's Reybanpac division is the third largest exporter of Ecuadorian bananas—behind the Dole Food Company's UBESA subsidiary and Truisfruit, which is a branch of the Grupo Noboa (Table 11).

Eight years old when his father died, Noboa started laboring from dawn past dusk three years later, a prelude to a lifetime of sixteen-hour days on the job. The future tycoon benefited from a series of business associations, starting with a position in Marcos's Sociedad General that came his way when he was twelve. Toward the end of his life, he tried to arrange a smooth succession at the Grupo Noboa, not least by grooming capable executives who were unrelated by blood or marriage. One such executive was Roberto Baquerizo,

Table 11: Top Ten Exporters of Ecuadorian Bananas, 2012

Company	Market share (%)
UBESA (Dole)	10.4
Truisfruit (Grupo Noboa)	7.8
Reybanpac (Favorita)	4.9
Comersur	4.1
Oro Banana	3.9
Asoagribal	3.6
Brundicorpi (Chiquita)	3.4
Ecuagreenprodex*	2.9
Coragrofrut *	2.9
Sentilver	2.2

* Owned by Russian fruit importers.
Source: AEBE, 17.

who was taken along by his boss to offices and other installations around the world in 1993 after having distinguished himself in various managerial assignments. But even though an effective team was in place at the top of the company the following year, when Noboa passed away, a distracting fight over his estate broke out immediately among his heirs.

The dispute stemmed from Noboa's decision not to divide his wealth equally among his six children. The older of his two sons and one of his four daughters are not mentioned in press reports about the inheritance. Each of the other three daughters received 150 million dollars—including Isabel, who in 2000 published an adulatory biography of her father. In contrast, assets worth 7.5 million dollars went to the younger of Noboa's two sons, Alvaro, who already had grown wealthy as an independent real estate investor. Some individuals who knew the father speculate that he wanted Alvaro to take over the Grupo Noboa, although he "thought it best to force his son to acquire it through hard work," and Alvaro maintains that the relationship with his father was "wonderful." In any event, he contested the will, which led to legal maneuvering that cost his sisters and him 20 million dollars and did not end until a London court ruled in his favor in 2002.[5]

Another distraction for the Noboas was Alvaro's political career. That career got underway in 1996, two years after his father's death, when he was appointed to head the government board responsible for monetary policy. Two years later, he campaigned for the Ecuadorian presidency, which he lost narrowly to Jamil Mahuad. He then founded his own party as a prelude to unsuccessful presidential bids in 2002 and 2006. The pursuit of high office, which never tempted Luís Noboa, required time and effort that might otherwise have been devoted to the family business.

One apparent consequence of the inheritance struggle and political distractions is that customers were lost in Japan and other places after Alvaro Noboa achieved effective control of the family conglomerate in 1997. In addition, major financial setbacks have been suffered at the hands of political foes. In May 2013, for example, fiscal authorities answering to Rafael Correa, who won the 2006 election,[6] confiscated Grupo Noboa assets with a combined value of approximately 136 million dollars to settle a debt of 94 million dollars in unpaid taxes and accrued interest. The most important of these assets was the Hacienda Clementina, which Luís Noboa had purchased in 1980 and which at the time of its confiscation had an estimated value of 118 million dollars.[7]

As the travails of Alvaro Noboa demonstrate, unfortunate choices by individual businessmen and women can cost their own enterprises dearly. Such choices also used to be a potential hazard for Ecuador's tropical fruit sector as a whole. In 1954, for example, four firms handled three out of every four bananas shipped overseas from the *costa* (Table 4) and the exit or collapse of any of the four would have been a serious blow. As recently as the 1990s, the Grupo Noboa, Dole, and Reybanpac exported more than one in every two Ecuadorian bananas (Table 9) and the disappearance of any of those three companies would have been debilitating. But today, their combined share of the market is under 25 percent (Table 11). Even if the largest of the three—Dole, with a market share of 10 percent—stopped operating, Ecuador's banana industry would not be thrown off stride, not for long anyway.

While Noboa and Wong drew on a long tradition of export-oriented commerce in Guayaquil as well as business services available in the port city to break valuable entrepreneurial ground during the 1950s, 1960s, and 1970s, the two men now have many imitators, including in Ecuador's northern neighbor. A little more than fifty years ago, United Fruit organized banana production in the Urabá region of Colombia and for a while monopolized foreign shipments. However, local growers, who produced all the Colombian bananas the multinational firm exported, objected strenuously when the firm attempted in the late 1960s to cut farm-gate prices. Those growers had direct ties to Medellín, a politically influential city not too far inland, and the Unión de Bananeros de Urabá (UNIBAN) that they organized to compete against

United Fruit received subsidized credit and other backing from the central government. UNIBAN's bananas, marketed under the Turbana brand name, subsequently won over European and North American consumers, although guerrilla warfare hindered production beginning in the 1980s and European protectionism reduced exports during the final decade of the twentieth century.[8] Also, UNIBAN joined Chiquita in making sizable investments right before the collapse of the Soviet Union and its satellites in the expectation of a demand surge once communism ended, although the surge never happened because Noboa and Wong had cornered the market east of the old Iron Curtain years before. The Colombian firm is still in business, though, and recently added Whole Foods to its list of regular customers in the United States.[9]

The imitators of Noboa and Wong also include foreign importers seeking their own banana supplies. As a rule, these enterprises do not look to Central America and other parts of the Caribbean Basin, where they would have to compete against Chiquita, Dole, and Del Monte. They turn instead to western Ecuador, where harvests are bounteous and no single producer or exporter has significant market power. As indicated in Table 11, Russian importers currently purchase more than 5 percent of the *costa*'s output—on their own, not through transnational firms headquartered in the United States or through local intermediaries. Similarly, Imperial Ukrainian Fruit buys Ecuadorian bananas for delivery to Odessa.[10]

However, the overwhelming majority of the firms and individuals currently in the business Noboa and Wong pioneered are from Guayaquil. The trade data reported in Table 12 indicate that Ecuadorian exporters still follow the example provided decades ago by their two countrymen. In addition to being shipped overseas in enormous quantities, tropical fruit harvested in the *costa* reaches a far-flung mix of countries: from Algeria to Argentina, from Norway to New Zealand, and in North America as well. Thus, Ecuador's entrepreneurs show no sign of losing their commercial touch and their country remains a force for competition in the global banana industry.

Those same entrepreneurs seem unfazed by recent developments beyond their control in the international marketplace, even the announcement in March 2014 that Chiquita and its former subsidiary, Fyffes, intended to reunite. Together with Dole and Del Monte, these two firms handle up to 70 percent of the world's banana trade, so the proposed merger raised the antennae of antitrust agencies in Europe and the United States. U.S. officials were

Table 12: Ecuadorian and Colombian Shares of Selected Markets, 2009 (%)

Importing nation or region	Ecuadorian share	Colombian share
North America		
Canada	34	27
United States	28	13
South America		
Argentina	57	0
Chile	97	0
Western Europe		
Austria	33	9
Belgium	21	39
Germany	33	37
Italy	43	19
The Netherlands	15	1
Norway	37	20
Spain	32	17
Switzerland	31	16
United Kingdom	5	24
Eastern Europe		
Poland	48	20
Romania	64	4
Serbia	91	4
Former Soviet Union		
Russia	93	1
Ukraine	89	4
Middle East and North Africa		
Algeria	98	0
Turkey	84	4
Asia and the Pacific		
Japan	5	0
New Zealand	35	0

Source: comtrade.un.org.

also concerned that ChiquitaFyffes (as the combined enterprise would have been called) was to be headquartered in Ireland, where corporate income tax rates are relatively low. In Central America, the negotiating power of ChiquitaFyffes would have been "huge," as an Ecuadorian grower observed. But as the same *bananera* hastened to add, the *costa*'s farmers would still be able to choose among a large number of buyers; consequently, the merger would not have had any effect on operations like hers.[11]

A Troublesome Populist

The same cannot always be said of political developments in Ecuador. There are precedents in the country for the mistreatment of leading commercial figures, as exemplified by a military junta's harassment of Luís Noboa more than forty years ago. Also, the pursuit of import substituting industrialization (ISI) before the mid-1980s demonstrates the government's inclination at times toward public policies that harm the agricultural sector, including the banana industry. With this history in mind, the industry has kept a wary eye on the national capital since Correa's inauguration in January 2007, in which Hugo Chávez of Venezuela and Evo Morales of Bolivia were given pride of place along with Iran's Mahmoud Ahmadinejad.

An economist with a postgraduate education in the dismal science, Ecuador's current president describes his guiding principles as "leftist Christian." He caught a major break in 2003—two years after earning a Ph.D. at the University of Illinois and taking a job at a private university in Quito—when vice president Alfredo Palacio took him on as an advisor. Palacio's eagerness to finance universal health care, which he had promised voters during the previous year's campaign, meshed perfectly with Correa's stance that payments to foreign creditors ought to be curtailed for the sake of increased social spending. Nothing tangible came of the partnership immediately, although the young economist made frequent use of the public platform the vice president gave him.[12]

Two years later, Palacio ascended to the presidency, after the national congress had removed the previous chief executive, and assigned his protégé to the finance ministry. Within a few weeks, a stabilization fund into which some of the government's oil earnings had been deposited and from which withdrawals had been permitted solely to maintain macroeconomic stability was abolished. Correa had been criticizing the fund for years, arguing that holders of Ecuadorian bonds were the fund's lone beneficiaries—inasmuch as the value of those bonds in secondary markets was enhanced by the fund's existence—and that oil revenues should be dedicated exclusively to social programs. With the stabilization fund gone, Palacio's finance minister trained his sights elsewhere. He denounced the International Monetary Fund (IMF) and World Bank for making the reform of national economic policies a prerequisite for credit and threatened to withhold debt service payments to the two multilateral institutions if they did not fulfill their lending commitments. When the World Bank decided in July 2005 that a 100 million dollar loan would not be disbursed, Correa "set himself proverbially ablaze" in an angry letter to its president, Paul Wolfowitz. This display damaged relations with major lenders, so Palacio had no choice other than to demand the resignation of his finance minister.[13]

The 106 days spent in the presidential cabinet gained Correa fame and support throughout the country. "Wrapping himself in the national flag to confront Washington [based] multilateral agencies, supposedly on behalf of the dispossessed of Ecuador," he had an approval rating of 57 percent, twenty points better than Palacio's rating, which positioned him well for a presidential campaign.[14] In addition, he had taken advantage of the opportunities that came his way as a government minister to forge ties with likeminded leaders elsewhere in Latin America: most prominently Chávez, with whom Correa had discussed the sale of Ecuadorian bonds as an alternative to going to the IMF or private investors—without previously securing his president's permission to do so. Less than a year after his departure from the cabinet, he ran for chief of state as a "Bolivarian" ally of the Venezuelan strongman. He lost the first round of the election, in October 2006, but prevailed over Alvaro Noboa in a two-man runoff the following month.

By any measure, Ecuador's foreign debt burden was light when Correa took the oath of office. With repayments to creditors regularly exceeding new disbursements, outstanding obligations were contracting. Meanwhile, oil prices had been rising steadily since 2002, which boosted gross domestic product (GDP). Furthermore, interest rates were low due to expansionary monetary management in the United States. Under these circumstances, Ecuador's interest payments as a share of GDP had declined from 26 percent in 2000 to 2 percent seven years later as external debt fell from 70 percent to 20 percent of GDP. But even in the absence of financial stress, Correa's government reduced its obligations by 3.2 billion dollars in a way that Arturo C. Porzecanski, an economics professor at American University, characterizes as "unprincipled."[15] This financial maneuver caused Ecuador to be counted with Argentina among the world's "rogue sovereign debtors."[16]

The debt repudiation also earned Correa a place of honor in the Bolivarian camp of leftwing populists organized and headed by Chávez. Sebastián Edwards, an economist from Chile as well as a professor at the University of California at Los Angeles, describes the populists' playbook succinctly, noting that they mobilize backing from "the working class as well as significant sectors of the middle class" as they take on these groups' "oppressors"—namely, "the oligarchy, corporations, financial capital, the business sector, and foreign companies." Edwards also points out that the blueprint for Bolivarian

governance is largely the creation of legal academicians led by Roberto Viciano-Pastor of the Universidad de Valencia, in Spain. Rather than shielding
individuals from an overbearing state, which is a fundamental purpose of
the U.S. Constitution, the constitutions designed by Viciano-Pastor and his
colleagues for Venezuela, Bolivia, and Ecuador after the elections of Chávez,
Morales, and Correa, respectively, feature myriad "aspirational" rights—for
economic security, health care, a clean environment, and on and on. All these
rights are advanced by heads of state who are little encumbered by institu-
tional checks and balances.[17] The Bolivarian playbook and constitutional
blueprint suit the Ecuadorian president to a tee.

Correa has used his executive powers to enlarge the public sector and
to revive a state-centered strategy for economic development his country
started to move away from thirty years ago. The latest attempt at this revival
is "smart" ISI, which became a subject of common complaint within weeks of
its roll-out in November 2013. As was to be expected, consumers grumbled
about shortages of foreign goods—including hamburgers sold in fast-food
outlets, not just luxury items. In addition, various firms registered their dissatisfaction because the imported inputs they required to produce domestic
substitutes for foreign goods were often unavailable.[18]

Financing difficulties have mounted also, owing to a swollen state payroll
as well as a vast improvement in roads, dams, and other infrastructure that
even Correa's detractors concede will have lasting economic rewards. In the
wake of debt repudiation, multilateral institutions and private banks have refrained from footing the bill, which so far runs to tens of billions of dollars.
Nor has Ecuador attracted much foreign direct investment (FDI); in 2013,
this investment amounted to 703 million dollars, which was 0.4 percent of
FDI for the entire Western Hemisphere south of the United States.[19] Instead,
taxes have been collected energetically, much more than was formerly the
case, and the government has captured a huge share of domestic savings—for
example, by obliging its Instituto Ecuatoriano de Seguridad Social (IESS) to
invest in state bonds and nothing else. Through the middle of 2014, it also
benefited from high prices for crude oil. Additionally, large sums have been
borrowed from China, which is now Ecuador's largest creditor. The East
Asian nation has committed more than 12 billion dollars since 2009, with all
financing secured with presales of oil.[20]

Now that the funds received in return for mortgaging untapped fossil
fuels exceed Ecuador's external debt in 2007, when Correa was inaugurated
and before 3.2 billion dollars in foreign obligations were trimmed away, there

is widespread unease about the country's dependence on China.[21] This un-ease is not enough to cause the president and his associates to bring public spending into line with tax revenues; even before oil prices plunged in the second half of 2014, that year's fiscal deficit was projected to equal 3.1 percent of GDP.[22] Nevertheless, Ecuador returned to traditional financing sources, as reflected by the suspension of all criticism directed at institutions such as the IMF and World Bank. In June 2014, the news surfaced that Goldman Sachs had lent the Ecuadorian government 400 million dollars, using Ecuadorian gold valued at 580 million dollars as collateral. Several days later, the government sold bonds worth 2 billion dollars and with a yield of 7.95 percent, apparently generous enough to reassure private investors who perhaps ought to worry more about the recovery of principal.[23]

Just as Correa now courts international capital, after railing against it throughout his career and earlier in his presidency, he no longer muses about creating a state agency responsible for all banana exports, as he did as recently as March 2011.[24] Such hints might have been nothing more than a sop to his far-left supporters—led by Ricardo Patiño, who once served the Sandinista government in Nicaragua[25] and in 2013 was in charge of the agency that re-lieved the Grupo Noboa of the Hacienda Clementina. But if Correa ever gave serious consideration to replacing dozens of private exporters with a single bureaucracy answering to him, he also knew that a proposal along these lines would arouse determined opposition. The stakes—hundreds of millions of dollars every year in overseas sales, tens of thousands of jobs, and livelihoods for thousands of farm households—are too large for the banana trade to be nationalized without protest.

Rather than voicing fears of nationalization, representatives of the tropi-cal fruit sector point these days to recent support from the government. For example, a tax of eight cents per exported box (weighing 18.9 to 19.5 kilo-grams, depending on its foreign destination) that was instituted in 1998 to pay for the reconstruction of roads and bridges after heavy storms that year was reduced in 2013 to nine-tenths of a cent per box, which covers inspection costs and related expenses.[26] This tax reduction is an encouraging sign since governmental assistance is essential in the struggle against tariffs and other trade barriers in nations that purchase Ecuadorian bananas.

At present, the banana industry is not focusing primarily on the United States, which has waived duties since 1991 on imports from Andean allies in the War on Drugs. These waivers no longer apply to Colombia and Peru, thanks to bilateral trade treaties those two countries have negotiated with the

United States, or to Bolivia, which has pulled out of counter-narcotics operations, and the renewal of Ecuador's preferences is iffy. Moreover, Correa has
adamantly opposed a trade pact with the United States, both on the campaign
trail in 2006 and since then as president. Ecuadorian *bananeros* do not press
the issue, however, because clawing a larger share of the U.S. market away
from Chiquita, Dole, and Del Monte would be a tall order even if banana
imports were never taxed or restricted.

Europe, now the leading outlet for Ecuadorian fruit exports, is of much
greater concern. In 2009, Correa pulled out of joint trade talks that Colombia, Peru, and his country had been conducting with the EU. Since then, Ecuador's northern and southern neighbors have signed bilateral accords, as
Mexico and all Central American nations have done. Each and every one of
these accords mandates a steady reduction in EU duties on banana imports.
Also, preferential access to the European market ended in December 2014
because living standards in Ecuador have risen far above the maximum level
the EU sets for application of concessionary tariffs.[27] Compounding the loss
of competitiveness resulting from these developments are the cost increases
experienced in the *costa* because large *bananeros* are being forced to obey
minimum wage laws and because the authorities have become much less tol-
erant about the hiring of temporary and contract laborers instead of permanent employees, who can unionize and have other rights.[28]

In 2012, Correa came out in favor of a trade treaty with the EU and, after
many months of preparation, negotiations got underway in January 2014.
Even though these negotiations were the responsibility of Patiño, who had
become foreign minister and was widely regarded as lukewarm at best about
an Ecuador-EU pact, the initial round of talks went well. Subsequent talks
bogged down, primarily because the Ecuadorians pressed for limited en-
forcement of intellectual property rights (IPRs) in their country and because
they did not want to do away with rules favoring national suppliers in governmental procurement.[29] But before the middle of the year, the minister of
international commerce, Francisco Rivadeneira, was in charge of the negotiations. Much more an advocate of trade liberalization than Patiño, Rivadeneira reached an agreement with the EU in July.[30]

By no means can Ecuador now be grouped with nations such as Australia
and New Zealand, where minimal barriers to international commerce follow
directly from a broad commitment to free markets.[31] Correa insists he is no
convert to "neoliberalism," to use a term favored by Latin American leftists.
His statement about Ecuador's pact with the EU, that "we don't believe in free

trade but we do believe in trade for mutual benefit," is peculiar in the eyes of anyone who understands the theory of comparative advantage, which holds that voluntary commercial exchange is always mutually beneficial. Regardless, Ecuador's president has chosen pragmatism over anti-market ideology. Conceding that his country imports less from Europe than it exports there, Correa now urges Ecuadorians "to be realistic" and to accept a bilateral treaty so as "to avoid the greater evil of being left without tariff preferences."[32]

The leaders of the tropical fruit sector applaud this concession to economic reality, appreciating full well that some of Correa's top allies remain hostile to neoliberalism and are in a position to undermine the trade treaty. In late 2014, for example, Patiño provoked a dispute with Germany, which ordinarily would back the treaty enthusiastically within the EU, by ordering that financial and other ties be severed between environmental groups in Ecuador and Europe's largest economy—all in the name of protecting national sovereignty.[33] If the dispute delays ratification of the bilateral trade accord, the foreign minister will shed crocodile tears, one must suppose.

A shakeup in the presidential cabinet in early 2015 left Patiño in place as foreign minister, but with Rivadeneira removed from the ministry of international commerce—a change that dissatisfied the banana industry and other exporting sectors. However, worries about matters such as the EU trade treaty are rarely expressed publicly, since Correa, like Chávez and other leftwing populists, has made his country less democratic, not more so. Newspapers that do not toe the government's line have been harassed, television stations have been nationalized, and the default response of Ecuador's president to criticism of any sort has been volcanic.[34] With Correa's political party poised to amend the constitution so that he can run for reelection in 2017,[35] the executive director of the Asociación de Exportadores de Banano del Ecuador (AEBE) has voiced full-throated support for steps the government has taken to maintain Ecuador's preferential access to the European market. AEBE's senior representative knows those steps could be reversed, especially if he failed to issues press releases about how "extremely happy and satisfied" he is with the stance of his country's president.[36]

Panama Disease, Again

Serious though they are at times, domestic political challenges facing Ecuador's banana industry are usually tractable. Pathogenic threats, in contrast, are potentially mortal. The damage done by Black Sigatoka is being contained at present. However, expenses are going up along with environmental damages as evolution of the airborne fungus, *Mycosphaerella fijensis*, obliges farmers to apply pesticides more and more heavily.[37] More ominous is the appearance on the far side of the world of a new race of the soil-borne fungus, *Fusarium oxysporum* Schlect. f. sp. *Cubense* (FOC), that plagued the tropical fruit business for decades beginning in the late 1800s.

Cavendish bananas resist Race 1 of the FOC fungus, which drove the Gros Michel variety to extinction as a commercial crop more than forty years ago. However, experts have known for a long time that the Cavendish variety is susceptible to other FOC strains responsible for Panama Disease. Diminished yields in a number of subtropical locations, including eastern Australia, South Africa, and the Canary Islands, were traced years ago to Race 4 of the fungus. Also, Race 4 has been implicated in the poor harvests suffered by highland farmers in Jamaica with poorly drained fields and by growers in Guadeloupe after a volcanic eruption rendered the island's soils more acidic. However, risks of Panama Disease were reckoned to be modest in Cavendish plantations located close to sea level and not too far from the equator.[38]

This view was "shattered" during the early 1990s, when the existence of a Tropical Race 4 (TR4) was confirmed. Commercial plantations were damaged and output was reduced in the absence of other causal factors in northern Australia as well as on various Indonesian islands and the Malay Peninsula.[39] Like Race 1 of the FOC fungus, TR4 persists for many years in infected soils and there are no chemical countermeasures. With the value of the annual Cavendish harvest reduced by 400 million dollars so far in the Philippines alone,[40] one Malaysian newspaper has likened the new edition of Panama Disease to the human immunodeficiency virus (HIV).[41]

TR4 is no longer confined to Southeast Asia and the Pacific, and recent reports that the fungus has shown up in Jordan and Mozambique have prompted warnings that an "eventual collapse" in worldwide production is "inevitable," with parallels drawn to the potato famine that devastated Ireland during the 1840s.[42] The combination of monocultural excess and microbial virulence, food writer Michael Pollan points out, made Ireland "exquisitely vulnerable, . . . dooming potatoes and potato eaters alike"[43] and in some respects the famine serves as an object lesson about the harm that might be wrought by TR4—especially as the fungus spreads across Africa, where bananas and plantains are staple foods in many countries, and once it reaches Latin America, the source of most tropical fruit exports. Only one potato variety was raised and consumed in Ireland, just as the Cavendish variety now accounts for all but a tiny share of the global banana trade. Also, the pathogen responsible for the potato famine, *Phytophthora infestans*, is hard to eradicate, as is TR4.

However, there is a critical difference between the tragedy that befell the Emerald Isle 170 years ago and the potential consequences of TR4. Direct genetic manipulation, commonly referred to as biotechnology, was beyond imagining when *Phytophthora infestans* crossed the Atlantic Ocean and, indeed, remained inconceivable for another century or more. Even conventional breeding, which involves the sexual crossing of related varieties to produce desirable hybrids, was primitive by today's standards. The fungus arrived in Ireland ten years before Friar Gregor Mendel began experimenting with garden peas in an Austrian monastery, and more time would pass before his insights about genetic inheritance would begin to guide improvement of crops and livestock and control of agricultural pests. Far from exemplifying agriculture's current vulnerability when confronted by pathogenic onslaughts, then, the Irish potato famine underscores the helplessness that existed as long as farmers could not enlist the aid of modern science.

Conventional breeding based on Mendel's insights has limitations where crops that do not reproduce sexually are concerned. The difficulties are exemplified by attempts at the Fundación Hondureña de Investigación Agrícola (FHIA)—the government agency that operates the research center United Fruit established at La Lima, Honduras, in 1958—to create satisfactory substitutes for the Cavendish without resort to biotechnology. To begin the process, bulb-like corms for several thousand banana plants are placed in the ground. Nine months later, when the plants are flowering, workers apply pollen from other varieties with preferred characteristics, thereby producing hybrid fruit. After another three months, the fruit is harvested and local women employed by FHIA peel tens of thousands of bananas by hand. Once the fruit is fermented, softened, and pulped, the women carefully remove whatever seeds they can find. The recovery rate is infinitesimal: about one seed for every ten thousand bananas. Moreover, the vast majority of seeds are incapable of providing viable embryos, so are useless for breeding.[44]

Remarkably, this approach yields positive results on occasion. During the 1980s, for example, James Rowe, a United Fruit scientist and long-time director of research at La Lima, created the Goldfinger banana: the culmination of many years of painstaking effort. Goldfinger's appealing traits are various, not least resistance to both Black Sigatoka and Panama Disease.[45] However, the fruit does not taste like the bananas customers are accustomed to, which highlights a fundamental challenge. As Dan Koeppel points out in his book, *Banana*, breeders are expected to come up with varieties that not only withstand harmful fungi, but also are amenable to controlled ripening, grow on plants that are not easily knocked down by tropical storms, and have "tough skin, good taste, (and) high yields."[46] Other attributes are prized by banana exporters and marketers, such as tight (as opposed to splayed) bunches of fruit and long shelf life. Different characteristics are important for bananas and plantains that small farmers in the tropics and subtropics raise to feed their families—including small plant size, which facilitates harvesting, and broad leaves that provide shade for coffee and other interplanted crops.[47]

Between the time required to breed a TR4-resistant version of (or substitute for) the Cavendish variety and the continuing evolution of the FOC fungus, the collapse of the global banana industry some writers warn about might actually happen. Koeppel, who opposes the alternative of direct genetic manipulation even though it is much speedier than conventional breeding, does not downplay the risk, speculating that imported bananas might disappear in temperate-zone settings such as the United States.[48] In addition, he recognizes the hunger that will result if TR4 and other diseases are not checked. In Sub-Saharan Africa and other parts of the world, more than 400 million impoverished individuals get at least 15 percent of their calories from bananas and related foods; for many of these people, substitute sources of nutrition are lacking.[49]

Koeppel is also forthright about the flimsy basis for rejecting genetically modified (GM) foods, even as he sympathizes with those who "cringe" at the idea of agricultural biotechnology.

> People become uncomfortable. Even scared. When they learn about modifying a Polynesian banana to contain extra quantities of vitamin A, they approve. When they learn that the marker genes come from fishes (it's true), they're horrified. It doesn't matter that none of this foreign genetic material would actually get into a growing banana plant (no more than a socket wrench would get into your car's oil supply after you've visited a Jiffy Lube).[50]

To judge by voluminous sales of GM foods in the United States and other countries, a large segment of the population is not in fact "horrified" by direct genetic manipulation. There are also millions of parents in places like Uganda whose children lack vitamin A and who would be overjoyed if this deficiency were eliminated by fortification of existing diets, even if the bananas eaten by their children contained a fish gene. But in affluent parts of the world, biotechnology's opponents are numerous and vociferous enough to give major fruit companies pause. "In our core markets, in America and Europe, a genetically modified banana would never be marketable," a Chiquita spokesman opines.[51]

This attitude is lamentable given how biotechnology is likely to be employed in the search for disease resistance. Considerable progress in mapping the banana genome has been made.[52] Also, University of Florida Professor Randy Ploetz, the first to identify TR4, estimates that 30 to 35 percent of all the world's banana varieties resist that strain of the FOC fungus.[53] Thus, the most promising way to save bananas, for subsistence farmers and the tropical fruit industry and its customers alike, is not to introduce genes from unrelated organisms, which is impossible with conventional breeding based on sexual reproduction and which is how Koeppel and other opponents of GM foods normally characterize agricultural biotechnology. Instead, genes can be moved from close relatives with resistance to the Cavendish and other varieties that are already being cultivated. This kind of genetic manipulation, which should be unobjectionable because it merely accelerates crop improvement of the sort banana farmers have been doing for millennia,[54] is called cisgenesis.[55]

There is still the issue of who pays. Multinational agribusinesses have little commercial stake in bananas and plantains produced as nontraded food crops, so research and development targeted on those farm products will depend on the support of national and multilateral aid agencies as well as organizations such as the Bill and Melinda Gates Foundation. Chiquita, Dole, or Del Monte could easily afford biotechnological improvement of Cavendish bananas and other traded fruit. Any of the three firms might even have the wherewithal to win consumers' acceptance of GM bananas on its own, which would require a sizable marketing campaign as well as the loss of some customers for an undefined period as everyone got used to the idea of cisgenesis for the sake of disease resistance. The problem with these undertakings is that there would be spillovers. A company that comes up with a new banana variety, thanks to direct genetic manipulation or some other means, must consider the possibility that its innovation will be adopted by competing firms that have made no financial contribution. Appropriation difficulties, or free riding, likewise discourage technological innovation in Ecuador's banana industry. But then, technological innovation has never been its strong suit.

CHAPTER 11

Creative Destruction?

A century ago, United Fruit's monopoly in the banana business was undisputed. One of North America's leading companies—in any industry, not just the food sector—it possessed vast tropical plantations, the largest private fleet of ships in the Western Hemisphere, and a host of other productive assets. At most, Standard Fruit, Samuel Zemurray, and other U.S. competitors nibbled around the edges of markets dominated by The Octopus. It was inconceivable that Latin Americans would export bananas on their own in significant quantities.

Yet the company suffered bankruptcy after the turn of the twenty-first century and The Octopus's time as an independent firm is now at an end. In October 2014, a pair of Brazilian conglomerates, the Cutrale Group and the Safra Group, won the assent of shareholders to buy the enterprise created by Lorenzo Baker, Minor Keith, and Andrew Preston and take it private.[1] Chiquita's trademark, which is universally recognized, will still exist. So will its operations in various parts of the world, though only as subsidiaries of another business—a South American business, at that. Generations of *El Pulpo*'s admirers and critics would be astonished.

Few of those admirers and critics ever came fully to grips with the competitive pressure exerted by South American exporters—Ecuadorian exporters, above all others. However, the second-smallest Spanish-speaking republic in the continent was highlighted in a study of the tropical fruit business published nearly fifty years ago by the Harvard Business School: "From an insignificant position at the end of World War II, Ecuador became the world's largest exporter, with an export volume that reached three or four times that of the closest competitor." The authors of the same study also put their collective finger on a distinctive feature of the country's banana industry, which is its "open-market, nonintegrated production structure."[2]

Competitive markets for exports have always been the rule, not the exception, in western Ecuador. During the mid-1800s, for instance, various merchants from the region peddled straw hats to aspiring gold miners crossing
the Panamanian Isthmus on their way to California. A few decades later, the
costa was the world's leading source of cacao. The cacao boom left practically
all the best farmland within reach of Guayaquil and other seaports in local
hands, which impeded establishment of a vertically integrated banana operation similar to those that existed for a long time in Colombia and Central
America. To forestall monopolization, the authorities in Quito placed limits
on foreign landholdings during the 1930s, shortly after United Fruit started
acquiring Ecuadorian real estate. Requirements to purchase bananas from independent planters were also imposed on every exporter, including *El Pulpo*.

An open market is a favorable setting for productive entrepreneurship—
more so than a vertically integrated monopoly, not to mention a government
ministry. Competing against other exporters, foreign and domestic, Luís
Noboa and Segundo Wong mastered one of the five entrepreneurial contributions to economic progress identified in the early 1900s by Joseph Schumpeter,[3] which is to venture into new markets. Other businessmen and -women
have followed their example, finding customers without fail for all the bananas their countrymen grow, so the *costa* has been the world's top exporter
of tropical fruit for more than six decades. Additionally, banana development
has transformed Ecuador from a primarily Andean country, with most of the
population inhabiting mountain valleys overshadowed by snowcapped vol-
canoes, into a predominantly coastal nation dominated by Guayaquil, where
three million people now live.

The accomplishments of Ecuador's banana industry and its enterprising
leaders have had an impact far beyond the country's borders. In line with
another of Schumpeter's five entrepreneurial contributions, which is to reorganize industries and markets, the countless tons of bananas exported by
Noboa, Wong, and others like them undermined United Fruit's former monopoly. That monopoly existed as long as practically all the bananas sold in
North America came from the Caribbean Basin and as long as The Octopus
controlled all but a small portion of supplies from that same region. For consumers in the United States and other importing nations, the destruction of
United Fruit's monopoly was advantageous, in terms of cheaper bananas.

Of great importance in the *costa*'s previous economic progress, the align-
ment between the talents and capabilities of merchants in and around Guayaquil, on the one hand, and the requirements for export success, on the other,

will be a key factor in the future unfolding of the banana industry. Sales of Ecuadorian fruit in Russia, which have been sizable for many years, could decline due to low prices for the country's energy exports and associated devaluations of the ruble. Likewise, recent gains of the South American nation in the Middle East are in jeopardy because of war and terrorism. Developments such as these underscore the constant need to find new customers, which Ecuadorian exporters appreciate full well. Largely thanks to their efforts, banana shipments to China increased by 500 percent in 2014.[4]

At some future date, exporting prowess may not be enough for Ecuador to remain atop the global banana business. Between reduced harvests and increased expenditures on fungicides, the economic burden of Black Sigatoka is growing. Tropical Race 4 (TR4) of Panama Disease (or Fusarium Wilt) has yet to appear in Ecuador or anywhere else in the Western Hemisphere. But in spite of monitoring and quarantine efforts, this soil-borne fungus has to show up eventually. Chemical countermeasures are ineffective, so the only way to combat TR4 will be to develop banana varieties that resist the pathogen.

According to Randy Ploetz, who has studied TR4 since discovering it, the creation of resistant varieties would require spending millions of dollars on scientific salaries, laboratories and other facilities, and so on.[5] Though not inconsiderable, such an expenditure would be modest relative to the value of global production and exports and therefore is not blocking the development of bananas that can withstand TR4. A more serious impediment is the opposition in some quarters to biotechnology, which is the most promising way to come up with new agricultural varieties.

Some people condemn genetically modified (GM) foods owing to a pronounced caution about what goes into their stomachs, what might be released into the natural environment, or both. A few taking a stand against GM bananas, in particular, imagine they are striking a blow against a globalized and inessential food supplied exclusively by U.S. corporations with worldwide reach. This view is profoundly erroneous. Growers and merchants in places such as Ecuador have a vital interest in the banana trade. So do consumers around the world, as manifested in 1913 by the angry rejection of a tax on imported bananas proposed by U.S. president Woodrow Wilson and as revealed before the Soviet Union collapsed by the decision of stingy communist officials to purchase tropical fruit from Ecuador. However, those with the greatest stake in the fruit today are the hundreds of millions of individuals—impoverished and residing in Africa, for the most part—for whom locally produced bananas are a critical source of nutrition. Many of those individuals could go hungry because of an uncompromising rejection of bioengineering.

Some opponents of GM bananas may be implacable, even objecting if biotechnologists refrain from inserting genes from one unrelated species into another and limit themselves to cisgenesis—the transfer of genes from resistant banana varieties to the Cavendish and other crops that are an important part of the food supply, in this specific case. But in light of the costs and suffering that might easily result if pathogenic assaults are not halted, the case for harnessing agricultural biotechnology on behalf of bananas could hardly be more compelling. One impediment to this effort will remain, however, at least in the private sector.

More than other entrepreneurial contributions to economic progress, the introduction of a new product is often accompanied by large spillovers. A case in point is Ecuador's capture of many of the gains stemming from Standard Fruit's development of the Cavendish variety during the 1950s. The U.S. corporation undertook the necessary scientific work, converted its plantations, and substituted the new variety for Gros Michel bananas on supermarket shelves, at considerable risk to its bottom line. Switching to Cavendish a few years after Standard Fruit did so, the *costa*'s growers benefited much from the company's efforts, to which Ecuadorian scientists and centers of investigation contributed nothing.

Defending itself from plant pathogens—as opposed to relying on the breakthroughs of others—continues to be an unfamiliar undertaking for the world's leading banana exporter. Agricultural research has been a public sector enterprise since the early 1980s, one the government has never supported adequately.[6] If TR4 ever threatened the fruit industry in the *costa* as much as it currently harms banana production in the Philippines, Ecuador would have to invest quickly in specialized laboratories and postgraduate training for scientists. Moreover, such an investment would be made in the face of two major risks, one being that useful results may not materialize and the other being the good chance that any advances made by Ecuadorians would be appropriated by free-riding producers and exporters in competing nations.

It should not come down to this any time soon, notwithstanding some breathless reporting about TR4's spread outside of Southeast Asia and the Pacific. Ploetz observes that the pathogenic agent is stealthy, as demonstrated by its unexplained arrival in Mozambique, although it does not move with great speed from plantation to plantation, much less from country to country.[7]

With no sign of the disease anywhere in the Western Hemisphere, Ecuadorian entrepreneurs are choosing not to grapple with the difficulties of improving productive technology and creating new products. Rather, their energies are still concentrated where they always have been. The recent upswing in fruit shipments to China proves that the ability of those entrepreneurs to seize export opportunities is undiminished. So do the hundreds of millions of dollars earned every year by exporting other valuable, though perishable, goods, such as shrimp and cut flowers.

The tropical fruit business is the subject of a large number of books and articles, most of which advance a narrative about the plundering of banana republics south of the Río Grande by multinational firms based in the United States. But Ecuador has never been thus plundered. United Fruit, Standard Fruit, and other foreign companies have made impressive contributions and homegrown entrepreneurs have taken the lead in developing the *costa*'s capacity to supply the world with tropical fruit. More than that, individuals such as Noboa and Wong have outmatched their foreign competitors, including U.S. multinationals on more than one occasion, in a series of overseas markets. Confronted with these accomplishments, exponents of the banana republic narrative sometimes distort the history of the tropical fruit industry in Ecuador. More often, they simply ignore that history.

While Ecuador has never been the fiefdom of a foreign corporation, it resembles the countries around it in terms of the rarity of creative destruction based on technological improvement. This sort of creative destruction is a major driver of modern economic growth, and its relative absence in Latin America is indicated by the small number of international patents originating in countries such as Argentina, Brazil, and Chile.[8] In Ecuador, inadequate investment in the scientific base underpinning the banana industry creates the risk of a catastrophic decline in production due to unchecked plant pathogens. Tiny at present, this risk could grow during the years to come, raising the possibility of a wholesale switch in the *costa* away from bananas and the reconfiguration of marketing networks.

Ecuador has endured the collapse of a critical export before—during the early 1900s, when cacao harvests were devastated by Witches' Broom and Frosty Pod Rot and the *costa* ceased to be the world's leading supplier of the principal dry ingredient of chocolate. However, a more likely consequence today of a weak scientific base is that the country will continue to depend on technology spilling over from somewhere else in the world and paid for by others. The chances are slight that the South American nation will lead a successful initiative to save bananas and the global banana business from TR4 and other plant diseases. But if pathogenic threats are turned back, the country's growers and exporters, reliably entrepreneurial as they are, will end up benefiting at least as much as their competitors.

APPENDIX: ECUADORIAN BANANA PRODUCTION AND EXPORTS, 1961–2013

Year	Area harvested (hectares)	Output (metric tons)	Exports (metric tons)	
1961	114,000	2,597,000	985,300	
1962	111,000	2,486,000	1,100,000	
1963	122,000	2,473,000	1,340,000	
1964	169,000	3,300,000	1,382,000	
1965	210,000	3,304,000	1,200,000	
1966	186,688	2,522,090	1,264,801	
1967	202,716	2,556,830	1,262,800	
1968	195,095	2,765,120	1,251,516	
1969	190,170	3,031,110	1,189,625	
1970	193,560	2,911,340	1,246,332	
1971	181,050	2,742,950	1,350,600	
1972	170,740	2,581,640	1,406,800	
1973	161,907	2,495,930	1,368,223	
1974	151,779	2,676,410	1,356,706	
1975	109,860	2,544,330	1,384,486	
1976	107,300	2,570,930	937,259	
1977	100,540	2,450,690	1,317,733	
1978	76,864	2,152,190	1,223,785	
1979	67,547	2,031,560	1,170,104	
1980	70,494	2,269,480	1,290,621	
1981	63,999	2,009,850	1,229,555	
1982	65,009	1,998,750	1,261,284	
1983	59,306	1,642,070	909,956	
1984	60,646	1,677,570	924,355	
1985	65,188	1,969,560	1,075,027	
1986	111,827	2,316,440	1,364,697	*Principal destinations of exports*
1987	119,500	2,386,500	1,374,319	(countries, with percentages of total exports in parentheses)
1988	127,230	2,576,100	1,516,700	USA (57); Italy (7); Chile (5); Japan (5); Belgium (4)
1989	130,650	2,576,220	1,725,936	USA (57); Belgium (7); Japan (5); Italy (5); Chile (5)
1990	143,230	3,054,570	2,156,617	USA (60); Japan (6); Italy (5); Chile (5); Belgium (3)
1991	168,500	3,525,300	2,662,750	USA (45); Germany (14); Belgium (10); South Korea (7); Italy (5)
1992	184,920	3,994,640	2,682,831	USA (67); Germany (13); Italy (11); Belgium (9); Japan (6)

Year	Area harvested (hectares)	Output (metric tons)	Exports (metric tons)	
1993	203,590	4,422,010	2,563,223	
1994	221,270	5,085,920	3,007,925	USA (28); Italy (16); Germany (11); Belgium (11); Argentina (8)
1995	227,910	5,403,300	3,665,182	USA (25); Italy (14); Germany (13); Belgium (9); Russia (8)
1996	225,927	5,726,620	3,866,079	USA (23); Italy (14); Germany (10); Belgium (9); Russia (7)
1997	211,227	7,494,120	4,462,099	USA (22); Italy (15); Germany (12); China (10); Russia (10)
1998	206,931	5,463,440	3,855,643	USA (35); Italy (15); Russia (9); Germany (8); Belgium (7)
1999	193,601	6,392,020	3,966,126	USA (31); Italy (14); Germany (8); Belgium (7); Russia (6)
2000	252,571	6,477,040	3,993,968	USA (21); Russia (14); Italy (12); Germany (10); Argentina (7)
2001	228,985	6,077,040	3,990,427	USA (24); Italy (13); Russia (12); Germany (11); Belgium (7)
2002	229,622	5,611,440	4,199,156	USA (25); Italy (22); Russia (21); Germany (12); Belgium (5)
2003	233,813	6,453,810	4,664,814	Italy (25); USA (21); Russia (21); Germany (11); Belgium (5)
2004	226,521	6,132,280	4,521,458	Italy (26); Russia (23); USA (22); Germany (10); Belgium (5)
2005	221,085	6,118,430	4,764,193	Russia (24); Italy (24); USA (22); Germany (11); Belgium (4)
2006	209,350	6,127,060	4,908,564	USA (23); Russia (23); Italy (22); Germany (10); Belgium (5)
2007	197,410	6,002,300	5,174,565	Russia (25); USA (20); Italy (19); Germany (8); Belgium (7)
2008	215,521	6,701,150	5,270,688	Russia (26); USA (19); Italy (18); Germany (10); Belgium (8)
2009	216,115	7,637,320	5,700,696	Russia (23); USA (22); Italy (18); Germany (9); Belgium (6)
2010	215,647	7,931,060	5,156,477	USA (22); Russia (21); Italy (17); Germany (9); Belgium (7)
2011	191,973	7,427,776	5,778,170	Russia (21); USA (18); Italy (13); Germany (10); Chile (7)
2012	210,894	7,012,244		
2013	188,658	5,995,527		

Source: FAO, *FAOSTAT Online.*

NOTES

Introduction

1. Chapman, 21, 161.
2. Koeppel, 227, 238.
3. Bucheli, 159–61, 168–77.
4. Striffler, 9.
5. Gelles.

Chapter 1. The Octopus

1. Noboa-Pontón, 49; Benjamín Urrutia (Noboa's long-time attorney), personal communication, 19 March 2004.
2. Benjamín Urrutia, personal communication, 19 March 2004.
3. Noboa-Pontón, 49–50.
4. Freedman.
5. Read, 182–83.
6. Langley and Schoonover, 34.
7. Cohen, 41–42.
8. McCann, 16–17.
9. Cohen, 43.
10. Read, 184.
11. Cohen, 46–47.
12. Taylor, 76.
13. Koeppel, 56.
14. Soluri, 33.
15. Read, 199.
16. Jenkins, 22–27.
17. Bucheli, 25–27.
18. Koeppel, 67–68.
19. Cohen, 12.
20. McCann, 18.
21. Cohen, 19–21.
22. McCann, 18.
23. Cohen, 24–25, 27–28.

24. Soluri, 32–33.
25. Bulmer-Thomas, 29.
26. Cohen, 75–76.
27. Soluri, 42.
28. Cohen, 91–96.
29. Bulmer-Thomas, 15.
30. Upham-Adams, 54–63.
31. It is biologically inaccurate to refer to a banana plant as a tree, which by defini-
tion sprouts from a seed. Instead its pseudo-stem, which bears leaves as well as a fruit-
bearing stem, grows out of a bulb-like corm, which is planted underground. Portions of
a corm containing secondary shoots can be cut off and transplanted, thereby extending
monoculture to new fields and different places.
32. Ploetz 2000.
33. Soluri, 178–80.
34. Ibid., 70.
35. McCann, 39–40.
36. Fox, 83.
37. McCann, 21–22.
38. Fox, 83–84.
39. Cohen, 139–40.
40. Striffler, 47–49; Soluri, 131–41.
41. Karnes, 68.
42. Thompson, 29, 97, 137, cited by Bulmer-Thomas, 339.
43. Bushnell, 180.
44. Kepner and Soothill, 76.
45. Pablo Neruda, "La United Fruit Co.," from *Canto General* (Santiago, 1950); lead
author's translation.
46. Bucheli, 88–94, 96–100.
47. Bulmer-Thomas, 109, 133.
48. Soluri, 172.
49. Bulmer-Thomas, 109.
50. Rabe, 46.
51. Ibid., 45–46.
52. Cohen, 192–94.
53. Rabe, 54–63.
54. Arthur, Houck, and Beckford, 5.
55. McCann, 26–27.
56. Schumpeter 1942, 83.

Chapter 2. *El Pulpo*'s South American Rivals

1. Hayek, 83–84, cited by Sabel, 1–2.
2. Hausmann and Rodrik, 605–6.

3. Schumpeter 1934, 66, cited by Baumol, 896–97.

4. Consumers gain from technological advances as prices are driven down because of falling costs of production. Those advances benefit consumers most in competitive markets, in which prices track production costs the closest. But even in a monopoly, in which the linkage between prices and costs is not as tight, there are gains for consumers if production costs decline, because of technological improvement or for any other reason.

5. Soluri, 19–21.

6. Bulmer-Thomas, 16.

7. Ibid., 12.

8. Arosemena, 113.

9. Schodt 1995, 106.

10. Bucheli, 150–51.

11. Parsons, 206–7.

12. Yellow Sigatoka is one of a number of leaf spot diseases that afflict bananas.

13. Preston, 81.

14. Parsons, 203.

15. Dr. Egbert Spaans (formerly of Earth University, Guácimo, Costa Rica), personal communication, 3 March 2007.

16. Bucheli, 168–69.

17. Sanbrailo.

18. John Sanbrailo (executive director, Pan American Development Foundation), personal communication, 4 June 2012.

19. Estrada-Ycaza, 151–53.

20. Baumol, 894–97.

21. Estrada-Ycaza, 34.

22. Baker.

23. Roberts, 63–73.

24. Arosemena, 271.

25. Xavier Marcos (director, Ingenio San Carlos) and confidential source, personal communication, 14 June 2004.

26. Bucheli, 161.

27. Poma-Mendoza, 65–78.

28. Eric Mattson (former United Fruit manager), personal communication, 15 November 2005.

29. Ibid.

30. Esteban Quirola-Figueroa, personal communication, 1 July 2005.

31. César Malnati (former banana grower and associate of United Fruit), personal communication, 10 July 2005; Gisela Wong (daughter), personal communication, 15 June 2004; Rafael Wong (son), personal communication, 7 June 2004; Vicente Wong (son), personal communication, 17 June 2004.

32. Noboa-Pontón, 29, 41–42; Benjamín Urrutia, personal communication, 19 March 2004.

33. Noboa-Pontón, 35–36.
34. Benjamín Urrutia, personal communication, 19 March 2004.
35. Noboa-Pontón, 41–46.
36. Ibid., 54–55.
37. Ibid., 57–58.
38. Bucheli, 161.
39. Ibid., 196.
40. Acosta, 91.
41. Baumol, 894.
42. Bucheli, 17–18, 19–20.
43. Schodt 1995, 108.

Chapter 3. Never a Banana Republic

1. Rodríguez-Clare, 855.
2. Soluri, 216–17.
3. Deininger et al., 56–64.
4. Ellis, cited by Bucheli, 152.
5. Aime and Phillips-Mora, 1012.
6. Roberts, 109–10.
7. Parsons, 210.
8. Arthur, Houck, and Bedford, 149.
9. Castillo.
10. Ibid.
11. Ibid.
12. Ibid.
13. Striffler, 34.
14. Ibid., 34.
15. Parsons, 213.
16. Orellana-Albán, 3; Felipe Orellana-Albán (former director, Programa Nacional del Banano), personal communication, 16 November 2005.
17. Carbo, 106.
18. May and Plaza, 17.
19. Schodt 1987, 48–49.
20. Pineo 1988, 709.
21. Schodt 1987, 51–52.
22. Rodríguez, 131–32.
23. Seidel, 87.
24. Rodríguez, 145.
25. Ibid., 158–162.
26. Cárdenas, 53.
27. Acosta, 92.

28. Roberts, 152–53.

29. Striffler, 34–37.

30. "Fruit Companies Interested in Export of Bananas from Ecuador," 28 April 1933, File 822.6156 /14, NA RG 59.

31. San Andrés, 84.

32. Dispatch No. 1563, 3 October 1934, File 822.3971/108, NA RG 59.

33. Schodt 1995, 115.

34. File 822.00 General Conditions/108 10-3-34 NA RG 59.

35. File 822.6156/28 7–9-36 NA RG 59.

36. Striffler, 30.

37. Schodt 1987, 74.

38. Velasco-Ibarra completed a four-year term in office only once—during the 1950s, when economic progress resulting from the banana boom created a respite from Ecuador's chronically fratricidal politics.

39. Registro Oficial No. 159, 6 Abril 1936.

40. File 822.6156/31 5-25-37 NA RG 59.

41. Franklin, 293–94.

42. Ibid., 295–99.

43. Registro Oficial No. 223, 23 Julio 1938.

44. Bucheli, 153.

45. Ibid., 152.

46. Ibid., 152.

47. Ibid., 152–53, 156–57.

48. Posada-Carbó, 53–54.

49. Bucheli, 158.

50. Ibid., 62.

51. Parsons, 203.

52. Ingenio San Carlos; Xavier Marcos and confidential source, personal communications, 14 June 2004.

53. Parsons, 213.

54. May and Plaza, 76.

Chapter 4. Good Governance, for a Change

1. Karnes, 159–62.

2. Ibid., 162–64.

3. Schodt 1995, 109.

4. Karnes, 249–55, 259.

5. Valles, 102.

6. Arthur, Houck, and Beckford, 97, 178.

7. Schodt 1995, 110–11.

8. CEPAL, 170, cited by Wunder 2001, 169.

9. Fowler.

10. Bulmer-Thomas, 73.

11. The implicit tariff of 25 percent is found by subtracting the fifteen pesos exporters receive for every dollar they are forced to exchange at the official rate from the twenty pesos they would receive if they could convert currency at the free-market rate and then dividing the five peso difference by twenty pesos.

12. Preston, 79.

13. Comité Ejecutivo de Vialidad.

14. Office of the Coordinator of Inter-American Affairs, 137–38.

15. Schodt 1995, 121.

16. Ibid., 121.

17. Larsen.

18. Linke, 123.

19. Enrique Ponce-Luque (brother-in-law and business associate of Luís Noboa), personal communication, 15 November 2005.

20. Rabe, 45.

21. Soluri, 42–52, 102, 166.

22. Bucheli, 90.

23. Ibid., 174.

24. Parsons, 213.

25. Schodt 1995, 113.

26. Ibid., 118.

27. Parsons, 206.

28. Schodt 1995, 118.

29. Valles, 117.

30. Parsons, 206.

31. Ibid., 204.

32. Preston, 78.

33. Redclift, 49.

34. Riofrío, 11.

35. Parsons, 204–5.

36. Preston, 81.

37. Redclift, 48.

38. Arthur, Houck, and Beckford, 57.

39. Bucheli, 62.

40. Schodt 1995, 122.

41. Bucheli, 167–68.

Chapter 5. South American Entrepreneurs Go Global

1. Botero and Guzmán, cited by Bucheli, 155.

2. Bucheli, 154.

3. Ibid., 154–55.

4. Simón Cañarte (former president, Asociación de Exportadores de Banano del Ecuador), personal communication, 21 June 2005.

5. Ibid.

6. Ibid.

7. Bucheli, 159–60.

8. Valles, 16–17.

9. The most celebrated member of the family, diplomat Raoul Wallenberg, rescued tens of thousands of Hungarian Jews from the Nazis in 1944, but disappeared early the following year as Soviet forces swept into Eastern Europe.

10. CIDA, 329–32.

11. Eric Mattson, personal communication, 11 October 2005; Per Olaf Marback (former associate of Folke Anderson), personal communication, 27 August 2005.

12. Linke, 113.

13. Arosemena, 130.

14. José Antonio González (agronomist and plantation owner), personal communication, 29 June 2005.

15. Cueva-Silva, 164.

16. Eric Mattson, personal communication, 15 November 2005.

17. Schodt 1995, 116.

18. Eric Mattson, personal communications, 11 July 2005, 7 January 2006; Fernando Ortega (plantation owner), personal communication, 5 June 2004.

19. Report, "General Conditions," by W. H. Mills to U.S. Department of State, 21 April 1961, NA RG 59 File 822.00/4-21-61.

20. Memorandum from A. Allen to A. Rábida, 27 February 1961, NA RG 84 File 922.2376/3-29-63.

21. Hurtado, 81.

22. Benjamín Urrutia, personal communication, 19 March 2004; Enrique Ponce-Luque, personal communication, 15 November 2005.

23. Kurt Maier (former general manager of Noboa's shipping subsidiary, Naviera del Pacífico), personal communication, 16 November 2005; Estrella Terán (Noboa's secretary), personal communication, 20 November 2005.

24. Noboa-Pontón, 93.

25. Benjamín Urrutia, personal communication, 19 March 2004.

26. McCann, 30–31.

27. Shillo Adir, personal communication, 31 August 2005.

28. Noboa-Pontón, 83.

29. Eric Mattson, personal communications, 7 March, 9 July, 1 October 2005.

30. Noboa-Pontón, 84.

31. Pérez-Pimentel, 46.

32. Noboa-Pontón, 84.

33. Benjamín Urrutria, personal communication, 6 November 2003.

34. Shillo Adir, personal communication, 31 August 2005.

35. Lautaro Aspiazu (former United Fruit manager in Ecuador), personal communication, 14 June 2004.

36. Shillo Adir, personal communication, 31 August 2005.

37. Kurt Maier, personal communication, 16 November 2005.

38. Noboa-Pontón, 84.

39. Eric Mattson, personal communication, 31 July 2005 and 27 January 2006; Kurt Maier, personal communication, 16 November 2005.

40. Eric Mattson, personal communication, 27 January 2006; Ronan Raes (manager of Noboa's office in Antwerp), personal communication, 16 March 2006.

41. Kurt Maier, personal communication, 15 November 2005; Eric Mattson, personal communication, 3 June 2005; Ronan Raes, personal communication, 16 and 17 March 2006.

42. Eric Mattson, personal communication, 27 July 2005.

43. United Nations, 2395.

44. Memorandum from A. Little, U.S. Embassy in Quito, to Secretary of State, 18 October 1960, NA RG 59 File 822.0049/10-18-60.

45. Francisco Swett (Guayaquil businessman and former Minister of Finance in Ecuador), personal communication, 29 August 2006.

46. Francisco Swett, personal communication, 20 August 2006.

47. Ibid.

48. Eric Mattson, personal communications, 15 May 2004, 16 September 2005, 25 March 2006.

49. Francisco Swett, personal communication, 29 August 2006.

50. Rafael Wong, personal communication, 7 June 2004.

51. Pérez-Pimentel, 47–48.

52. Ibid., 48.

53. Estrella Terán, personal communication, 20 November 2005.

Chapter 6. Keeping Up with Technological Advances

1. Valles, 136–37.

2. Clarence-Smith, 178.

3. Valles, 19.

4. Schodt 1995, 119.

5. Ibid., 119.

6. Parsons, 206.

7. Valles, 117.

8. Parsons, 205–8.

9. Ibid., 205.

10. Valles, 120.

11. Acosta, 83.

12. Valles, 122–23.

13. File 822.6156/24 11–24-34 NA RG 59.

14. Preston, 84.

15. Ibid., 84.

16. Eric Mattson, personal communication, 15 May 2005.

17. Teodoro Alvarado-Olea (ANBE vice president), report to ANBE board of directors, 16 July 1956.

18. IFAC.

19. John Kirchner (emeritus professor of geography, California State University at Los Angeles), personal communication, 3 October 2004; Luís Felipe Duchicela (former United Fruit manager), personal communication with John Sanbrailo, 8 September 2004.

20. Vicente Santistevan, personal communication, 13 November 2003.

21. Sergio Seminario, personal communication, 31 May 2004.

22. Parsons, 209.

23. Preston, 82.

24. Desrosiers, cited by Preston, 82.

25. Valles, 122.

26. Preston, 82.

27. Arthur, Houck, and Beckford, 140.

28. Noboa-Pontón, 110.

29. César Malnati, personal communication, 20 July 2005; Esteban Quirola-Figueroa, personal communication, 1 July 2005.

30. In the late 1950s, researchers affiliated with Standard Fruit and United Fruit identified another benefit of covering stems of bananas with plastic bags, which was that pesticides could be used more effectively and with less of an environmental impact. Molds, for example, could be controlled with smaller quantities of pesticides sprayed inside bags. This practice also prevented harmful chemicals from being carried off by wind and rain.

31. Anonymous.

32. Toral.

33. Rosengarten, 132–34.

34. Malo, 494–500.

35. Ibid., 502–4.

36. José Antonio González, personal communication, 17 November 2005.

37. Malo, 538–41.

38. Ibid., 550–52.

39. Noboa-Pontón, 96.

40. Valles, 153.

41. Arthur, Houck, and Beckford, 149–50.

42. Karnes, 282–87.

43. Ibid., 289.

44. Arthur, Houck, and Beckford, 151.

45. Ibid., 152.

46. Bennett and Arneson.

47. Valles, 153–54.

48. Ibid., 154.

49. Ibid., 101.

50. Roche, 43.

51. Valles, 114.

52. Esteban Quirola-Figueroa, personal communication, 1 July 2005.

53. Ruff.

54. Felipe Orellana-Albán, personal communication, 16 November 2005.

55. Spurrier-Baquerizo 1998, 18.

56. "Bi-weekly Economic Review, January 28–February 10, 1961," NA RG 59 File 822.00/2-10-61.

57. Spurrier-Baquerizo 1998, 5, 18.

58. Bucheli, 166–67.

Chapter 7. Agrarian Reform, Unionization, and a Policy Tilt Against Agriculture

1. Rabe, 45–46.

2. Schodt 1987, 84.

3. Zevallos, 49–52.

4. Redclift, 31–32.

5. Schodt 1987, 121–22.

6. Ibid., 127.

7. Zevallos, 95.

8. Ibid., 92, 128.

9. Acosta, 83.

10. Striffler, 47–48.

11. Ibid., 42.

12. In his book about the global banana industry, Peter Chapman misses few opportunities to portray United Fruit in the worst possible light. In one of the five short passages he devotes to Ecuador, for example, he points out that there was "no pressure" in the country to build schools and clinics on banana plantations, which is not far from the truth, and states that the company "wondered whether it should bother" (161). However, Chapman does not see fit to report that United Fruit in fact constructed a first-rate hospital at El Tenguel.

13. Striffler, 3, 41, 47.

14. Ibid., 42, 45, 48–49.

15. Ibid., 47

16. Ibid., 45–46.

17. Ibid., 44–45, 48.

18. Pineo 2007, 136.

19. Cohen, 128–30.

20. Malo, 100.

21. Arthur, Houck, and Beckford, 147.

22. Ibid., 140.

23. May and Plaza, 170–71.

24. Soluri, 175.

25. Ibid., 174.

26. Ibid., 175–76.

27. Arthur, Houck, and Beckford, 53.

28. Soluri, 175–77.

29. Arthur, Houck, and Beckford, 148.

30. Soluri, 176, 178.

31. Bucheli, 162, 171–73.

32. By no means was Ecuador the only country where United Fruit was obliged to dispose of its plantations. In Guatemala, for example, all the company's agricultural holdings were purchased in 1972 by Del Monte, which had gotten into the banana business five years earlier because it wanted to thwart a possible takeover by The Octopus and because the 1958 consent decree prohibited acquisitions that would enlarge United Fruit's banana business (Taylor, 82).

33. Norma Plaza de García (former Registradora de Compañías, Registro de Propiedad, Provincia del Guayas), personal communication, 22 June 2005.

34. Uggen, 79.

35. Ibid., 79.

36. NA RG 59 File 822.2378/7-11-61.

37. NA RG 59 File 822.2376/7-11-61.

38. Lautaro Aspiazu, personal communication, 14 June 2004.

39. Striffler, 102–3.

40. Ibid., 105.

41. César Malnati, personal communication, 10 July 2005; Sergio Seminario, personal communication, 31 May 2004.

42. Striffler, 107–9.

43. Lautaro Aspiazu, personal communication, 14 June 2004.

44. Striffler, 65–79.

45. Ibid., 86–87, 90, 92.

46. Ibid., 84, 92.

47. Ibid., 4, 8.

48. Benjamín Urrutria, personal communication, 6 November 2003; José Antonio González, personal communication, 29 June 2005.

49. Juan Casals, personal communication, 11 June 2004.
50. Striffler, 130–36.
51. Ibid., 136–39.
52. Ibid., 140.
53. Ibid., 140–43.
54. Actual verification of this occupational malady did not occur until the late 1960s, several years after the switch from manual to aerial fumigation, when Portuguese doctors inspected the lungs of vineyard laborers (Cortez-Pimentel and Marqués, cited by Soluri, 125–26), who had much less contact with Bordeaux Spray than people who worked with the fungicide on banana plantations.
55. Soluri, 153–54.
56. Marquardt, 24–25.
57. Rafael Wong, personal communication, 7 June 2004.
58. Estrella Terán, personal communication, 20 November 2005.
59. Pier, 65–67, 72–75.
60. Esteban Quirola, personal communication, 1 July 2005.
61. Schodt 1987, 57.
62. Gardner, 35.
63. Schodt 1987, 105, 111.
64. Southgate 2011, 143.
65. Aráuz, 427–28.
66. Schodt 1987, 107.
67. Ibid., 91–92.
68. Whitaker and Greene, 26.
69. Whitaker and Alzamora, 177–78.
70. Schodt 1995, 107.
71. Ruff.
72. Scobie, Jardine, and Greene, 43–44.
73. Ibid., 37.
74. Spurrier-Baquerizo 1984.
75. Schodt 1987, 111.

Chapter 8. Resurgence

1. Wunder 2001, 169.
2. Brenes and Madrigal, 100.
3. Ibid., 100.
4. Karnes, 290–94.
5. AEBE.
6. FAO, 23.
7. Benjamín Urrutria, personal communication, 6 November 2003; José Antonio González, personal communication, 29 June 2005.
8. Noboa-Pontón, 105.

9. Benjamín Urrutia, personal communication, 19 March 2004.

10. Pérez-Pimentel, 60–64.

11. Arosemena, 135.

12. Noboa-Pontón, 114–16.

13. Arosemena, 137–38.

14. Rafael Wong, personal communication, 7 June 2004.

15. Noboa-Pontón, 135.

16. Scobie, Jardine, and Greene, 38.

17. José Antonio González, personal communication, 17 November 2005.

18. Striffler, 193.

19. Spurrier-Baquerizo, 1990.

20. Brenes and Madrigal, 106.

21. Schodt 1995, 106–7.

22. Ibid., 107.

23. Esteban Quirola-Figueroa, personal communication, 1 July 2005.

24. Kurt Maier, personal communication, 16 December 2005.

25. SICA.

26. Noboa-Pontón, 109.

27. Anonymous.

28. Vega.

29. Rosenberry, 60.

30. Tangermann 2003a, 20–21.

31. Ibid., 21–22.

32. Ibid., 27.

33. Ibid., 27–28.

34. Ibid., 34–35.

35. Ibid., 35–36.

36. Ibid., 36–37.

37. Tangermann 2003b, 46–47.

38. Intent on hemming in outside competitors as it expanded its business in the EU, Fyffes lobbied the Irish government vigorously in support of the COMB, even though Ireland was about as open to banana imports through the early 1990s as Germany was (Tangermann 2003a, 34).

39. Josling, 171.

40. Ibid., 181.

41. Ibid., 185–86.

42. Ibid., 176.

43. Kurt Maier, personal communication, 31 May 2006; Francisco Swett, personal communication, 21 August 2006.

44. PNB, 16–29, 31.

45. UNCTAD, 27.

46. Eric Mattson, personal communication, 8 February 2006.

47. Rafael Wong, personal communication, 7 June 2004.

48. For example, the brief history that economist Timothy Taylor provides of the global banana industry is generally accurate, although each of his two observations about Noboa's business is off target. First, Taylor characterizes the Ecuadorian's business as "parastatal," not privately owned (67). Second, he suggests that Noboa started exporting bananas during the mid-1960s, rather than ten years earlier (79). Taylor does not mention Wong or his companies at all.

49. Duchicela's ancestor, named Atahualpa, was executed in 1533 in spite of having offered his Spanish captors a roomful of gold and twice as much silver.

50. Luís Felipe Duchicela, personal communication, 1 July 2005.

51. Josling, 189.

52. Ibid., 190.

53. Ibid., 190.

54. Tangermann 2003b, 60–61.

55. Ibid., 63; Alfredo Pinoargote (formerly Ecuador's ambassador to the EU), personal communication, 19 October 2006.

56. Tangermann 2003a, 19.

57. Bishop, 2.

58. Pier, 21, 24–40, 42–44, 57–59.

59. Ibid., 90–91.

60. Ibid., 84–85, 88–89.

61. Ibid., 80–82.

62. Ibid., 5–6, 20, 45, 79–80, 95.

63. Brenes and Madrigal, 113.

64. Ibid., 106.

65. Pier refrains entirely from exploring the contradictions of fair agricultural trade. For example, the word "farm" rarely appears in her report. Nor does she ever describe Ecuadorian growers as family farmers, even though practically all of them fit that description. Instead, Pier invariably refers to their properties as plantations, which presumably are indistinguishable from the large estates where most of Costa Rica's bananas are harvested. Rather than clarifying the challenge of fair agricultural trade, this choice of words obfuscates key issues.

Chapter 9. The Environmental Impact

1. Brenes and Madrigal, 112.

2. Soluri, 200.

3. Wunder 2001, 167–68.

4. Parsons, 206.

5. Cepal, 43–48, cited by Wunder 2001, 167.

6. Wunder 2001, 173.

7. Ibid., 174–76.

8. Ibid., 178.

9. Wunder 2003, 32–33.

10. Southgate and Whitaker, 16–17.

11. Wunder 2003, 234–35.

12. Southgate 1992, 227.

13. Wunder 2001, 182.

14. Preston, 82.

15. Churchill, 308.

16. De Bellaire et al., 331.

17. Soluri, 197, 199–200.

18. Spurrier-Baquerizo 1987; Jorge Coronel (former quality control manager for Dole in Ecuador), personal communication, 1 July 2005; Benjamín Rosales (businessman and banana grower), personal communication, 19 June 2005.

19. Spurrier-Baquerizo 1987.

20. Spurrier-Baquerizo 1990.

21. Jorge Coronel, personal communication, 1 July 2005; José Antonio González, 29 June 2005.

22. Bennett and Arneson.

23. Jorge Chang, Ph.D. (agricultural scientist), personal communication, 16 May 2004.

24. José Antonio González, personal communication, 22 June 2006.

25. Benjamín Rosales, personal communication, 19 June 2005.

26. Jorge Mendoza-Mora (agricultural researcher), personal communication, 7 June 2004.

27. Jorge Chang, Ph.D., personal communication, 16 May 2004.

28. Soluri, 210–210.

29. Benjamín Rosales, personal communication, 19 June 2005.

30. Churchill, 308.

31. Jorge Coronel, personal communication, 1 July 2005; José Antonio González, 29 June 2005.

32. Soluri, 212.

33. Thrupp, 744–47.

34. Soluri, 208.

35. Ibid., 212.

36. Pier, 24–37.

37. Southgate and Whitaker, 95.

38. Hasson et al., 116.

39. Hechler.

40. Kim; Ecuador is at the center of another attempt to punish a major U.S. company financially for alleged environmental wrongdoing which has resulted in a judicial finding of misconduct on the part of plaintiffs' counsel. In March 2014, a federal judge ruled that the attorney who had won an award of more than nine billion dollars in Ecuador against Chevron Corporation for pollution in the eastern part of the country supposedly

caused by Texaco, which Chevron acquired in 2001, had engaged in "illegal and wrong-ful conduct," for which "there is no 'Robin Hood' defense" (Neumeister). Barrett (2014) provides a comprehensive account of this legal donnybrook, which has dragged on for more than two decades.

41. Reuters (2011).

42. Bennett and Arneson.

43. Churchill, 322–34.

Chapter 10. Continuing Challenges, New Risks

1. Striffler, 47.

2. Sergio Seminario, personal communication, 31 May 2004.

3. Cohen, 24–25, 27–28.

4. McCann, 26–27.

5. Freedman.

6. Dan Koeppel provides a tendentious interpretation of the 2006 election in his book, *Banana*, about the global tropical fruit industry. He notes that U.S. officials "were watching the election closely and that the election of Correa, who promised to close a U.S. military base in Ecuador, would be considered troublesome." Also, there are dark hints in *Banana* that the officials' attention "contained echoes of the past" (Koeppel, 227). However, the book reinforces the standard banana republic narrative less by its take on the 2006 election than by its complete neglect of the losing candidate's father. Luís Noboa created a multinational company and traded many more bananas than any other Latin American. No matter. Koeppel never mentions him, not even in passing.

7. Alvaro 2013.

8. Bucheli, 171–77.

9. Rogers.

10. AEBE, 17.

11. Evans and Mock.

12. Porzecanski, 259.

13. Ibid., 260.

14. Ibid., 260.

15. Porzecanski (2010, 256, 265–66) describes Ecuador's repudiation of its financial obligations and the antecedents of this repudiation in detail. Correa set things in motion in November 2008 by labeling the debt of 3.2 billion dollars, which Ecuador had re-ceived on concessionary terms in 2000 when a severe macroeconomic crisis threatened to unleash hyperinflation, "immoral and illegitimate." This pronouncement drove down the value of that debt in secondary markets. Since indebted governments are barred from those markets, a private bank in Guayaquil purchased some of the debt at a two-thirds discount from its face value and then resold its purchases to the government at a modest profit. At this point, remaining creditors were intimidated, so in early 2009 practically all of them accepted Correa's offer to cash in their debt, at prices that differed little from depressed secondary values. The upshot was that the Ecuadorian government

reduced its external obligations from a little more than ten billion dollars to about seven billion dollars, at a cost of about one billion dollars.

16. Ibid., 252.

17. Edwards, 167.

18. EIU, 48–49.

19. Alvaro 2014.

20. Ibid.

21. Krauss and Bradsher.

22. EIU, 7.

23. Alvaro 2014.

24. Fresh Fruit Portal 2011.

25. Porzecanski, 262.

26. Eduardo Ledesma-García (executive director, Asociación de Exportadores de Banano del Ecuador), personal communication, 24 April 2014.

27. EIU, 43–44.

28. Eduardo Ledesma-García, personal communication, 24 April 2014.

29. EIU, 43–44.

30. Gill.

31. Southgate, Graham, and Tweeten, 253.

32. Gill.

33. Reuters 2014.

34. In February 2014, for example, a cartoonist was fined $90,000 for a sketch published in *El Universo*, an opposition daily, that state authorities ruled was "defamatory" (EIU, 27–28). Likewise, indigenous leaders and organizations that once supported Correa but now object to the government's plans for large-scale mineral extraction and the centralization of public institutions have been vilified countless times in weekly presidential addresses, which all radio and television stations must broadcast live. More than a few of those leaders and organizations have been prosecuted criminally, including for terrorism and sabotage (Martínez-Novo, 120).

35. EIU, 24–26.

36. Fresh Fruit Portal 2014.

37. De Bellaire et al., 331.

38. Ploetz 2005.

39. Ibid.

40. Guilford.

41. Peed.

42. Guilford.

43. Pollan, 205–6.

44. Peed.

45. Office of the Gene Technology Regulator, 47–48.

46. Koeppel, 179.

47. Ibid., 204.

48. Ibid., 234.

49. Guilford.

50. Koeppel, 212.

51. Peed.

52. D'Hont et al., 216.

53. Randy Ploetz, personal communication, 31 March 2014.

54. Perrier et al., 11312.

55. We are grateful to Dr. Alice C. L. Churchill, a microbiologist at Cornell University and an expert on Black Sigatoka (or Black Leaf Streak Disease), for introducing us to this term.

Chapter 11. Creative Destruction?

1. Gelles.

2. Arthur, Houck, and Beckford, 5.

3. Schumpeter 1934, 66, cited by Baumol, 896–97.

4. Fresh Fruit Portal 2015.

5. Randy Ploetz, personal communication, 31 March 2014.

6. Whitaker, 313–14.

7. Guilford.

8. Lederman et al., 9–10.

REFERENCES

Acosta, Alberto. 2004. *Breve historia económica del Ecuador*. 2nd ed. Quito: Corporación Editora Nacional.

Aime, M. C. and W. Phillips-Mora. 2005. "The Causal Agents of Witches' Broom and Frosty Pod Rot of Cacao (Chocolate, *Theobroma cacao*) Form a New Lineage of Marasmiaceae." *Mycologia* 97: 1012–22.

Alvaro, Mercedes. 2014. "Ecuador Sells $2 Billion in 10-Year Bonds." *Wall Street Journal*, 17 June.

———. 2013. "Ecuador Tax Agency to Auction Assets of Alvaro Noboa Next Week." *Wall Street Journal*, October 17.

Anonymous. 1992. "El mejor bananero del mundo." Archivo de Guayas, Guayaquil.

Aráuz, Luís Alberto. 2009. *Derecho petrolero ecuatoriano*. Quito: Comité de Empresa de los Trabajadores de Petroproducción.

Arosemena, Guillermo. 1991. *El fruto de los dioses: El cacao en el Ecuador, desde la colonia hasta el ocaso de su ndustria*. Guayaquil: Editorial Graba.

———. 1993. *Comercio exterior del Ecuador*. Guayaquil: Self-published.

Arthur, Henry B., James P. Houck, and George L. Beckford. 1968. *Tropical Agribusiness Structures and Adjustments: Bananas*. Boston: Graduate School of Business Administration, Harvard University.

Asociación de Exportadores de Banano del Ecuador (AEBE). 2014. *Bananotas*, January–February.

———. 2006. "Historia del Banano." http://www.aebe.com.ec.

Baker, Christopher P. 2009. "Putting on the Style." http://www.christopherbaker.com/html/body_panama_hats.html.

Barrett, Paul M. 2014. *Law of the Jungle: The $19 Billion Battle over Oil in the Rain Forest and the Lawyer Who'd Stop at Nothing to Win It*. New York: Crown.

Baumol, William J. 1990. "Entrepreneurship: Productive, Unproductive, and Destructive." *Journal of Political Economy* 98: 893–921.

Bennett, R. S. and P. A. Arneson. 2003. "Black Sigatoka of Bananas and Plantains." http://www.apsnet.org/edcenter/intropp/lessons/fungi/ascomycetes/Pages/BlackSigatoka.aspx.

Bishop, Andrew S. 2001–2002. "The Second Legal Revolution in International Trade

Law: Ecuador Goes Ape in Banana Trade War with European Union." *International Legal Perspectives* 12: 1–36.

Botero, Fernando and Alvaro Guzmán. 1977. "En enclave agrícola en la zona bananera de Santa Marta." *Cuadernos Colombianos* 8.

Brenes, Esteban and Kryssia Madrigal. 2003. "Banana Trade in Latin America." In *Banana Wars: The Anatomy of a Trade Dispute*, ed. Timothy E. Josling and Timothy G. Taylor. Wallingford: CABI.

Bucheli, Marcelo. 2005. *Bananas and Business: The United Fruit Company in Colombia, 1899–2000.* New York: New York University Press.

Bulmer-Thomas, Victor. 1987. *The Political Economy of Central America Since 1920.* Cambridge: Cambridge University Press.

Bushnell, David. 1993. *The Making of Modern Colombia: A Nation in Spite of Itself.* Berkeley: University of California Press.

Carbo, Luís Alberto. 1978. *Historia monetaria y cambiaria del Ecuador.* Quito: Banco Central del Ecuador.

Cárdenas, José C. 1980. *La Economía y los problemas del desarrollo en el Ecuador.* Quito: Editorial Universitaria.

Castillo, J. Cicerón. "1922 Report on Bananas." Hoover Institution Archives, Stanford, Calif.

Chapman, Peter. 2007. *Bananas: How the United Fruit Company Shaped the World.* Edinburgh: Cannongate.

Churchill, Alice C. L. 2011. "*Mycosphaerella fijensis*, the Black Leaf Streak Pathogen of Banana: Progress Towards Understanding Pathogen Biology and Detection, Disease Development, and the Challenges of Control." *Molecular Plant Pathology* 12: 307–28.

Clarence-Smith, William G. 2000. *Cocoa and Chocolate, 1765–1914.* London: Routledge.

Cohen, Rich. 2012. *The Fish That Ate the Whale: The Life and Times of America´s Banana King.* New York: Farrar, Strauss, and Giroux.

Comisión para América Latina (CEPAL). 1954. *El desarrollo económico del Ecuador.* México: Naciones Unidas.

Comité Ejecutivo de Vialidad. 1952. "Siete años de incesante labor: El plan de carreteras, las obras portuarias, realizaciones y proyectos." Guayaquil.

Comité Interamericano de Desarrollo Agrícola (CIDA). 1965. *Tenencia de la tierra y desarrollo socio-económico del sector agrícola del Ecuador.* Tercera Parte. Washington, D.C.: Unión Panamericana.

Cortez-Pimentel, J. and Fernando Marqués. 1969. "Vineyard Sprayer´s Lung: A New Occupational Disease." *Thorax* 24: 678–88.

Cueva-Silva, Jaime. 1964. *La Comercialización del banano ecuatoriano.* Quito: AECA.

De Bellaire, Luc de Lapeyre, Eric Fouré, Catherine Abadie, and Jean Carlier. 2010. "Black Leaf Streak Disease Is Challenging the Banana Industry." *Fruits* 65: 327–42.

Deininger, Klaus and Derek Byerlee with Jonathan Lindsay et al. 2011. *Rising Global Interest in Farmland: Can It Yield Substantial and Substainable Benefits?*. Washington, D.C.: World Bank.

Desrosiers, Russell. 1958. "The Control of Sigatoka Disease on the Gros Michel Banana by Low Volume Spraying in Ecuador." Quito.

D'Hont, Angélique et al. 2012. "The Banana (*Musa acuminate*) Genome and the Evolution of Monocotyledonous Plants." *Nature* 488: 213–17.

Economist Intelligence Unit (EIU). 2014. *Country Report Ecuador, May 2014*. London.

Edwards, Sebastian. 2010. *Left Behind: Latin America and the False Promise of Populism*. Chicago: University of Chicago Press.

Ellis, Frank. 1983. *Las Transnacionales del Banano en Centroamérica*. San José: Editorial Universitaria Centroamericana.

Estrada-Ycaza, Julio. 1995. *Guía histórica de Guayaquil*, vol. 1. Guayaquil: Banco del Progreso.

Evans, Peter and Vanessa Mock. 2014. "Chiquita and Fyffes to Merge, Creating New Global Top Banana." *Wall Street Journal*, March 10.

Food and Agriculture Organization (FAO). 1971. *The World Banana Economy*. Rome: FAO.

Fowler, Glenn. 1987. "Galo Plaza, Ex-Ecuador Leader." *New York Times*, January 29.

Fox, Dennis N. 2002. *Totally Bananas: The Funny Fruit in American History and Culture*. Philadelphia: Xlibris.

Franklin, Albert. 1943. *Ecuador, Portrait of a People*. New York: Doubleday Doran.

Freedman, Michael. 2003. "Slippery Situation." *Forbes*, March 17.

Fresh Fruit Portal. 2011. "Ecuador Could Nationalize Banana Exports." March 22. http://www.freshfruitportal.com/2011/03/22/.

———. 2014. "Important Breakthrough for Banana Exports." July 21. http://www.freshplaza.com/article/124011.

———. 2015. "Ecuador May Become China's Main Banana Exporter." January 12. http://www.freshplaza.com/article/133196.

Gardner, Frank J. 1972. "Ecuador Eyes No. 2 Rank Among Latin Oil Exporters." *Oil & Gas Journal* (April 17): 35.

Gelles, David. 2014. "Chiquita Will Not Buy Irish Banana Producer, Clearing Way for Move to Brazil." *New York Times*, October 24.

Gill, Nathan. 2014. "Ecuador President Backtracks and Signs Trade Accord with EU." *Bloomberg News*, July 17.

Guilford, Gwenn. 2014. "How the Global Banana Industry Is Killing the World's Favorite Fruit." *Quartz*, March 3.

Hasson, K. W. et al. 1995. "Taura Syndrome in *Penaeus vannamei*: Demonstration of a Viral Etiology," *Diseases of Aquatic Organisms* 23: 115–26.

Hausmann, Ricardo and Dani Rodrik. 2003. "Economic Development as Self-Discovery." *Journal of Development Economics* 72: 603–33.

Hayek, Friedrich August. 1949. *Individualism and Economic Order*. London: Routledge and Kegan Paul.

Hechler, David. 2009. "The Kill Step." *Corporate Counsel*, October 1.

Hurtado, Osvaldo. 1985. *Political Power in Ecuador*, encore edition. Boulder: Westview.

Ingenio San Carlos. 1997. "En el centenario del Ingenio San Carlos, 1897–1997." Guayaquil.

Instituto Francés de Investigaciones Agronómicas en el Ecuador (IFAC). 1960. "Las Bananeras en el Ecuador: Misión J. Champion 1959." Guayaquil.

Jenkins, Virginia Scott. 2000. *Bananas: An American History*. Washington, D.C.: Smithsonian Institution Press.

Josling, Timothy E. 2003. "Bananas and the WTO: Testing the New Dispute Settlement Process." In *Banana Wars: The Anatomy of a Trade Dispute*, ed. Timothy E. Josling and Timothy G. Taylor. Wallingford: CABI.

Junta Nacional de Planificación y Coordinación Económica. 1963. *Programa de Banano*. Quito.

Karnes, Thomas L. 1978. *Tropical Enterprises: The Standard Fruit and Steamship Company in Latin America*. Baton Rouge: Louisiana State University Press.

Kepner, Charles D., and Jay Soothill. 1935. *The Banana Empire: A Case of Economic Imperialism*. New York: Vanguard.

Kim, Victoria. 2010. "Judge Throws Out Verdict Awarding Millions to Dole Workers." *Los Angeles Times*, July 16.

Koeppel, Dan. 2008. *Banana: The Fate of the Fruit That Changed the World*. New York: Hudson Street.

Krauss, Clifford and Keith Bradsher. 2015. "China's Global Ambitions, with Loans and Strings Attached." *New York Times*, July 24.

Langley, Lester D., and Thomas Schoonover. 1995. *The Banana Men: American Mercenaries and Entrepreneurs in Central America, 1880–1930*. Lexington: University Press of Kentucky.

Larrea, Carlos. 1987. *El Banano en el Ecuador: Transnacionales, modernización, y subdesarrollo*. Quito: Facultad Latinoamericana de Ciencias Sociales.

Larsen, Harold. 1948. "Report on the Economy of Ecuador." International Bank for Reconstruction and Development, Washington, D.C.

Lederman, Daniel, Julián Messina, Samuel Pienknagura, and Jamele Rigolini. 2014. *Latin American Entrepreneurs: Many Firms but Little Innovation*. Washington: World Bank.

Linke, Lilo. 1960. *Ecuador: Country of Contrasts*. 3rd ed. Oxford: Oxford University Press.

Malo, Simon E. 1999. *El Zamorano*. New York: Simbad.

Marquardt, Steve. 2002. "Pesticides, Parakeets, and Unions in the Costa Rican Banana Industry, 1938–1962." *Latin American Research Review* 37: 3–36.

Martínez-Novo, Carmen. 2014. "Managing Diversity in Postneoliberal Ecuador." *Journal of Latin American and Caribbean Anthropology* 19: 103–25.

May, Stacy and Galo Plaza. 1958. *The United Fruit Company in Latin America*. Washington, D.C.: National Planning Association.

McCann, Thomas. 1976. *An American Company: The Tragedy of United Fruit.* New York: Crown.

Neumeister, Larry. 2014. "NY Judge Rules for Chevron in Ecuador Case." *AP, The Big Story*, March 4.

Noboa-Pontón, Isabel. 2000. *Luís Noboa Naranjo: Profile of a Winner.* Quito: Grupo Editorial Norma.

Office of the Coordinator of Inter-American Affairs. 1947. *Historical Reports on War Administration.* Washington, D.C.: Government Printing Office.

Office of the Gene Technology Regulator, Australian Government. 2008. *The Biology of Musa L. (banana).* http://www.ogtr.gov.au/.

Organization of American States (OAS). 1975. *Sectoral Study of Transnational Enterprises in Latin America: The Banana Industry.* Washington, D.C.: OAS

Orellana-Albán, Felipe. 1952. *La industria bananera en el Ecuador.* Quito: Editorial Ecuador.

Parsons, James J. 1957. "Bananas in Ecuador: A New Chapter in the History of Tropical Agriculture." *Economic Geography* 33: 201–16.

Peed, Mike. 2011. "We Have No Bananas: Can Scientists Fight a Devastating Blight?" *New Yorker*, January 10.

Pérez-Pimentel, Rodolfo. 2003. *Diccionario biográfico del Ecuador*, vol. 19. Guayaquil: Universidad de Guayaquil.

Perrier, Xavier et al. 2011. "Multidisciplinary Perspectives on Banana (*Musa* spp.) Domestication." *Proceedings of the National Academy of Sciences* 108: 11311–18.

Pier, Carol. 2002. *Tainted Harvest: Child Labor and Obstacles to Organizing on Ecuador´s Banana Plantations.* New York: Human Rights Watch.

Pineo, Ronn F. 1988. "Reinterpreting Labor Militancy: The Collapse of the Cacao Economy and the General Strike of 1922 in Guayaquil, Ecuador." *Hispanic American Historical Review* 68: 707–36.

———. 2007. *Ecuador and the United States: Useful Strangers.* Athens: University of Georgia Press.

Ploetz, Randy C. 2000. "Panama Disease: A Classic and Destructive Disease of Banana." *Plant Health Progress online series*, December 4.

———. 2005. "Panama Disease: An Old Nemesis Rears Its Ugly Head; Part 2, The Cavendish Era and Beyond." *APS Net*, October.

Pollan, Michael. 2002. *The Botany of Desire: A Plant's-Eye View of the World.* New York: Random House.

Poma-Mendoza, Vicente A. 2004. *El banano en el oro.* Machala: Agencia Editorial P&C.

Porzecanski, Arturo C. 2010. "When Bad Things Happen to Good Sovereign Debt Contracts: The Case of Ecuador." *Law and Contemporary Problems* 73: 251–71.

Posada-Carbó, Eduardo. 1996. *The Colombian Caribbean: A Regional History.* Oxford: Oxford University Press.

Preston, David A. 1965. "Changes in the Economic Geography of Banana Production in Ecuador." *Transactions of the Institute of British Geographers* 37: 77–89.

Programa Nacional del Banano (PNB). 1993. *Banano.* Guayaquil.

Rabe, Stephen G. 1988. *Eisenhower and Latin America: The Foreign Policy of Anticommunism.* Chapel Hill: University of North Carolina Press.

Read, Robert. 1983. "The Growth and Structure of Multinationals in the Banana Export Trade." In *The Growth of International Business*, ed. Mark Casson. London: Allen and Unwin.

Redclift, M. R. 1978. *Agrarian Reform and Peasant Organization on the Ecuadorian Coast.* London: University of London Press.

Reuters. 2011. "Dole Food Company Signs Definitive Settlement Agreement with Provost and Umphrey Regarding Banana Workers' Alleged Exposure to DBCP." October 4.

———. 2014. "Ecuador Halts Environment Deals with Germany over Rainforest Visit." December 19.

Riofrío, S. 1995. *Banana en cifras . . . y otras novedades.* Guayaquil: Acción Gráfica.

Roberts, Lois J. 2010. *El Ecuador en la epoca cacaotera: Respuestas locales al auge y colapso en el ciclo monoexportador.* Quito: Gráficas Iberia.

Roche, Julian. 1998. *The International Banana Trade.* Cambridge: Woodhead.

Rodríguez, Linda. 1985. *The Search for Public Policy.* Berkeley: University of California Press.

Rodríguez-Clare, Andrés. 1996. "Multinationals, Linkages, and Economic Development." *American Economic Review* 86: 852–73.

Rogers, Matt. 2010. "Most Definitely a Different Banana." *Whole Foods Market Blog.* February 26.

Rosenberry, Bob. 1990. "World Shrimp Farming: Can the Western Hemisphere Compete with the Eastern?" *Aquaculture Magazine* 16: 60–64.

Rosengarten, Frederic. 1991. *Wilson Popenoe: Agricultural Educator, Educator, and Friend of Latin America.* Lawai: National Tropical Botanical Garden.

Ruff, Samuel. 1984. "Agricultural Progress in Ecuador: 1970–82." Foreign Agricultural Economic Report 208. Washington, D.C.: U.S. Department of Agriculture.

Sabel, Charles. 2012. "Self-Discovery as a Coordination Problem." In *Export Pioneers in Latin America*, ed. Charles Sabel et al. Washington, D.C.: Inter-American Development Bank.

San Andrés, José. 1961. *Recopilación de leyes, estudios y estadísticas del banano ecuatoriano.* Guayaquil.

Sanbrailo, John. 2012. "Ecuador: Never a Banana Republic." *Latin Business Chronicle*, May 29.

Schodt, David W. *Ecuador: An Andean Enigma.* Boulder, Colo.: Westview, 1987.

———. 1995. "State or Market: The Development of the Ecuadorian Banana Industry." In *Foreign Direct Investment in a Changing Global Political Economy*, ed. Steve Chan. New York: St. Martin's.

Schumpeter, Joseph A. 1934. *The Theory of Economic Development*. Cambridge, Mass.: Harvard University Press.

———. 1942. *Capitalism, Socialism, and Democracy*. New York: Harper and Row.

Scobie, Grant M., Veronica Jardine, and Duty D. Greene. 1991. "The Importance of Trade and Exchange Rate Policies for Agriculture in Ecuador." *Food Policy* 16: 34–47.

Seidel, Robert. 1994. "American Reformers Abroad." In *Money Doctors, Foreign Debts, and Economic Reforms*, ed. Paul W. Drake. Wilmington, Del.: Scholarly Resources.

Servicio de Información Agropecuaria (SICA). 2004. "El Rol del Banano en la Economía Ecuatoriana," Ministerio de Agricultura y Ganadería, Quito.

Soluri, John. 2005. *Banana Cultures: Agriculture, Consumption, and Environmental Change in Honduras and the United States*. Austin: University of Texas Press.

Southgate, Douglas. 1992. "Policies Contributing to Agricultural Colonization of Latin America's Tropical Forests." In *Managing the World's Forests*, ed. Narendra P. Sharma. Dubuque, Iowa: Kendall/Hunt.

———. 2011. "National Interests, Multinational Actors, and Petroleum Development in the Ecuadorian Amazon." *Whitehead Journal of Diplomacy and International Relations* 12: 137–51.

Southgate, Douglas, Douglas H. Graham, and Luther Tweeten. 2011. *The World Food Economy*. 2nd ed. Hoboken, N.J.: Wiley.

Southgate, Douglas and Morris Whitaker. 1994. *Economic Progress and the Environment: One Developing Country's Policy Crisis*. New York: Oxford University Press.

Spurrier-Baquerizo, Walter. 1984. *Weekly Analysis* (March 8): 1–6.

———. 1987. *Weekly Analysis* (November 6): 1–5.

———. 1990. *Weekly Analysis* (May 22): 1–6.

———. 1998. *Fifty Years of Bananas*. Guayaquil: ACORBAT.

Striffler, Steve. 2002. *In the Shadows of State and Capital: The United Fruit Company, Popular Struggle, and Agrarian Restructuring in Ecuador, 1900–1995*. Durham, N.C.: Duke University Press.

Tangermann, Stefan. 2003a. "European Interests in the Banana Market." In *Banana Wars: The Anatomy of a Trade Dispute*, ed. Timothy E. Josling and Timothy G. Taylor. Wallingford: CABI.

———. 2003b. "The European Common Banana Policy." In *Banana Wars: The Anatomy of a Trade Dispute*, ed. Timothy E. Josling and Timothy G. Taylor. Wallingford: CABI.

Taylor, Timothy G. 2003. "Evolution of the Banana Multinationals." In *Banana Wars: The Anatomy of a Trade Dispute*, ed. Timothy E. Josling and Timothy G. Taylor. Wallingford: CABI.

Thompson, Wallace. 1926. *Rainbow Countries of Central America*. New York: Dutton.

Thrupp, Lori Ann. 1991. "Sterilization of Workers from Pesticide Exposure: The Causes and Consequences of DBCP-Induced Damage in Costa Rica and Beyond." *International Journal of Health Services* 21: 731–57.

Toral, Zalatiel. 1970. "Monografía de la Provincia del Guayas," Archivo de Guayas, Guayaquil.

Uggen, John F. 1993. *Tenencia de la tierra y movilizaciones campesinas: Zona de milagro*. Quito: Andean Center for Latin American Studies.

United Nations. 1964. *United Nations Commodity Trade Statistics, Series D, Volume XIV*. New York: United Nations.

United Nations Conference on Trade and Development (UNCTAD). 2001. *Investment Policy Review: Ecuador*. Geneva: United Nations.

Upham-Adams, Frederick. 1914. *Conquest of the Tropics: The Story of the Creative Enterprises Conducted by the United Fruit Company*. Romance of Big Business 1. Garden City, N.Y.: Doubleday.

Valles, Jean Paul. 1968. *The World Market for Bananas, 1964–72: Outlook for Demand, Supply, and Prices*. New York: Praeger.

Vega, Henry. 2009. "2009 Ecuador Fresh Flower Industry Situation." USDA Foreign Agricultural Service, EC9006. Quito.

Whitaker, Morris D. 1990. "The Human Capital and Science Base." In *Agriculture and Economic Survival: The Role of Agriculture in Ecuador's Development*, ed. Morris D. Whitaker and Dale Colyer. Boulder, Colo.: Westview.

Whitaker, Morris D. and Jaime Alzamora. 1990. "Irrigation and Agricultural Development." In *Agriculture and Economic Survival: The Role of Agriculture in Ecuador's Development*, ed. Morris D. Whitaker and Dale Colyer. Boulder, Colo.: Westview.

Whitaker, Morris D. and Duty Greene. 1990. "Development Policy and Agriculture." In *Agriculture and Economic Survival: The Role of Agriculture in Ecuador's Development*, ed. Morris D. Whitaker and Dale Colyer. Boulder, Colo. Westview.

Wunder, Sven. 2001. "Ecuador Goes Bananas: Incremental Technological Change and Forest Loss." In *Agricultural Technologies and Tropical Deforestation*, ed. Arild Angelsen and David Kaimowitz. Wallingford: CABI.

———. 2003. *Oil Wealth and the Fate of the Forest*. London: Routledge.

Zevallos, José. 1985. "Oil, Power, and Rural Change in Ecuador, 1972–1979." Ph.D. dissertation, Land Tenure Center, University of Wisconsin, Madison.

INDEX

1925 coup d'état, 44–45, 54
1938 banana industry decree, 48–49, 51–52, 53, 55, 75, 116
1958 consent decree, 18, 76, 113, 115–16, 193n32
Adir, Shillo, 79–82, 88, 157
Afrikanische Frucht, 72, 74–75
agrarian reform, 17–18, 53, 106–8, 113–14, 117–18, 120
agricultural credit and lending, 50, 62–64, 67, 76, 90, 140, 161–62
Amable-Calle, Manuel, 32–33, 157
Anderson, Folke, 73–74, 94, 116, 134
antitrust issues, 9, 18, 76, 112–13, 116, 157, 162–63. *See also* 1958 consent decree
Antwerp, Belgium, 82–83, 102, 104, 139
appropriation difficulties, 20–21, 23, 173, 177. *See also* intellectual property rights
Arbenz, Jacobo, 17–18, 106, 114
Argentina, 163, 165, 178, 182
Arosemena, Carlos Julio, 114–15
Asociación Nacional de Bananeros Ecuatorianos (ANBE), 64, 93, 95–96, 102–3, 132
Associate Growers' Program, 111–12
Astral Fruit Company, 74, 80, 94, 107, 116
Australia, 168, 170

backhauling. *See* transoceanic shipping
Baker, Lorenzo, 8–9, 14, 22, 25, 43, 174
banana boxes, 86, 100–105, 123, 127, 130, 132–33, 167
Banana Distributors, 79–81
banana export duties, 12, 17, 42, 48–49, 122–23, 125, 128, 147, 152, 167
Banana Framework Agreement (BFA), 137–39. *See also* Common Organization of the Market for Bananas

banana import tariffs, 10, 49, 72, 135–39, 141, 167–69, 176
banana industry economic linkages, 132–34. *See also* multiplier models
banana industry taxes, 16–17, 25, 48, 122, 161
banana prices, 10, 49, 54, 64, 67, 76, 79, 89, 100, 123, 129, 135–36, 140, 161
banana republics, 1–2, 16, 38–39, 120–21, 178, 198n6
Banco Comercial y Agrícola (BCA), 41, 44–45
Banco Nacional de Fomento (BNF), 62–64, 67, 90, 98
Baumol, William J., 29–30, 36
Belgian Fruit Lines, 82–83
Belgium, 72, 82–84, 134–35, 163, 181–82
Benlate, 151, 155
biotechnology, 5, 156, 171–73, 176–77
Black Leaf Streak Disease. *See* Black Sigatoka
Black Sigatoka, 101, 145, 150–54, 156, 170–71, 176, 200n55
Bogotá, Colombia, ix (map), 16, 38
Bordeaux Spray, 95, 119, 150–51, 194n54
Boston, Massachusetts, 8, 15, 42, 44, 81
Boston Fruit Company, 8–9
Bolivia, 164, 166, 168
Brazil, 5, 91, 174, 178
Bruns, Willy, 75, 116, 126–27, 134
Bucheli, Marcelo, 2, 16, 26, 37, 49–51, 66

cacao, 30–31, 37, 40–44, 53, 59–60, 63, 69, 73, 77, 89–90, 92, 116, 134, 175, 178
Calderón, Juan B., 70–71
California, 13, 30, 41, 76, 96, 155, 175
Canada, 84, 118, 131, 163
Cañarte, Simón, 71, 76
Canary Islands, 83, 137, 170

Cartagena, Colombia, ix (map), 25, 37
Castillo, J. Cicerón, 41–42
Castle and Cook, 126–27, 130
Cavendish bananas, 13, 22–23, 28, 40, 67, 90,
    100–104, 111, 117–18, 125, 147–49, 156,
    170–73, 177
Chapman, Peter, 2–3, 192n12
Chávez, Hugo, 164–66, 169
Chester, Clarence L., 46
Chile, 21, 25–26, 29, 34, 44, 71, 131, 163, 178,
    181–82
China, 1, 58, 139, 144, 166–67, 176, 178, 182
Chiquita Brands International. 2, 5, 23, 28,
    38–39, 81, 104, 130, 138, 140, 142–43, 160,
    162–63, 168, 173–74. See also United Fruit
    Company
Ciénaga, Colombia, ix (map), 16, 25, 70
coffee, 11–12, 16, 46, 63, 77, 91, 172
Coleman, Francis V., 46–47
Colombia, ix–x (maps), 12, 24–25, 27–28, 37,
    67, 81, 83–84, 89, 91, 125, 129, 135, 137,
    151, 163, 167–68; labor strife and its after-
    math in, 16–17, 53; local entrepreneurs in,
    2, 23, 26, 32, 70–71, 104–5, 161–62; pro-
    duction contracts, 39, 49–50, 69; United
    Fruit in, 26, 37–39, 49–50, 62, 67, 69–71,
    83, 112, 161–62
Comité Ejecutivo de Vialidad, 59–60
Common Organization of the Market for
    Bananas (COMB), 136–41, 195n38
Compañía Naviera del Pacífico, 128, 139
Comproba, 85–86
concessions and land grants, 9, 14, 16–17, 25,
    42, 48, 62, 125–26
Cooperativa Juan Quirumbay, 114–17
Cornejo, Carlos, 117–18
Correa, Rafael, 161, 164–69, 198n6, 199n15,
    199n34
Costa Rica, 9, 11, 17, 24–25, 65–66, 104, 119,
    121, 123–26, 129, 137, 143–45, 151–52,
    154–55, 196n65
costs of land clearing and banana production,
    63, 89, 91–92, 99, 101, 111, 123, 151, 153, 168
creative destruction, 19, 175, 178
countertrading and bartering, 85–86, 104
Cuba, 54, 106
currency overvaluation, 56–58, 67, 103, 123,
    125–26, 129, 149, 188n11
Cutrale Group, 174
Cutter, Victor M., 41, 44

Cuyamel Fruit Company, 11–12, 62, 159
Czechoslovakia, 85–86

D'Antoni, Joseph, 100
Dávila, Francisco, 35, 72
deforestation, 63, 67, 89–90, 146–50
Del Monte Corporation, 23, 28, 38–39, 128,
    130, 140, 143, 162, 168, 173, 193n32
Denmark, 84, 135, 136
Desrosiers, Russell, 95
dibromochloropropane (DBCP), 154–55
Dole Food Company, 23, 28, 38–39, 126–27,
    130–31, 140, 142–43, 152–53, 155–56,
    159–62, 173. See also Standard Fruit and
    Steamship Company
Dollar Diplomacy, 12
drainage, 27, 41, 91, 94, 96, 111, 170
Dupont Corporation, 151, 155

Ecuador, ix–x (maps), 2–5, 23, 43–45, 47–48, 53,
    55–56, 58–63, 65–67, 89–90, 106–7, 117–23,
    125, 131–34, 164–67, 174; banana exports
    from, 2, 8, 25–26, 46, 64, 74, 84, 89, 103, 124,
    129, 163; environmental and geographical at-
    tributes of, 3, 25–30, 37, 40–41, 91–92; foreign
    fruit companies in, 2–4, 14, 21, 38–43, 45–48,
    50–52, 55, 74–75, 77–80, 92–94, 108–10,
    113–16, 126–27, 130, 157–58, 178; health
    and environmental issues in, 142–55; local
    entrepreneurs of, 3–4, 18–19, 23–24, 29–37,
    51, 66, 71, 76–78, 80–83, 85–88, 96–97, 103–4,
    127–29, 131, 158–62, 175–76, 178–79; plant
    diseases and switching banana varieties in,
    94–96, 99–104, 177–79; trade disputes and
    negotiations of, 139–41, 167–69
El Salvador, xi (map), 24, 99
Elders and Fyffes. See Fyffes
Enríquez-Gallo, Alberto, 48, 52, 55, 75, 116
entrepreneurial innovation and specializa-
    tion, 20–21; in Ecuadorian banana sector,
    3–4, 18–19, 23–24, 32–33, 36–37, 68, 81,
    90, 131, 133–34, 136, 159, 161–62, 175,
    177–79; in worldwide banana business,
    22–23, 103; taxonomy of, 21–22; unpro-
    ductive and destructive, 29–30
Esmeraldas, Ecuador, x (map), 60, 63, 74, 94,
    121–22, 151–52
Estrada, Victor Emilio, 35
European Economic Community (EEC), 72,
    84, 135

European Union (EU), 72, 126–28, 136–42, 168–69, 195n38

exchange rates, 5. *See also* currency overvaluation.

Export-Import Bank, 60–61, 147

Exportadora Bananera Noboa, 74–75, 126, 130–31, 140

Exportadora de Frutas Ecuatorianas, 74–75

fair trade, 142–44, 196n65

Favorita Fruit Company, 142–43, 159–60

Febres-Cordero, León, 98, 129, 149, 152

fertilization, 63, 82, 91, 94, 150. *See also* soil properties

Fiji, 101, 150

Flota Bananera Ecuatoriana, 128, 133

Flota Mercante Gran Colombia, 81, 128, 132

flower exports, 31, 134, 178

France, 54, 72, 83–84, 135–36

free riding, 23. *See also* appropriation difficulties

Fundación Hondureña de Investigación Agrícola (FHIA), 152, 171

Fusarium oxysporum Schlect. F. sp. *Cubense* (FOC) virus. *See* Panama Disease

Fusarium Wilt. *See* Panama Disease

Fyffes, 9–10, 138, 140, 162–63, 195n38

General Agreement on Tariffs and Trade (GATT), 137–38. *See also* World Trade Organization

General Fruit, 82–83

genetically modified (GM) foods. *See* biotechnology

Germany, 1, 72–73, 75, 83–84, 87, 89, 133–36, 163, 169, 181–82, 195n38

González, Anacreonte, 72–73

Grace Steamship Lines, 46, 80–81

Great Britain, 9, 54, 71–72, 83, 136. *See also* United Kingdom

Gros Michel bananas, 13, 22, 28, 32, 40, 63, 66–67, 74, 85, 90–94, 100–103, 125, 146–48, 157, 170, 177

Grupo Básico program, 130, 152–53

Guadeloupe, 95, 121, 135, 137, 170

Guatemala, xi (map), 14, 17–18, 25, 61, 65–66, 92, 99, 104, 106, 121, 125–26, 137–39, 193n32

Guayaquil, Ecuador, x (map), 7, 31–35, 44, 48, 51, 71, 74, 76, 99, 103, 110, 119, 124, 126–27, 132–33, 148–49, 151–52, 159, 175; as a commercial hub, 3, 21, 25, 29, 82, 87, 132; entrepreneurial specialization in, 19, 24, 30, 36–37, 77–78, 134, 161–62, 175, 199n15; shipping facilities of, 41, 46, 59, 61

Gulf Corporation, 121–23

Hacienda Clementina, 73, 75, 108, 116, 120, 161, 167

Haiti, 54

Hamburg, Germany, 28, 73, 75, 82, 139

highways, 4, 41, 45–46, 55, 59–63, 73–74, 87, 91, 111, 124, 147, 150, 166–67

Honduras, xi (map), 10–12, 14–17, 24–25, 39, 56, 61–62, 65–66, 69, 92–93, 97, 99, 111–12, 121, 125–26, 129, 138–39, 151, 171

Hubbard, Ashbell, 11, 159

Human Rights Watch, 142–43, 145, 155

Humboldt Current, 26, 28

hurricanes. *See* tropical storms

Hurtado, Jaime, 119–20

import-substituting industrialization (ISI), 4–5, 67, 122–23, 125–26, 164, 166

inflation, 5, 44–45, 55–58, 66–67, 123, 149, 199n15

Ingenio San Carlos, 51, 98

Institut National de la Recherche Agronomique (INRA), 93, 96

Instituto Ecuatoriano de Reforma Agraria y Colonización (IERAC), 117–18

Instituto Nacional de Colonización (INC), 63–64, 113–14, 117

intellectual property rights (IPRs), 20–21, 141, 168

International Monetary Fund (IMF), 164–65, 167

Iran, 139, 164

Ireland, 163, 170–71, 195n38

irrigation, 3, 27, 41–42, 91, 94, 111, 123, 125, 152–53

Italy, 21, 72, 84, 135, 163, 181–82

Jamaica, 8–10, 54, 83, 121, 136, 170

Japan, 75, 81–85, 161, 163, 181

Keith, Minor, 9–10, 14, 22, 24–26, 39, 43, 174

Kemmerer, Edwin, 44–45

Kennedy, John F., 106, 114

Koeppel, Dan, 2–3, 172–73, 198n6

land disputes, 115–18
land ownership, 4, 14, 17, 33, 39, 47–48, 50–52, 53, 62–67, 90, 106–7, 111–12, 116–17, 127, 157
land redistribution. See agrarian reform
Laniado, Marcel, 98
Luxembourg, 72, 84, 135

Machala, Ecuador, x (map), 32, 41, 46, 60, 121, 126, 130, 148
malaria, 28, 55
Marcos, Juan F., 7, 31–32, 34–35, 76–77
Marcos, Juan X., 31–32, 34–36, 51, 61, 76–81, 87–88, 94, 96, 98, 157–58
Martinique, 95, 121, 135
McCann, Thomas, 14, 18
Mexico, 53–54, 137–40, 168
Mobile, Alabama, 10–11, 35
monopolization. See antitrust issues
Mozambique, 170, 177
multiplier models, 133–34

Naranjo de Noboa, Zoila, 7, 34
The Netherlands, 29, 72, 83–84, 135, 163
New Orleans, Louisiana, 9–11, 24, 26, 70–71, 73, 76, 78–79, 93
New York, New York, 8, 11, 26, 28, 46, 67, 70, 79–81, 89, 93, 102, 127, 157
New Zealand, 21, 23, 83, 131, 162–63, 168
Nicaragua, xi (map), 12, 17, 25, 99, 137, 155–56, 167
El Niño. See tropical storms
Noboa, Alvaro, 160–61, 165
Noboa, Luís, 7–8, 61, 66, 75–78, 87–88, 96, 99, 103–4, 120, 127–29, 132–33, 143, 152, 157–61, 196n48, 198n6; business conducted in Europe by, 82–83, 86–87, 104, 127, 134, 136, 139, 162; business conducted in Japan by, 75, 83; business conducted in United States by, 76, 79–82, 127–28; early life and career of, 7, 32, 34–35, 127, 159; entrepreneurial specialization of, 19, 21, 81, 90, 125, 175, 178. See also Exportadora Bananera Noboa
Norway, 84, 135, 162–63

The Octopus. See United Fruit Company
organic bananas, 152–53
organized labor. See unions

Páez, Federico, 48
Palacio, Alfredo, 164–65
Pan American Agricultural School, 97–99
Panama, ix (map), 11–13, 25, 27–28, 30, 65–66, 104, 121, 125–26, 129, 175
Panama Canal, 12, 19, 28, 37, 40, 71, 77, 83, 89, 92, 99
Panama Disease, 13–14, 22–23, 40, 54, 74, 99–100, 102, 111, 113, 150, 169–71, 176. See also Tropical Race Four
Panama hats, 30, 175
Parsons, James J., 27, 51, 62–65, 90
Patiño, Ricardo, 167–69
Peru, x (map), 25–27, 32, 59–61, 107, 122, 167–68
pesticides, 5, 142, 145–46, 150–56, 170, 191n30. See also Benlate; Bordeaux Spray; dibromochloropropane
petroleum, 41–42, 121–24, 148–49, 166
Philippines, 83, 85, 129, 170, 177
Pier, Carol, 142–43, 155, 196n65
plastic bags, 96, 130, 132, 145, 155, 191n30
Plaza, Galo, 54–55, 58–59, 61–62, 64, 66–67, 126
Ploetz, Randy, 173, 176–77
Poland, 131, 140, 163
Ponce-Luque, Enrique, 76
Popenoe, Wilson, 97–98
port facilities, 10, 61–62, 71, 74, 86, 111, 127–28
post-harvest handling, 59, 92–93, 102. See also banana boxes
Prague, Czech Republic, 85–86
Preston, Andrew, 8–9, 11, 14, 22, 25, 43, 174
production contracts, 39, 49–51, 65–66, 69–71, 75, 104, 115, 130, 140, 143. See also Associate Growers' Program; Grupo Básico program
Programa Nacional del Banano (PNB), 102–3, 128, 132, 151–52
Puerto Bolívar, Ecuador. See Machala, Ecuador
El Pulpo. See United Fruit Company

Quevedo, Ecuador, x (map), 33, 60, 74–75, 94–95
Quirola, Esteban, 33, 65, 96–98, 102, 104, 113, 120, 128, 132–33, 144, 152
Quito, Ecuador, x (map), 30, 42, 44, 47–48, 55, 60, 65, 85, 95, 115, 132, 164

railroads, 9–13, 16–18, 24, 28, 41–42, 46–47, 61–62, 69, 73, 91
research and development, 14, 20–21, 23, 90–91, 93–95, 100, 103, 171–73, 177, 191n30. *See also* biotechnology
Rey Banano del Pacífico (Reybanpac), 128, 130–31, 139–40, 159–61
rice, 1, 31. 55, 58, 71, 76–77, 97, 109, 133, 158
Río Guayas, Esmeraldas, x (map), 29, 41, 59–60, 71, 78, 99, 155
Rivadeneira, Francisco, 168–69
Rockefeller, Nelson, 54–55, 60
Rodríguez-Clare, Andrés, 38–39
Rodríguez-Lara, Guillermo, 107, 127–28
Rome, Italy, 83, 139
Rowe, James, 171
Russia, 139, 144, 162–63, 176, 182

Safra Group, 174
Salen, Sven, 82–83, 88, 134, 157
San José, Costa Rica, 9, 25
Santa Marta, Colombia, ix (map), 25, 37, 50, 70, 73, 83
Santo Domingo, Ecuador, x (map), 60, 63–65, 146, 148
Schodt, David, 54, 64, 131–32
Schumpeter, Joseph, 19, 20–22, 24, 29–30, 175
Scobie, Grant M., Veronica Jardine, and Duty D. Greene, 123–24, 129
Servicio Interamericano de Cooperación para la Agricultura (SICA), 95–96
shrimp, 31, 134, 155, 178
soil properties, 27, 41, 91, 94, 147, 170
Soluri, John, 14, 39, 112, 145, 154–55
Somalia, 72, 121, 135
South American Fruit Company (SAFCO), 25–26, 32, 46, 157
South Korea, 139, 181
Soviet Union, 85–87, 128, 162, 176, 189n9
Spain, 83, 133, 136, 163, 166
Standard Fruit and Steamship Company, 17, 53–54, 62, 65–66, 71, 79, 111–12, 126, 151, 154; early years of, 10, 24, 37, 174; Ecuadorian operations of, 74–75, 77–78, 80, 94, 96, 102, 126–28, 130, 158, 178; technological advances by, 13, 23, 100, 111, 177, 191n30. *See also* Dole Food Company
Striffler, Steve, 2–3, 36, 42, 47, 108–10, 113, 115–18, 130

sugar, 25, 51, 94, 97–98, 103–4
Sutherland, Thomas, 111–12
Sweden, 72–73, 82, 84, 134–35

Tamayo, José Luís, 40–45, 47, 55, 126, 157
Tampa, Florida, 71, 76
Tangermann, Stefan, 141–42
Taura-Vainillo plantation, 47, 113–14
Tegucigalpa, Honduras, xi (map), 12, 25
El Tenguel plantation, 45–47, 52, 93–94, 108–11, 113–17, 140, 147, 157, 192n12
Texaco, 121–23, 198n40
transoceanic shipping, 8–13, 15, 21–22, 25–26, 28–29, 31, 37, 40–41, 46, 54, 71, 73, 75–83, 87, 89, 104, 128, 132–33, 139–40, 174
transportation infrastructure. *See* highways, port facilities, railroads
Treaty of Rome, 135
Tropical Fruit Company, 71, 76
Tropical Race Four (TR4), 170–73, 176–77, 179
tropical storms, 3, 18, 28, 40, 67, 100, 102, 111, 124, 125, 129, 151, 167, 172
Tropical Trading and Transport Company, 9
Unión de Bananeros de Urabá (UNIBAN), 161–62

Unión de Bananeros Ecuatorianos (UBESA), 74–75, 83, 116, 126–27, 130, 159–60
Unión de Países Exportadores de Banana (UPEB), 123, 125–26
unions, 15–17, 79–80, 107–8, 110, 112, 115, 118–20, 122, 142–44, 168
United Fruit Company, 10, 40, 43–44, 79–80, 86, 95, 153–54, 191n30; and the banana republic narrative, 1–2, 15–16, 111, 178, 192n12; in Central America, 17–18, 24–25, 39, 61–62, 65–66, 104, 106, 111–12, 125–26, 151, 171; in Colombia, 2, 16–17, 26, 37–39, 49–50, 62, 67, 69–71, 83, 112, 161–62; dealings with organized labor, 15–16, 107, 110; early years of, 3, 9–10, 22, 43; Ecuadorian operations of, 3–4, 26, 39–43, 45–48, 50–52, 55, 60, 74–75, 92–94, 102, 108–11, 113–17, 126, 147, 157–58, 175, 192n12; past monopolization of the banana business, 8–10, 14, 18–19, 23, 39, 69–71, 76, 80–81, 112–13, 115–16, 157,

162–63, 174–75, 193n32; and Samuel Zemurray, 11, 14–15, 18, 35, 159; varietal replacement by, 85, 100–101. *See also* Chiquita Brands International
United Kingdom, 72, 84, 163. *See also* Great Britain
United States, 10, 40, 45, 58, 71, 94–95, 135, 154–56, 165; banana consumption in, 1, 10, 90, 111; banana markets in, 8–9, 11, 22, 79–80; banana shipments to, 26, 39, 53–54, 59, 77, 84, 90, 93, 128, 131, 162–63, 172, 175; Latin American policies of, 11–12, 18, 167–68; opposition to European restrictions on banana imports, 138–41. *See also* antitrust issues; Dollar Diplomacy; Standard Fruit and Steamship Company; United Fruit Company

Urabá región, Colombia, ix (map), 62, 112, 161

Vaccaro, Joseph, 10, 22
Valery bananas. *See* Cavendish bananas
Van Parys, Leon, 82–83, 88, 104, 127
Van Weert, Henri, 83, 139
Velasco-Ibarra, José María, 47–48, 61, 85, 106–7, 114, 127, 132, 187n38
Venezuela, ix (map), 137, 164, 166

vertical integration, 9–11, 22, 61, 69, 111–17, 128, 159, 175
Vives, Pepe, 32, 35, 72

wages, 15–16, 25, 34, 40, 92, 99, 102, 108, 110, 112, 133, 147, 168
Wallenberg family, 73, 75, 108, 116, 189n9
Wong, Segundo, 87–88, 119–20, 139–40, 143–44, 158–59, 161–62, 175, 178, 196n48; early life and career of, 33, 159; Ecuadorian investments and businesses of, 103–4, 128, 132, 142–43, 152; trade with Soviet Union and its satellites by, 85–87, 128, 136, 162
World Bank, 60–61, 147, 164–65, 167
World Trade Organization (WTO), 137–43. *See also* General Agreement on Tariffs and Trade
Wunder, Sven, 125, 146–49

yellow fever, 9, 28, 37
Yellow Sigatoka, 27, 54, 74, 94–97, 101, 119, 145, 150–53, 185n12
Yerovi, Clemente, 61–62
Yugoslavia, 86, 126, 131

El Zamorano. *See* Pan American Agricultural School
Zemurray, Samuel, 11–12, 14–15, 18, 22, 35, 46–47, 97–98, 110, 159, 174

ACKNOWLEDGMENTS

This book has been sixty-five years in the making, tracing back as it does to the coauthor's journey to Guayaquil, Ecuador in July 1950. Accompanied by her two small children, Lois Roberts arrived on a vessel belonging to the Standard Fruit and Steamship Company to join her husband, who a few months earlier had agreed to serve as a private pilot for Juan X. Marcos—the port city's leading businessman.

The husband made a quick start on a rewarding career that would keep him in Ecuador the rest of his life. But after growing up in Los Angeles and residing in a San Fernando Valley suburb, Lois was little prepared for all she encountered in Guayaquil, not least the juxtaposition of ostentatious wealth and widespread squalor. In October 1951, she returned with her son and daughter to Los Angeles, where she completed her undergraduate education while holding down various jobs. Determined to teach about the foreign culture she had experienced firsthand, Lois ended up earning a Ph.D. at the University of California at Los Angeles, writing a dissertation about Ecuador's cacao boom during the late 1800s and early 1900s.

More than ten years ago, Lois began investigating the banana industry, initially with Carlos Icaza-Estrada—a young historian from Guayaquil who conducted interviews, prepared a bibliography, and helped with the writing before heading off to college in the United States. His mother, Cecilia Estrada de Icaza, meticulously edited a Spanish-language manuscript about Ecuadorian entrepreneurs involved in the development of their country's tropical fruit sector: titled *Empresarios ecuatorianos del banana* and published in Quito, Ecuador, in 2009 by the Corporación para el Desarrollo de la Educación Universitaria.

Of the many people interviewed by Carlos, Lois, or both, none provided more insights and information than Eric Mattson, a Swede who had multiple employers during the many years he spent in Ecuador and had connections with banana importers in Western Europe, behind the old Iron Curtain (where he had done business while based in Vienna), and in the Far East. Another Scandinavian who was generous with his time and knowledge was Kurt Maier, a sea captain from Norway who managed shipping and port operations for Luís Noboa, Marcos's long-time partner and a key figure in this book. Other associates of Noboa also made themselves available for interviews: brother-in-law Enrique Ponce-Luque, attorney Benjamín Urrutia, Antwerp-based Kevin Bragg, and secretary Estrella Terán. So did Shillo Adir, an importer of tropical fruit in New York City whose long association with Noboa began when he facilitated the Ecuadorian's entry into the U.S. market, and Vicente Santivestan, Marcos's private secretary for many years.

Esteban Quirola-Figueroa, a major banana producer in western Ecuador, was interviewed. So were growers José Antonio González and Benjamín Rosales-Valenzuela, as well as the offspring of pioneering Ecuadorian exporters—Simón Cañarte and Gisela, Rafael and Vicente Wong. Also consulted were representatives of state institutions dedicated to agricultural research and other parts of the Ecuadorian government: Pedro Cubillo-Aguayo, Jorge Mendoza-Mora, Felipe Orellana, and Luís Tazán. Lois interviewed former employees of the United Fruit Company (now Chiquita Brands International): Joseph Montgomery as well as Luís Felipe Duchicela—a direct descendant of Incan royalty who had a long career with the U.S.-based multinational after growing up on its principal Ecuadorian estate. In addition, my coauthor and I appreciate what we learned from Sergio Cedeño, Enrique Gallardo, as well as Jacques Kohn—a Holocaust refugee whose business career began with exports of balsa and other material during the Second World War. Crucial insights were also shared by Eduardo Ledesma-García, executive director of the Asociación de Exportadores de Banano del Ecuador.

Contacts with many of these informants were arranged by a pair of individuals. One is Mariano González-Portes, a leading agribusinessman and one of a handful of Ecuadorian ministers of agriculture to complete a four-year term (beginning in August 1992). The other is Russell Crawford, an associate of González-Portes as well as Lois's son—the same son who as a youngster landed in Guayaquil in July 1950.

The two of us are especially grateful for the assistance of John Sanbrailo, whose long and distinguished career with the U.S. Agency for International Development included two tours as director of its mission in Ecuador. Since his retirement from the agency, John has been executive director of the Pan American Development Foundation, which is a branch of the Organization of American States. He supported Lois's research by sending interns to track down bibliographic materials and in other ways. By the same token, John had backed my previous work in Ecuador unfailingly. He also had the idea of complementing Lois's talents as a historian with my competence in economics (such as it is).

John recommended Marcelo Bucheli's history of United Fruit in Colombia. Bucheli, a faculty member at the University of Illinois, provided valuable advice as Lois and I began this collaborative project. Anthropologist Robert Wasserstrom has been a close associate of mine for many years as well as an excellent source of scholarly guidance during the preparation of this book. Carlos Camacho, an Ecuadorian economist with whom I have worked on a number of projects since the early 1990s, provided a lot of information about his country's economy, especially the agricultural sector. Three scientists were generous with their insights about banana diseases: Alice Churchill of Cornell University, Jim Lorenzen of the Bill and Melinda Gates Foundation, and Randy C. Ploetz of the University of Florida. Special thanks is due Paul Barrett, a senior writer at *Bloomberg Businessweek*, who shared more than a few writing tips (which I tried my best to follow) as he completed *The Law of the Jungle*—a blockbuster account of the legal aftermath of oil industry pollution in eastern Ecuador. Likewise, my coauthor greatly appreciates the proofreading and other editorial assistance provided by Brian Medley—Lois's one-time student at the Naval Postgraduate School in Monterey, California.

Concentrated work on this book began in earnest in October 2011, when I began a sabbatical at the University of Hohenheim on the outskirts of Stuttgart, Germany. My hostess there was Martina Brockmeier, an economist who specializes in international trade; she and her secretary, Clara Sifi, arranged an ideal academic environment for me. The two of them also made my wife and me feel right at home, for which we shall be forever grateful. Martina's doctoral students—Beyhan Bektasoglu, Tanja Engelbert, Vladimir Korovin, Kirsten Urban, and Fan Yang—were unfailingly congenial and always willing to hear me think out loud about the banana industry, Ecuador, etc. I also appreciated the countless conversations with postdoctoral researchers—especially Matthias A. Siebold, who like me has a deep interest in South America thanks to a fortunate marriage made in the Andes.

From my base at Hohenheim, I started making presentations on Lois's and my book-in-progress. The first seminar, arranged by Philipp Aerni in December 2011, was at the University of Bern, in the Swiss capital. Joachim von Braun kindly invited me to make a presentation at the University of Bonn in March 2012, which was followed four weeks later by a seminar at Berlin's

Humboldt University arranged by Harald von Witzke. Back in the United States, I gave a pair of talks at Ohio State University, where I have been on the faculty since 1980. Additionally, there were presentations at four other places in the United States: in October 2012 at the University of Minnesota, thanks to Paul Glewwe and C. Ford Runge; the following month at the University of Kentucky, where I was hosted by Yoko Kusunose and Jack Schieffer; in February 2013 at the University of Wisconsin, where Jean-Paul Chavas and Ian Coxhead made the necessary arrangements; and in April 2013 at Cornell University, where my hosts were Ralph Dean Christy and David R. Lee. The feedback I received during each of these seminars, from professors and students who are too numerous to be identified here, was invaluable.

Since embarking on this project with Lois, I have gained much from consultations with my Ohio State colleagues. Particularly useful have been the conversations with Trevor Arscott, an emeritus professor of agronomy whose professional career began on banana plantations in Honduras owned by Standard Fruit. Several professors in the Department of Agricultural, Environmental, and Development Economics have reviewed draft chapters, suggested readings, or helped in other ways: Joyce Chen, D. Lynn Forster, Claudio González-Vega, Douglas H. Graham, Mark Partridge, Ian Sheldon, Stanley Thompson, and Carl Zulauf. Librarian Florian Diekmann was endlessly resourceful about digging up trade data and all the other information I requested. Chen Xiang, a doctoral student in the Department of Geography, prepared the book's maps. A pair of undergraduate students provided significant assistance. Sam Goldberg, from Oberlin College, tracked down a lot of data and prepared many of the book's tables. Keith Taylor, Jr., from Pennsylvania State University, brought some great literature to my attention on topics such as experimentation with alternative banana varieties. Alex McAlvay, a doctoral candidate in the Department of Botany at the University of Wisconsin, furnished useful insights into plant diseases.

As the first couple of chapters of this book were starting to take shape, I sought the advice of Seth Ditchik. Now an editor at Princeton University Press, Seth kindled my interest in the global food economy several years ago by signing me up to write a book on the subject for Blackwell Publishing. He suggested that I submit a proposal to Erin Graham at the University of Pennsylvania Press. Lois and I are grateful that the proposal was accepted and for the guidance provided by Erin and all her colleagues: William Finan, who took charge of this book after Erin's departure from Penn Press and is now Editorial Director at Brookings Institution Press; Editor-in-Chief Peter

Agree; Acquisitions Assistant Amanda Ruffner; Managing Editor Alison Anderson; two anonymous reviewers; and an anonymous copy editor.

More than anyone else, our families have been endlessly supportive: Lois's children, Anne and Russell Crawford and Susan Weinman (who searched and photocopied U.S. consular dispatches and other archival material); my wife Myriam Posso; and Myriam's and my children, Elizabeth and Richard Southgate. This book is dedicated to you: Anne, Russell, and Susan and Myriam, Elizabeth, and Richard.